LOVE

AROUND THE HOUSE

Elizabeth Baker

This book is designed for your personal reading pleasure and profit. It is also designed for group study. A Leader's Guide with helps and hints for teachers is available from your local bookstore or from the publisher at $2.25.

VICTOR BOOKS

a division of SP Publications, Inc., Wheaton, Illinois

Offices also in Fullerton, California • Whitby, Ontario, Canada • London, England

Recommended Dewey Decimal Classification: 261.83442
Suggested subject headings: Behavior; Emotions; Love; Marriage

Library of Congress Catalog Card Number: 78-52781
ISBN: 0-88207-603-5

VICTOR BOOKS
A division of SP Publications, Inc.
P.O. Box 1825 • Wheaton, Illinois 60187

This book is dedicated with gratitude
to my own husband, Bill. A man
whose quiet ways and steadfast faithfulness
have done much to teach me
about its subject.

Contents

1

LOVE

and Human Need

I once came up with a theory that the need to be loved was basically a weakness in human character and should be eliminated from the growing Christian. We should love others but never should we desire to be loved in return. I thought it was a logical theory and I could support it with several parts of Scripture. It sounded good, even pious!

It seemed to me that eliminating the need of being loved from one's life would also eliminate most of the pain, since many of our deepest hurts come when we love someone who doesn't love us in return. *How safe we would be!* We couldn't be lonely if we needed no one. We couldn't be disappointed in people if we wanted nothing from them. We couldn't be hurt by the absence of love if we never needed love in the first place.

Today I excuse my long-ago reasonings by saying I was young then and could not be expected to know much about life, yet the theories I formed set my heart for viewing the world from one narrow angle, and for shutting out much sunlit truth that I desperately needed to know. I thought that to be without the need of love would be a safe and sheltered place and I wanted that place to be my dwelling forever. This sheltered place was to become a burden that nearly crushed me for the next 15 years.

Need For Support

Perhaps my foolish attitude was most pointedly illustrated about 10 years ago when I lost a baby five months into my pregnancy. We then had one child, age four, but we very much wanted a large family. As one pregnancy after another ended in early miscarriage, it looked as though our hopes would never be reality. I knew that this pregnancy would probably be my last chance for another child and as the hours of labor began to drag on, and the certainty of the baby's death became obvious, a great need for emotional support and tenderness grew inside me. My need to be loved was showing and I despised the feeling. It was weakness, and I would fight it. Although labor was well advanced, I encouraged my husband to leave. I remember biting the insides of my cheeks until they bled while I smiled a shaky smile and waved him good-bye, saying there was no need for him to stay. I was determined I would need no one. I would give instead of take. I would offer him an opportunity of a good night's rest and make all the need for understanding and tenderness go away by refusing to admit it existed.

After the miscarriage I learned the baby had been deformed, but I would not cry. Tears must only be shed for the grief of others. They told me

I needed surgery immediately and they were calling my husband to come in and sign the legal forms. I insisted there was no need to wake him up at 3 A.M. for such a foolish reason. I would sign the forms myself. But it was against hospital regulations because I had already received drugs, so they called him anyway.

It is easy to see what disastrous effect such a misguided theory can cause in a life. Marriage, parent-child relationships, emotional stability, even physical health were all adversely affected through the years because one stubborn woman refused to admit that being loved was a good thing for the heart and something placed there by God.

The Results of Forgetting How to Cry

Concluding that wanting to be loved was basically a weakness in human character, I fought mightily to deny that this need existed. For years I chased my goal with Spartan determination. I was fully persuaded that mine would be a heart that could freely shed tears in sympathy for others' grief but never waste a drop on personal pain. I was determined that I would love others deeply, yet never admit that the need to be loved existed inside myself. I would hold personal love and grief at arm's length. They would be analyzed but never embraced. I would never cry again. Not I! I would never admit to needing anything or anyone. But a funny thing happened to me on my way to Never Never Land. When I killed the ability to cry, I lost the ability to laugh. When I ignored loneliness, instead of satisfaction I found an inexplicable deadness of spirit.

During the last winter we spent in Oklahoma, a

beautiful early winter snow settled peacefully on the prairie one night while we slept. At that time we had two children and a new baby (sometimes doctors' theories shatter too!). None of the children remembered having seen snow, so when they woke to find the white wonderland stretching outside the windows for miles in every direction, they danced with delight. Bill was off work that day and breakfast was scarcely over before he and the two children were in the backyard building a snowman.

After they had been out for some time, I made coffee and cocoa, then went to the window in the back door, and wiped away the fog with a dish towel. The three were laughing and chasing each other around the faceless snowman until they tripped and rolled in the snow. Gasping for breath and pink-cheeked, our little girl tried to stuff snow down her father's coat collar. I watched them play and was mildly awed by the fact that I felt so separated from their laughter. It was not that I felt sadness, for I had long ago trained myself not to yield to that feeling. It was not as though I had some inner longing that made laughter a stranger to me. My heart was not sad—it was cold. Yes, that was the right word. Cold. I had not cried in years, but how long had it been since I had really laughed? I couldn't remember.

Looking but Never Touching

I was to recognize that cold feeling of separation again and again. Sometimes in a crowd when everyone was laughing, I allowed my mouth to smile, although my heart could not. It was like viewing life through a glass window. Always looking but never touching.

The problem with well-laid theories is that they are worse than useless if they ignore truth. The fact that we all need to be loved is truth, and though it took many years, God finally got it through my hard head and cold heart that people who refuse to accept love soon forget how to give it, and those who will not cry soon forget how to laugh.

Holding love at a distance and refusing to admit that we ourselves need to be loved are futile attempts to keep pain at a distance and to guard ourselves against the hurt of not being loved. But such efforts will never succeed because they are not what God has planned for our lives. It is not *possible* for us to seal ourselves off from personal involvement with the needs and griefs of life and still minister God's love to others.

By *personal involvement* I do not mean giving money to the poor, or doing good deeds, or giving cold acts of charity. I mean that we follow the commandment and allow our hearts and emotions to be stirred as we "Rejoice with them that do rejoice and weep with them that weep" (Rom. 12:15). Everyone is not of the same emotional makeup and for some tears come easier than for others; but to *deeply care* is as much our calling as to *freely share* our worldly goods.

Jesus did not shut Himself off. The fact that He stepped out of the ivory palaces of heaven and came to live with us on earth assures us that He is a merciful and faithful High Priest to His people (Heb. 4:15). Since He has personally known rejection and suffered the trials and pain of living, He understands what we are talking about when we come to Him with our trouble or pain.

What The World Needs Now Is Love

A few years ago financial reverses forced me to get
a job, first as a door-to-door cosmetic saleswoman,
then as a secretary-bookkeeper in a local furniture
store. Home and children were all I had ever known
up until that time and I found the adjustment to
working with the public every day an extremely
difficult one to make. I did not like establishing
adult relationships. Letting the Lord teach me the
basic steps of motherhood and self-respect had been
difficult enough. Now I was confronted with an
entirely new set of circumstances. In no way was
I willing to cope with yet another time of learning;
I thought that surely the Lord's timing was off.
What I wanted was REST, not trial.

My career as a cosmetic saleswoman is bound to
be one of the shortest on record. It lasted less than
a week. There were two things about it that I could
not bear. One was walking up and introducing myself to strangers. Without exaggeration I really
believe that it would have been less frightening to
have introduced myself to hungry alligators. The
second frightening aspect was watching the people
once I met them.

Many of the houses in my district were poor, yet
strangely enough, these women were most anxious
to buy my perfumes and creams. I remember one
woman who invited me into her shabby living room
where the smell of stale grease was so strong my
stomach almost flipped; a dirty-faced baby lay on
his back on the floor nursing a half-empty bottle.
His diaper had obviously been wet a long time, but
he looked up at me and grinned. I gave the mother
a book showing our latest lines of color and scent
for the fashionable woman of today, and spread a

few brightly colored bottles on the cheap coffee table before us. While the mother tried the newest color in lip gloss, the baby became interested and toddled to the table to touch and smell the pretty things. From a small spray bottle I gave the mother a bit of a new perfume we were peddling, and noticing the baby's interest, I decided to squirt the little fellow behind his ear to make him laugh. But the instant I sprayed, the baby jerked his head around to see what the noise was and received the spray full in his open eye. He cried and clawed at the painful eye while I apologized profusely. After a brief inspection the mother sat him back down stating that I was to "never mind" because "he cries a lot anyway." The baby settled into a sniffing pattern and the mother ordered my largest bottle of perfume.

I thought things would be better when I covered the more prosperous sections of town, but I was wrong. There too I found loneliness and trouble. One house on my route was a charming old, two-story home that had been lovingly restored. I settled myself in the living room thinking that selling cosmetics might not be so bad after all; but after a pleasant visit and a modest sale I was standing at the door when the woman's husband entered the room. His legs were in heavy braces and he dragged himself along on crutches. The illness disturbed me but not as much as the thought of trying to explain my belief in an all-powerful God of love in light of this suffering.

When the opportunity for changing jobs arose, I jumped at the chance like a fish grabbing bait. But there too I met with people, and the problems and the troubles of life were ever present.

Everything but Love

I had been working only a few days, and still didn't have much idea of what I was supposed to be doing. While sitting at my desk one day, trying hard to look busy, I overheard a conversation across the room.

"She was only 23," the first man said.

My new boss shuffled his feet and studied the floor. "Only 23," he repeated. "She had everything in this world to live for . . . everything in this world."

I thumbed through the papers before me and wondered if perhaps that wasn't the young woman's problem. The *only* things she had to live for were the things in this world, and what this world was offering her was not reason enough to stay. Having gone *a little way* down that road myself in years past, I knew something of its crooks and turns. I suspected that rather than what the world might be offering her of youth, money, education, prospects of opportunities yet unborn, the young woman probably needed what only another person could offer her. Love. Would it have made a difference if someone had been able to convince her he was sincere when he said, "Don't take your life, I love you"?

It seemed as though everywhere I turned during those months I was confronted with some unpleasant memory I thought I had buried or some unanswered question I had tried to put from my mind. It was as though some giant shovel were digging up forgotten skeletons and saying, "You must deal with these things. You must deal with them NOW." Was it right for a Christian to need love and acceptance? How could one reconcile a God of love and a world of pain? How could both be equally real?

The Greatest Human Need

To stay alive at all costs, to put oneself first, to hang onto life with a place among the living is survival. And survival is said to be the strongest human instinct. The need to keep our hearts beating and lungs breathing; the need for life-supporting food, shelter, and water, holding to what we call *self*, is said to be the deepest need of natural man.

The second strongest instinct is said to be the sex drive. The physical and emotional need to mate is supposed to follow close on the heels of the need to survive. The world, it seems, would have us believe that our existence hinges on surviving and our pleasure hinges on sex. But I wonder if there isn't something that outweighs both these powerful needs. Could it be that the inborn need of man to love and be loved is stronger than either of these?

If we truly believed that no one existed who needed the love we might offer, and that no one would want to love us in return, how long would the need to survive keep us going?

I have heard of babies in large orphanages who die for no apparent reason. The babies were clean and well fed; yet they seemed to give up on life. One theory was that though these children had all they needed to sustain physical life, they were never picked up and cuddled, seldom or rarely talked to and smiled at. The busy nurses had so much to do trying to provide so many small bodies with physical care that they couldn't show each child the affection he needed. The babies died simply for lack of being loved.

Babies are not the only ones who demonstrate these feelings. Often, adults and teens find it easier to do without life than to live without love, as witnessed by continually rising suicide statistics.

Twenty million Americans, or roughly 10 percent of the population, have mental illness or personality disorders. Fifty percent of our hospital beds are filled with patients whose illnesses are related to mind and emotion, and 70 percent of all patients seen by private physicians have some type of emotional illness or personality disorder. The medical expenses and lost earnings for such problems amount to $2.8 billion dollars annually.[1] Although these statistics include both those born with mental defects (such as mental retardation) and those developing defects later in life, I can't help but wonder what these statistics might have been if each of these people, from early childhood, had been given a foundation of love.

Love is Life

The need to be accepted and cared for by another person is strong. Even in the tiniest baby the need of love is very real; it is implanted in him by the Divine Planner.

I may not admire Dr. Benjamin Spock's politics, or agree with his religious philosophy, but he is highly qualified in his field by reason of his many years' experience in child psychiatry plus years as a physician specializing in the care of young children. Spock says, "Every baby needs to be smiled at, talked to, played with, fondled—gently and lovingly—just as much as he needs vitamins and calories." [2]

Any mother knows the nutritional value of vitamins and calories. When food is withheld, the baby's body becomes shriveled and ill. When the baby's heart is denied love, and the natural, inbred need for love goes wanting, year after year, the spirit also becomes shriveled and ill.

Jesus said that in the last days the love of many people would become cold (Matt. 24:12). As hearts harden and children grow up in loveless homes, and as people isolate themselves, each into his own private shell, the result will be an ever-increasing number of shriveled spirits.

Not only children are hurt and twisted by a lack of love. Adults also can have their lives wrecked by their own refusal to take a chance on giving or receiving love. Lack of love in generations past may find its way down to us, when our parents treat us as their parents treated them and we in turn fail to show love to our children. Family members affect each other, as the boss gripes at daddy, daddy criticizes mother, mother yells at junior, and junior kicks the dog. Lack of love spreads from one to another like disease germs. It affects neighborhoods, towns, and nations.

But love spreads from one to the other too. Like the rays from a crackling fireplace can warm the cold feet outstretched before it, cold people and cold hearts exposed to love can find themselves strangely warmed.

The Beginning Steps

Love is the strongest power in the universe because its source, indeed its very substance, is God (1 John 4:8). Many of our deepest problems would vanish if we all could learn to truly love each other. The trouble we face day by day is in trying to roll with the punches when others express a lack of love toward us and in wondering how to give unselfish love to others even when we don't feel like it.

Loving like that is an art no man on earth can practice without God's help, and that is what this book is about. It won't answer your every question about love, but perhaps through a few of the things I have learned, when added to your own reflection, and the leadership of the Spirit, a tiny bit more of this priceless commodity can start spreading through a few more lives.

One of the necessary steps in learning to love others is seeing and respecting the need to be loved inside our own hearts. Jesus said the second greatest commandment was to love others as we love ourselves (Matt. 22:39). We are not to neglect or trample on self any more than we neglect or trample others. One of the most basic doctrines of the church has been the worth and dignity of human life. God has placed great value on each of us.

Give and Take

As Christians, we emphasize the *giving* side of love, spending most of our efforts to express love to others. But when we ignore the need inside ourselves to *be* loved, we are starving one of God's creatures by refusing the needed nourishment to our selfhood. I believe God meant this hunger to exist. He created us with the desire to be loved.

Wanting to be loved is firmly an integral part of every person. Each one has his own degree of need according to temperament, environment, or family background, but the desire is present in us all. We shouldn't feel ashamed, or think we're not the kind

of Christians we should be when our need to be loved starts showing. It is natural to feel pain when another snubs us; or be hurt when someone we love turns bitter toward us; or when we taste the salty tears of loneliness, and long for another human heart that could share the ragged, painful burden that is crushing our spirit, and really care. We are not being weak or worldly when we are lonely, or disappointed, or hurt. We are experiencing a need inside that God put within us when He made us in His own image. Loneliness, hurt, and sorrow are natural feelings and are not to be ignored. It is only when we let these feelings lead us into self-pity that they become sin. God means for those needs to be satisfied. They will be satisfied for those who leave their lives in His hands, not instantly, nor by magic, but slowly, sometimes one by one.

But we can never know satisfaction unless we first experience need. And we cannot love others unless we first recognize and feel the need to be loved within our own hearts. And to feel that need and to find it satisfied is one of the privileges of being Adam's children.

---

[1] Statistics on page 16 were taken from *Modern Home Medical Adviser,* edited by Morris Fishbien, M.D. Copyright 1969

[2] *Baby and Child Care.* Dr. Benjamin Spock

2

LOVE
and Truth

That year when God dropped all those questions and problems into my lap, I focused on the relationship between love and truth and why truth is so illusive. While considering this problem, the Lord pulled an experience from the distant past and used it to teach me a lesson.

Our family burst through the back door that night at a run. "Everybody grab something!" I shouted above the laughter, and for the next 10 minutes bedlam reigned. Nobody had mentioned having the preacher and his family in for coffee when we left for services earlier that evening, and we had left the house looking like Custer and the Indians had just passed through.

"Put the coffee on, Mama!" Bill nervously shouted from the bedroom as he quickly jerked off his tie and in the same breath exclaimed, "This bathroom is filthy!"

"Maybe no one will ask where it is," suggested Lori with a laugh as she hastened down the hall loaded with newspapers and trash from the living room floor.

"Who left this dish and apple core on the television?"

"Boys, grab those dirty socks and put away that blanket!"

Children, trash, adults, clothes, toys, and dirty dishes raced from room to room with lightning speed. As the headlights of a car turned into the drive I tossed the last armload of soiled clothes in the general direction of the utility room floor and closed the door behind me. Maybe no one would ask where the utility room was either.

With cheerful dignity we welcomed the pastor, his wife, and child into a neat, orderly room while the aroma of fresh coffee drifted in from the kitchen. After a few minutes of conversation he complimented, "I don't know how you do it. This house is spotless everytime I come in and you have four kids. We only have one and my wife can't keep the place straight. There is always junk lying around." He gave a reproving glance in the direction of his young wife and my heart bled for her embarrassment.

"You should have seen it 15 minutes ago," I confessed. "We all hit this place on a run, grabbing things and cleaning as we went so that it would look half decent when you came."

"Oh sure, sure," he dismissed my honesty with a wave of his hand.

"But it's the truth!" I insisted. "No one can keep an uncluttered house with preschool children underfoot."

Yet, try as I might, he would not believe me. He looked about at two neat rooms and passed judgment on his wife because their house was less than what he thought mine to be. I was sorely tempted to grab the gentleman by the nape of his neck and —preacher or not—march him through the unseen sections of the house! Oh, well, if he wanted to wash his hands before coffee was served he would find out for himself.

Even in the simplest, everyday situations we can be misled by seeing only part of a situation and claiming we know the whole truth.

John, the Gospel writer, is sometimes called the disciple of love. His writings contain nearly one and a half times as many references to love as all the other books of the New Testament combined. But the same Gospel and letters that talk so much about love also contain nearly one and a half times as many references to truth as all the rest of the New Testament combined.

Love and truth go hand and hand. We as Christians are encouraged to love in truth (1 John 3:18). But like love, truth can be an illusive item for a man made out of dust.

How dangerous is partial knowledge! We see only part of the whole, touch only a fragment of the truth, and pass judgment on others by what we think we see. Yet, we can never honestly say we know the whole truth about any situation or subject.

I often eat peanut butter, and if someone were to ask me if I knew the whole truth about peanut butter I would probably say "yes," but that statement would be inaccurate. I know some things about peanut butter but before I could say I knew the whole truth about it I would have to know everything there is to know about it. I would have to know its chemical breakdown, varieties of peanuts, the history of peanuts, and how it was manufactured. George Washington Carver began discovering some truth about a peanut and found everything from machine oil to cattle feed bound up in that little nut and who knows what still lies locked undiscovered beneath its shell? The whole truth is as illusive as smoke and I doubt that as long as we live we will ever know the whole truth about any subject, no matter how trivial.

We never know all truth because we never know all facts. We look at life as though it were being viewed through a keyhole. Turning our head from one side to another, we catch glimpses of truth scattered about, then using the God-given ability of human imagination we guess at the whole.

If I can never attain total knowledge and complete truth about a sticky mass of mashed nuts, why should I become discouraged when I fail to understand the inner workings of the Godhead, the mystery of evil, the power of love, or the unknown workings of my own mind and heart?

I suppose the hardest earthly truth to catch and hold is the truth about oneself. For instance, I am not a difficult person to get along with. Ask the grocery clerk who sees me every Monday at the check-out stand, and she will tell you I am always smiling. Ask my training union teacher who sees me for an hour on Sunday evenings and sometimes during the week. She is my friend and she will tell you how I accept criticism with a sweet spirit. If you don't believe them ask my husband. On second thought, perhaps you had better not ask him, because I live with him seven days a week and he gets a different view of me than the others.

The grocery clerk would not be lying when she said I always smiled. My friend would not be lying when she spoke of my sweet spirit, for to the limit of her knowledge that is true. But Bill sees me late in the evenings when my head and shoulders ache. He and the children know when I am as warm and as motherly as a soreheaded grizzly bear. And wonder of wonders, Bill loves me anyway!

Yet, even my husband does not know the whole truth about me. There are many long, dark tunnels in my mind that he has never entered. My soul has felt depths and heights he has never known about. I know myself better than Bill does because I have been more honest with my own heart than I have with him. But even I have problems knowing myself.

An Alka-Seltzer advertisement on television showed a woeful, pajama-clad, sick-looking gentleman seated on the edge of a bed shaking his head and moaning, "I can't believe I ate the whole thing!" I sympathize with that fellow because more than one time I have stood amazed as I looked in the mirror and moaned, "I can't believe I said that! What got into me?" or "Surely I didn't do that. Did I?" Those who have never been surprised at what they found inside themselves are those who have never been brave enough to examine their own hearts. So, it is not only other people who can't see the whole truth about us; I believe we never completely know ourselves either. We know only what we think ourselves to be as we judge by the light we have at the moment. Likewise, we know only part of the truth about others as we judge by what they say and do. Recognizing these facts can act as a buffer zone when the perfect mate we married starts showing human blood a month after the ceremony, and our imperfect mental image of what we thought he was has to bend a little to accommodate the change. Or, when the Spirit throws light into a long forgotten room of our own heart and we must react to some weakness or sin cowering in the corner.

A truth is a truth, whether I am aware of it or not. If I am crossing a bridge which has all the supports under it broken and rotting away, the fact that I don't know the timbers are rotten will not keep the bridge from collapsing. If I am aware of the truth about the bridge, it doesn't change the bridge, but it surely will make a difference in my actions! We may never know all truth about everything, but we are responsible to respond to the truth we do know. How foolish it is not to respond to undeniable reality.

Truth never changes. It is as constant as the tides and as persistent as time. But our opinions and mental images change with increased experience as our knowledge expands.

Jesus Is Truth
Since God holds all knowledge (1 John 3:20; Psalm 94:11), He has access to the whole truth about every individual and situation. He is not straitjacketed by what we call time, and He understands the motives of our hearts better than we can (1 Chron. 28:9), since He has complete knowledge. He is called the "Lord God of truth" (Ps. 31:5).

The truth about God has always been there, steady and unchanging, even though man is not always aware of it. Through what we call general revelation, man glimpses God through nature and conscience. Through special revelation he sees a little of the holiness of God through the Old Testament sacrifices and the laws of Moses. But the most truth man can know about God is provided through the life, death, and resurrection of Jesus Christ. Jesus came to tell us what God is like (John 1:17). Jesus claimed to be truth (John 14:6) and all of the unshakable, undeniable qualities of real truth apply to Jesus also.

When Jesus was on trial for His life before Pontius Pilate, in answering one of Pilate's questions He said, "I came into the world, to testify to the truth. Everyone on the side of truth listens to Me" (John 18:37, NIV).

There are times when a large chunk of truth is set down in front of us and we find ourselves dwarfed by the undeniable. We may wish this were not so; we can close our eyes and turn our head, but the truth is there just the same and deep inside we know it. This happened to Pilate when a few hours later that same night, after beatings and another trial before Herod, Jesus, the humble preacher who had said He was a king, once more stood before the rich and mighty procurator, Pilate.

The private meeting was held in the beautiful marbled halls of the governor's palace in Jerusalem. Jesus had been beaten, mocked, spat on, and His hands were tied with a rope. All outward appearances said that Pilate was more powerful than Jesus and outranked this Galilean peasant. History to that point would surely say that Pilate was the braver of the two men, for he was a seasoned soldier from Rome and had been in many battles and had carried out at least one massacre (Luke

13:1). Jesus had never killed a man or lorded His own authority over others. The only suggestion that Jesus was a king was the purple robe about His shoulders that, though fit for a king, had been placed on Him as a mockery, and the crown made of thorns that had been pressed onto His head. But as He stood there before the governor with an un-earthly calm and regal bearing, it was the governor who looked in awed amazement at the One who stood before him (Matt. 27:14).

It was true that Jesus probably had hands and a face that appeared much like any other Jewish carpenter. The blood, dirt, and spittal on Him were real. But there was more complete truth far beyond outward appearances that outweighed the smaller surface truths. The truth was that Jesus was who He said He was, the Son of God, the King. I think Pilate knew it and marveled greatly.

The truth of who Jesus is and what He has done in being our substitute on the cross is real. We can ignore it, refuse to believe it, swear it is not so, or build our lives as though this truth did not exist, but truth does not change or go away just because we refuse to admit it. I can say the moon is made of cheese all I want, and believe it with all my heart. But it won't change the makeup of the moon one bit. Truth can change me as I accept and act upon it, but I can never change truth. There is no way for sinful man to be reconciled to God except by acknowledging the truth about Jesus and acting on it (2 Thes. 2:10).

Truth and Circumstance
Circumstance. Such a big uncontrollable word! It falls in the category with death and time and all

those other awesome things that roll over us.
Things we cannot stop and cannot change. Things
that find their value not so much in what they are,
but in how we react to them. As God reaches
through these things and leads us by the Word and
the Spirit, and encourages us to react in the way
He would have us, we become His students. When
we learn to set our wills to respond as God would
have us respond, then His power undertakes to
perform.

Jesus never asked His followers to pretend there
were no problems, or pain, or evil in the world. He
never asked them to walk with their heads in the
clouds or to deny reality. On the contrary! One way
He often worked was to show them how big and
hopeless and ugly the problem really was. God
doesn't want His children to close their eyes to
trouble. Rather, He wants them to see circumstance as transcended by the reality of His love
and power.

The young man who worked for the prophet
Elisha woke early one morning in the city of
Dothan, rubbed his eyes and yawned as he looked
out over the city wall. The sight he saw gave him
the shock of his life. Stretching outside the walls
in every direction was a mighty host of Syrian
soldiers armed for war. Perhaps the lad wondered
what it would be like if the Syrians tried to starve
out the people of the city! What if they were
tortured? The young man ran to alert Elisha to the
situation and pleaded, "Alas, my master! What shall
we do?" (2 Kings 6:15, NASB) Elisha did not ask
the young man to ignore the truth. The invading
army was real, the swords were sharp and ready.
The plight of the city was real and the situation

desperate. Elisha denied none of these things. They were all true. But something else was also true. Another real piece of information existed that the youth did not have. Elisha asked that the Lord would provide the lad with the rest of the truth.

"And the Lord opened the eyes of the young man; and he saw: and behold, the mountain was full of horses, and chariots of fire round about Elisha" (2 Kings 6:17).

The Lord let him see the unseen but real army of the Lord filling up the mountain behind the Syrians. The Bible does not say what the young man felt or did once he knew the whole truth instead of only part, but I believe he wasn't frightened anymore. Why should he be since he was on the winning side?

The Truth Will Set You Free

Many things in this world could make us afraid and many things could bind us. Some are our habits that others can see and condemn, such as smoking or gambling. Some bind us inside our own mind, such as constant self-condemnation, obsession with sex, or a critical attitude toward others. We can also be bound by ghosts from our past—past sins that we can't forget. These things can bind us and make it harder to express love. We feel weighted down with things that refuse to change no matter how hard we fight them. We can find ourselves wanting to run from the battle, to break out of the chains that bind us and run away. We want to be free!

How often we hear people talk of "the good ol' days." Usually these were days when the person was a child, or a teen. Many people I know long to go back to yesterday, or find "freedom" on some deserted island, or on a mountain, or in a night club, or in a motel room. They would like to break free of the binding commonplace lives they lead.

God's solution to the "bound and tied" feeling of man is one which logical, modern man has trouble accepting. The solution He gave to a group of His followers was: "If you hold to My teaching, you are really My disciples. Then you will know the truth, and the truth will set you free" (John 8:31-32, NIV).

Freedom comes through recognizing the truth, and truth comes through obedience to the teachings of Jesus. The Holy Spirit guides us ever deeper into the truth (John 16:13). If we disobey we quench the Spirit and prevent His ministry of truth from taking hold in our lives.

There are many other paradoxes in the Christian life. We find our life by losing it (Luke 9:23-24). We get by giving (Luke 6:38). We find forgiveness by forgiving others first (Matt. 6:14-15). We find rest by willingly accepting the burden Jesus offers us (Matt. 11:28, 30). We find strength by accepting the fact that we are weak (2 Cor. 12:9). And we find freedom by binding ourselves to the commands found in the teachings of Jesus (John 8:31-32), because obedience to His commands is the key that puts us in a position to receive more of the truth.

The teachings of Jesus are a lot more than a list of thou-shalts and thou-shalt-nots. They are God's most explicit, clear, written instructions given to us as a guide leading us where we want to go. He did not give His commands because He wanted to tie us down, but because He wanted to teach us how to experience freedom.

While driving to Austin, Texas last year, I missed a road sign and ended up on the wrong highway. When I saw the sign showing Kilgore, Texas was straight ahead, I knew I was going the wrong direction and doubled back. Both the signs I saw and those I missed had been placed by the Texas Highway Department and I had little trouble believing what they said. In this case I took for granted that these people knew more about how I was to get to my mother's house than I did. I had never tried to drive that road before and I knew I couldn't get where I was going without proper directions.

There is a slight chance I may be a little stubborn around the edges. Someone once said I would stand all day and argue with a fence post. But I would have to be an outright fool to argue with a road sign when I don't know how to reach my destination on my own.

We know where we want to get. We want to love and be loved. We want peace of mind and satisfaction and freedom from the heavy, burdensome things of life. But getting where we want to go can be a difficult matter. God has laid down road signs in His Word and called them commands; the teachings of Jesus amplified the commands and showed even more clearly what they meant in spirit as well as letter. However, a lot of us are sitting around arguing with the road signs instead of following them by faith.

Obedience to the commands of God is the first step toward freedom because it opens the way for the Spirit to reveal more truth to us.

Perhaps it is selfishness that binds me. I see this trait in my life, and I don't like it. I do as He has instructed me to in His Word and I pray and ask

the Lord to change me so that I will enjoy giving.
So, prayer is my first act of obedience. For the next
several weeks the selfish feelings inside me may
seem to grow. I am irritated because the neighbor
got a new car and I can't have one. Little things
gall me worse than ever. I don't want to give my
time and attention to the other members of the
family and my mind begins to dwell constantly on
things I don't have. I may wonder, "What happened? Did I not ask Jesus to help me with these
selfish feelings? Things are getting worse, not
better."

One of the reasons for apparent failure is that
we give up on God too soon. Sometimes He shows
us more truth about our problem before He shows
us more truth about His solution. Sometimes it is
not that problems get bigger when we pray about
them, but that we see them more clearly when
viewed through the glass of prayer.

When I see my selfishness in all its strength and
ugliness, it makes me want to be free from it all
the more, and shows me that I can never break free
alone. Once this new element of truth has been
learned I am ready for more obedience.

The neighbor with the new car comes over and
asks to borrow my lawn rake. I don't really want to
give, but in obedience to the teachings of Jesus, I
lend it (Matt. 5:24). One week passes and the
neighbor hasn't brought back the rake. I get upset
with him. Two weeks pass and I don't like him anymore. Three weeks pass and I am telling the neighbors I don't like him. During the fourth week I go
to his house and get the rake but three days later,
here comes the neighbor. Full of apologies, he asks
to borrow the rake once more. I am still not too

happy with him but I can't deny what the teachings of Jesus say about forgiving another 70 times seven if that is necessary (Matt. 18:21-22), so I lend him the rake again. I don't do this because I love him, but because I love and obey Jesus.

Because I have obeyed, the Spirit begins to impress on my mind the fact that the things I own are not really mine but the Lord's. I may have heard preachers and teachers say this for years, but now I see it with my own spiritual eyes. It is easier to say that because I belong to the Lord, all my earthly possessions belong to Him, than it is to accept that my seven-year-old, rusty lawn rake wasn't mine to get upset over in the first place; it belongs to Him. That bit of truth was always real; however, it only made a difference in me when I experienced its reality in the day-to-day trial of living.

Through continued obedience the Spirit may even be able to show me some truth about my neighbor. Truth like, how much the Lord loves him and what makes my neighbor so careless with the property of others. I may see needs and possibilities in him that until this moment had slipped past me unnoticed. Even a glimmer of love may begin to stir. As the truth sets me free I begin to learn more of what the truth has to do with love.

3

LOVE
and Touch

The women of our church were once asked to help care for an elderly woman who was dying of cancer. I volunteered to help, but never having been involved with such a ministry before, I was a bit apprehensive. My shift would be in the middle of the night. I would be alone, and I hadn't the least idea what would be expected of me.

As I entered the hospital room, the woman I was to replace stood and stretched, her muscles weary from hours of sitting. She was older than I and her confident manner gave me the impression she had sat by many other sick beds.

After a brief greeting she explained, "The nurses' station is just down the hall and here is the emergency button in case you need help. They have given her a shot and she is asleep now, but she will be awake soon."

She was turning to leave when, still rather bewildered, I asked, "Isn't there something I am supposed to do for her?"

She smiled and said, "She will want you to hold her hand." And with only those instructions I was left alone. Soft and clean, wrinkled and aged, the woman's hand lay limp on smooth white sheets.

She soon woke and the first sign of consciousness was her reaching out for someone to touch. I took the chair beside the bed and wrapped her hand with my own. We were strangers, although I had been given her name, but through the next few hours we worked together as friends as death crept uncomfortably close. In moments of peace we would talk about the sweater I was knitting and the color yellow, but when the pain would come she always, always reached out trying to find someone living to touch. I am told that often the last willful act of terminal patients is to reach out for a hand to hold. There are times when communication with others by the sensation of touch can break through more clearly than words. These times prove the power of silent communication.

In a moment of tragedy a person may reach out and squeeze the hand of a dear friend and all of the longing and sympathy and sorrow would be communicated in that touch so that the friend would understand.

A few years later, in a moment of joy and triumph, the same person may reach again to squeeze the hand of his friend and though the act was exactly the same as before, what it communicated would be completely different.

Touching someone tells him you accept him and that he is worthy of your consideration. It is assurance that we care.

Loving touches are important and natural. When a little child skins his knee and comes running home with tears making clean rivers down dirty cheeks, is he only looking for a cloth to wipe the blood away? Or is he looking for mama's arms to hold him? He draws comfort and reassurance even if the pain is not yet gone. To him, the world will soon be right again simply because he feels his mother's touch. Even infants respond to such sensations. They soon learn their own mother's feel, and find comfort and assurance in it. But they often loudly object when they are placed in the arms of a stranger.

Although it must be used with propriety and common sense, touching is an important part of loving, especially within the family circle. Babies need to be played with and held. A welcome-home kiss and hug for Daddy are the kind of bricks that can build a strong wall of family solidarity. Sitting on a parent's lap while a story is being read, or getting tickled in the ribs, or kissed good night are some ways a parent can communicate to his child that he cares about him.

Not all people have the same need to be touched or the desire to touch another. But for most of us, being touched is important, and the lack of it can cause feelings of separation and loneliness among family members.

While I was counseling a young mother one time she remarked to me, "I would give anything if just once W----- would walk through the kitchen and give me a little love tap, or slap me somewhere as he passed!"

A tender touch can stir a long-dead heart and make it sing. A firm touch can strengthen a fearful heart and give it hope. A gentle touch can reassure the broken heart that life will someday be sweet again. A caressing touch can say, "I love you, I value your nearness."

One long-ago winter, a cold and lonely night settled about the house, dark and full of rain. I picked up an old volume of poetry my pastor had lent me and among its faded pages found a poem by Thomas Curtis Clark:

The touch of human hands:
Not vain, unthinking words,
Nor cold charity
Which shuns our misery;
We seek a loyal friend
Who understands,
And the warmth, the pulsing warmth
Of human hands.

Jesus ministered to others through the touch of His hands. Outcast lepers (Matthew 8:3), children (Luke 18:15-18), older people (John 5:5-9; Luke 13:10-13), fevered people (Mark 1:30-31), disciples (John 13:3-5) and more, knew what it was like to be touched by the loving hands of the Carpenter who was God incarnate. Through His touch came healing, comfort, and teaching as Jesus used His physical body to contact others in this physical world.

Jesus not only touched others, but He did not shy away when others touched Him (Mark 5:25-34; John 12:3; 13:24-26). Even when the disciple John was an old man, he still seemed to marvel that his hands had actually touched Jesus, the Word of life (1 John 1:1).

The sensation of touch is a gift from God and a vital part of reaching out to another person for a brief moment to know about him in a more intimate and tender way.

All forms of communication are frail bridges at best. Even the written word can be misinterpreted. How much easier to misread messages traveling by the sensation of touch. But touch is a form of communication and it can sometimes say things we wish would remain unsaid. This can be pointedly true in sexually oriented touches between a husband and wife. The things we feel inside (or don't feel!) can travel through our touch like water through a pipeline.

Many a wife has been made to feel as though she were nothing more than a convenience to her man, and that sex is just another thing she is expected to do for him like doing the dishes and the laundry. His touch to her seems to have changed from one that said, "I am considering your value" to one that said, "I am considering my need." From a touch of "I want you because I love you" to "I am taking because you owe me." There is a painful difference between being used because of what we can give and being loved because of who we are. Although it is not an instant answer to a complicated problem, if a man finds his wife distant and unresponsive to his touch, he would do well to consider the possibility that either his attitude toward his wife has changed, or perhaps she thinks it has changed and she has become merely his routine convenience instead of his beloved.

It takes two to communicate effectively, and the woman's touch is also important to the man. A man may turn to work, or drink, or mountain climbing or a hundred other forms of competition to prove to himself and others that he is a true man because his wife refuses to let him feel worthy and masculine at home as she withdraws herself from his touch. The most painful words in all the world are, "I don't love you anymore" and it is easy for a man to believe this is what his wife means every time he feels her pull away from his embrace.

Within the marriage relationship the woman is created with a longing that only the true and open love of her own husband can fill (Gen. 3:16) while man is created with a need to be respected and honored as a man. He needs assurance of his worth that is best satisfied through the love of a good wife (Prov. 31:11).

Marriages are often less than we want them to be because they are formed by two people who are less than what God wants them individually to be. Natural love which seemed so strong and real at first gets lost in the fog of daily living and, as each person gravitates toward self-centeredness, two hearts full of natural, God-planted need grow lonely.

Sexual Touch
Man was told before sin entered the world to populate the earth. Sex was not born of sin but of the will of God. It is another of those unasked-for gifts He gives and is part of natural love. Like all other elements of natural love, sex can easily lose the lovely qualities God meant for it to have and become only an act of selfishness. But it is a part of natural love, and natural love is a part of God's total plan for human joy and pleasure.

Sexual touch is different from other forms of physical encounter. It has a mystery found nowhere else on earth: the mystery of "one flesh."

God first created this mystery in the garden of Eden (Gen. 2:24) and Jesus reemphasized it when

He said, "At the beginning of creation, God 'made them male and female.' For this reason a man will leave his father and mother and be united to his wife, and they two will become one flesh. So they are no longer two, but one. Therefore what God has joined together, let not man separate" (Mark 10:6-9, NIV).

Any sexual encounter forms such a bond. It matters not whether the encounter was within the bonds of legal marriage or out of it, neither does it matter if emotional affection played a part in the affair. Even relations with a prostitute set in motion the principles of "one flesh" (1 Cor. 6:15-16).

It continually amazes me how authors, playwrights, and professional advice-givers, leave the impression that a sexual encounter can be walked away from like a casual friendship or passing acquaintance. They seem to think two people can meet and share each other in body and/or heart, and then as the passion wanes, drift to their own separate ways, leaving nothing but a bittersweet memory in their wake. Such nonsense is passed off as portraying "real life." But according to the Bible this idea could not be farther from the truth. It is as foolish to think of a sexual encounter as a passing thing with no permanent consequences as it would be to think a man could breathe water as fish do.

The same "one flesh" law that is so valuable in building a solid marriage and so lovely when kept within bounds God set for it becomes a life-destroying force when active outside those bounds.

Judging by what I read, many people (often Christians) have found themselves in the quagmire of being "one flesh" with more individuals than God intended. To their grief and dismay they learn that such encounters do not die as easily as they are born.

All sin pays the wage of death (Rom. 6:23), but it seems as though sexual sins have a stubbornness about them found in few other sins. In Bible examples, they hang on through years and sometimes generations. Paul's writing indicates something extremely deadly about this particular kind of sin that sets it apart from the other sins (1 Cor. 6:18).

The law of "one flesh" by sexual touch is real and will not change to adapt to our opinions. It will not bend to accommodate what we want to believe.

If left to our own self-effort and given only the justice of the law, our hope of ever being free from the sticky glue of past sins (any kind of sins) would be futile. But God can overrule the law by His great power, sovereignty, and mercy. He can make iron to float when according to nature it ought to sink (2 Kings 6:6). He can stop the burn of fire when by nature flesh ought to be consumed (Dan. 3:13-28). And He can make the guilty man clean again:

"Come now, and let us reason together, saith the Lord: though your sins be as scarlet, they shall be as white as snow. . . . If ye be willing and obedient" (Isa. 1:18-19). "With man this is impossible but with God all things are possible" (Matt. 19:26, NIV).

The Touch of Man to Creation

Have you ever seen a child turn his face up toward the snow, close his eyes, and let the frozen flakes brush across his cheeks? Ever see a child pick a daisy, then sit down in the grass to examine, smell and taste each petal?

I always thought those odd-shaped, ragged things growing in the lawn were weeds until my children taught me differently. To them the bright yellow dandelion blooms were treasures of gold on a sea of emerald green. Jesus said that the royal robes of Solomon were not as lovely as one wild lily and when I studied the little flowers, I had to agree with the children. Even weeds were valuable because they could bring lightness to the heart when one took time to really see them.

A child looks at life with fresh clean eyes; he touches and feels the wonders of God's creation with an uninhibited awe for the mystery of it all. But we adults are too rushed, too wise, and too old to be delighted by the wonder of being alive.

A friend of mine broke her arm and was forced to wear a cast for six weeks. When at long, long last the cast was removed she showed up at Sunday School all smiles. She talked of the clean fresh feeling of air tingling her tender skin as the cast was cut away and how very good cool water felt splashing on the arm once again. Because her skin had been sealed off for so long, all the sensations of touching and feeling were fresh and new to her, giving her real delight with the common, everyday occurrence of being whole and well.

Other sensations often seem as important as touching. Light. Color. Smell. Taste. It is not till unpleasant circumstances seal us off from these everyday things that we realize how pleasing they were to us.

Corrie ten Boom spent many months in a Nazi prison camp and in her book, *The Hiding Place* she recalls how hungry she became for such a common thing as color. After being placed in solitary for a month she cried, "At least in the other cells there had been bright bits of clothing; the baroness' red hat, Frau Mikes' yellow blouse. How I regretted now my own lack of taste in clothes." And when at last a package from home was given her she delighted in the blue of a sweater and the red of a towel. "How Nollie understood the gray color-hunger of prison! She had even wrapped the cookies in gay cellophane."

My doctor has a sign on his office wall. "Don't worry. Don't hurry. Take time to smell the flowers." Next time you wash your hands, take time to really feel the rush of cool water and be grateful for it. The next time a milkweed blooms in your lawn take a moment to blow on it and watch the silk umbrellas float away. The next time it snows, turn your face up toward it and close your eyes.

If your days are as busy as mine, you will more than likely retire tonight with some of the things you intended to do still waiting for your attention tomorrow. Big problems will follow you from week to week and so will daily annoyances, such as where to find a parking space when none is available, and remembering to smile when you don't want to, because the boss said it was good for business. Daily living can become a heavy thing that doesn't make too much sense anyway and no doubt everyone has times of depression.

But, what a waste it is when we hurry through each day, ignoring the physical world around us. We can easily condemn society for squandering God's gift of clean air and water, but how often do we condemn ourselves for squandering the daily delights that God has made available to us through touch and taste and sight and sound?

We cannot be grateful for blessings of which we are not aware, and being grateful to God for all He supplies is both a stabilizing factor for today and an encouragement for tomorrow.

Robert Louis Stevenson said, "The world is so full of a number of things, I am sure we should all be as happy as kings." And I believe he was right.

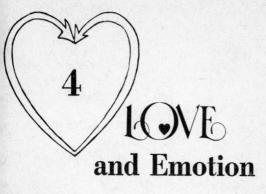

4

LOVE
and Emotion

Mary had been a Christian for many years. Active in the local church and growing in Christ, her life had been busy and happy, until the day infidelity butted its ugly head into her heart and her world fell into pieces. She knew that the Lord Jesus wanted her to reestablish a loving relationship with her husband once more. She made every effort, but found her path blocked by an impossible mountain —her total inability to feel any amount of love inside herself.

Mary yielded to her husband's embrace, said words of love when they were required, carried on her church work and household tasks with smoothness and dedication, yet her heart remained untouched. She had never been given to much emotional tenderness, nor did she place much value on feelings. Yet in those dark days when the feelings of love were altogether vanished, how to get those feelings back again became the central problem of her life.

Love Can Return

The warm feelings of love *are* important, and when
we lose them, it is only natural to want that joyful
sparkle to return. But getting it back is the problem. Can a dry marriage bloom again once the
feelings of love have gone? Can a stale spiritual life
find again the vitality it once knew? Can we learn
to love others from the heart when feelings of love
don't come naturally? Yes, to all three.

While writing under the inspiration of the Holy
Spirit, John gave the church at Ephesus (Rev.
2:1-5) the Lord's one rebuke because she had left
her first love. Her relationship to Jesus had grown
stale. She still did the works that looked like acts
of love but the warm, sweet closeness that had
existed at first was gone. She was like a woman
who still cleaned house and cooked for her husband
but took his presence for granted. She was meeting
responsibility on the surface but not feeling love in
the heart.

Jesus knew about this lost-love situation and He
had the solution. He advised these people, "Remember the height from which you have fallen!
Repent and do the things you did at first."

I could never explain all the whys and where-
fores of the Book of Revelation, but it does seem
to me that this Scripture gives the pattern to restore love that has grown stale, our love for Christ
and our love for the mate He has given us. The
first step is to admit something is missing.

In keeping with His ministry of exposing us to
the truth, the Holy Spirit often shows us when
something is missing in our relationship with God.
It might be a deep inner hunger to get alone with
God, like the desire to go home after a long journey,

or it could be an awareness that our sins do not grieve us as they once did. However He may choose to do it, the Spirit gets through to our spirit with the truth that something warm and real has slipped away. He can show this to us in human relationships too if we let Him. He may show our lack of compassion for some child, or remind us that, if we had more love for our husband or our wife, we would be more patient and less critical.

To know and admit that we are wrong is the first step to finding the solution. To know and admit that our love is not as warm as it should be is the first step toward restoring love gone stale.

The next step given to this church was, "Do the things you did at first." Love was to be restored by *doing* something. Note the close relationship between this statement and the one in Luke 12:34 when Jesus said, "For where your treasure is, there will your heart be also." Our "treasure" can be money, but it can also be time, a willingness to listen, cleaning another person's laundry, giving a compliment, patience, and a thousand other "gold coins" of encouragement and help. These acts of love for the purpose of investing treasure by creating love within our hearts is a practical way to restore lost love.

For example, a man could have started out his married life with a heart full of the emotions of love for his wife, but as time passed and business took more of his attention, thoughts of his wife were pushed farther back in his mind and the relationship grew stale. He no longer felt the way he once did toward her. Such a man doesn't have to live in that situation if he really wants to restore the warm love they once enjoyed. He regains lost love by investing treasure in the direction he wants his heart to go. Treasure of words and deeds, treasure of kind acts of consideration, and all of it given for the purpose of restoring something that was lost.

Husbands are particularly urged to watch that their emotional love for their wives does not grow cold. "Therefore take heed to your spirit, and let none deal treacherously against the wife of his youth" (Mal. 2:15). If we had no control over our spirits or feelings, and if they were intended to be our masters, it would have been foolish for God to tell us to "take heed" concerning them.

In her book, *Beyond Ourselves,* Catherine Marshall says that where the head is determined to go the heart is compelled to follow. I read these words six years ago and they have followed me ever since. I have seen this theory proven true in more ways than I could recount.

It may be in a relationship as mystical and spiritual as that between a human heart and his God. Or it could be as close and difficult as that between a husband and wife. It could be as loose and distant as that of a request for prayer for someone you have never personally met. By so doing, we can invest our treasure in the direction we want our hearts to go, especially if it is a direction pointed out by God's commands, and trust Him to place the emotional feelings of our hearts where our treasure is.

What if I Don't Feel Love?

Nearly all Christians can name some of the Ten Commandments found in the Old Testament. Even people who have never attended church regularly know a few of the "thou-shalt-nots" such as, "thou shalt not steal" or "thou shalt not kill." We can buy small replicas of the Ten Commandments engraved on charm bracelets. Once I got a set in a box of Cracker Jack. But if you study the whole Bible, you find another important commandment also. It is the command Jesus gave us just a few hours before He died. The Last Supper was over and His disciples clustered about in a saddened group, listening to Him tell about His imminent death. Jesus said, "A new commandment I give you, that ye love one another; as I have loved you" (John 13:34). It is as binding that we love others as it is that we don't murder. Such an idea causes problems for us because not everyone is lovable. In fact, most of us know some folks who aren't even likable! How can God expect us to love those we find difficult even to like? What about those who we feel are unworthy of our love?

At first glance it would seem as though God were squeezing the toothpaste tube at both ends. We must love others but we must love from pure motives. If I show love to people I don't even like, am I not a hypocrite? And if I don't show love, will I be branded rebellious for not keeping His commands? If we don't *feel* love, can we honestly and without hypocrisy *give* love? Yes, and there are several ways we can. One way is to love by proxy —not a far-out or complicated idea, for we do this almost every day. For example, Lonnie was a close friend of my husband. They went through military basic training together. He often double-dated with Bill and me. Several years later, when Lonnie and his wife were on their way to Spain, they stopped off at the home of Bill's parents. Though Lonnie and his wife were total strangers to Mom and Dad, they welcomed them warmly and gave them several good meals and a night's lodging. They didn't do this because they loved these strangers, but because they loved their son and their son loved these people.

God is our example in all phases of loving and He at times practices proxy love. David was called, "A man after God's own heart." David obeyed and loved God and God honored and loved David. Because God loved David, He extended extra mercy toward Solomon, David's son. Solomon turned aside to idols and deserved to have his kingdom taken from him, but God withheld punishment for a time because of His love for David. And when punishment finally came, it was not as severe as it would have been (1 Kings 11:6-13). David also practiced proxy love during his lifetime when he extended abundant kindness to Mephibosheth because he was the son of Jonathan (2 Sam. 9:7). This kindness was not earned by Mephibosheth but was given to him as pure grace because of David's love for Jonathan.

Every time we pray "in the name of Jesus" we are calling on God's proxy love. We want Him to hear us, not because we are good, or have earned His attention but because Jesus loves us and He is worthy to be heard.

We can show love to people whose habits or personalities irritate us, not because we feel love for them, but because Jesus loves them, and because He cares about them and has died for them. He has a place for them in His plan. Acting on God's behalf, functioning as His substitute, we can love others in His name, which is the most honorable motive for showing love.

Is Emotion Important?

Man is God's earthly masterpiece, created in His image (Gen. 1:26). Because we are, many of God's attributes are also ours. Like God, we have the ability to perform certain physical works, we have wills and decision-making abilities, and we have emotions.

We can't take credit for any of our abilities, since these are all gifts from our Father. We insult God when we take credit for these abilities, or when we pervert or destroy what He has given us. When a youth shoots his veins full of drugs so that his mind is permanently warped, he has shown a total lack of respect for the Creator. It is disrespectful to destroy the intelligence of one of His creations. We can easily see the sin and condemn the youth, but can we as easily see the wrong in denying, destroying, or warping the emotional side of man? Our emotions are a vital part of us, just as is our intelligence.

God created man with a body, a soul, and spirit (1 Thes. 5:23). Christians would not think of ripping out the soul or spirit of a man, yet in many, many Bible verses emotion and spirit seem so closely entwined as to be almost inseparable. Joy seems to be a function of the spirit (Luke 1:47), as does sorrow (1 Sam. 1:15); bitterness (Ezek. 3:14); jealousy (Num. 5:14); sadness (1 Kings 21:5); pride (Prov. 16:18); and grief (Isa. 54:6). To teach that feelings are unimportant, or that they should be totally ignored or suppressed, is to ignore a vital part of God's image which He has placed there for a purpose.

God feels emotion. He feels grief (Eph. 4:30; Psalm 95:10); love (John 3:16); pleasure (Deut.

6:15); anger (Deut. 9:20); delight (1 Kings 10:9); longing (Jer. 31:20) and other emotions. He created man with the ability to feel, for He created the spirit within a man (Zech. 12:1). We cannot dissect feeling from our lives and still remain the whole persons God meant us to be.

The world might be a much less complicated place if there were no such thing as emotion. If all matters were settled according to cold fact and no one was ever compelled to action by compassion or grief, most of our interpersonal and international problems might be eliminated. But the world would also be less alive. People would be like machines, and the word "heart" would mean only a functional blood pump.

How Reliable Is Emotion?
Emotion is a vital part of man but we dare not depend on it for total guidance or trust it will never betray us. Emotions can be swayed by everything from indigestion to a good book. Emotions are affected by the weather, the bank balance, and pregnancy. No one of intelligence would try to build a house on a foundation of shifting beach sand. Neither should anyone try to lean on emotion to build a life. The writer of Proverbs declared, "He that trusteth in his own heart is a fool" (Prov. 28:26).

We need something far more stable than feelings. We need a basis that will be the same regardless of indigestion, weather, or the bank balance. God has given us that stable basis, the Bible.

It is wonderful when we feel the presence of God lifting our burdens and refreshing our spirits, but if in a time of trouble we don't feel Him, we have something more certain than our emotions to assure us that He has never left us. The writer of Hebrews quoted Deuteronomy 31:6, "Never will I leave you; never will I forsake you" (Heb. 13:5). The longest chapter in the Bible, Psalm 119, is dedicated to the steadfastness and ability of the Word of God.

Few things on earth are as binding as a legal contract duly signed and sealed. In God's Word we have such a written legal document, signed and sealed with His own blood, confirmed both by miracles and the testimonies of thousands upon thousands who have put their trust in his contract and found it steadfast both for life and death.

Emotions stir our minds and hearts and compose a vital side of lives. We have the ability to touch others emotionally and God Himself stirs our emotions by His touch. And we can know our feelings have a foundation to rest on, His steadfast Word. "Forever, O Lord, Thy word is settled in heaven" (Ps. 119:89).

The Place of Emotions

Everything in creation seems to have a place and function. Ecologists claim that every form of life has a place in the food chain and when one link of the chain becomes extinct or is removed from a particular locality the whole chain could become weak and chaotic. God has a place and purpose for each species of animal. On a human and spiritual level, God has a place and purpose for each Christian within the Church, and a place and purpose for each member of the family unit. In the same way, God has a place and purpose for our emotional makeup.

Our problems begin when our personal makeup —our intellects, our emotions, and our wills—get out of control or function improperly. God has ordained that both body and emotions would be subject to the will. The will is like the steering mechanism in a car or the rudder on a boat. The will determines which course of action we take. When we give the rule of our lives over to the appetites of the body, we are living as enemies of the cross of Christ, whose "destiny is destruction, their god is their stomach" (Phil. 3:19, NIV). Likewise, when we give the rule of our lives to our emotions we have changed God's order and what results is emptiness, confusion, and defeat. The Bible compares a man who has no rule over his emotions (his spirit) to a city that is broken down and without walls around it (Prov. 25:28). Such a man is defenseless.

The commands of God are our road map, showing us the direction to take in our search for freedom and happiness. But often our emotions crave to go in direct opposition to God's commands. His commands tie us down and keep us from going in the direction we want. We are tempted to reason that if it feels good at the moment, if we want it, if it gives us pleasure, why not do it? But, like a kite, we don't find freedom by cutting ourselves loose from the string that holds us, or we would fall in a confused spiral to the ground. Kites cannot fly without the restraining cord. So we fulfill our purpose by keeping ourselves bound by God's restraints, which serve an even higher purpose for us than the string does for the kite.

Emotions are important, because they are one of the ways in which we are like God. Emotions were given to us to make our lives real and rich. But when, because of our fallen nature, emotions lead us to disobey God's commands, we must set our will to take the path God's Word lays down. In the end this is the only way to freedom and joy. So if the Son [Jesus] sets you free, you will be free indeed (John 8:36).

An Emotional Touch from God

All through the Bible we see God's Spirit touching things, nations, and people. He brooded over the face of the waters when earth was darkness and void, and out of the confusion brought life and light. In other places He reached down to pick out individual men for specific purposes and made them walk like giants on the earth. People like David, Abraham, Moses, Deborah, Mary, and scores of others were set apart by God when He touched them.

The birth of Christ Jesus was a new and intimate touch between God and man. God the Son wrapped Himself in human flesh and came to earth to live and walk among us. And in a most intimate and personal way, the Holy Spirit now lives and works on the earth in the lives of those who accept and welcome Him (1 Cor. 3:16; 1 John 4:12-13; 2 Cor. 6:16; Rom. 8:9). This touch from God sets us apart from the rest of the world, makes us children of God, and provides the possibility for an abundant, joy-filled life. The steps to reach out to God, who is already reaching for us, are both simple and profound:

1. Admit to Him that we are sinners (Rom. 3:23; Rom. 10:9; 1 John 1:9).

2. Have a sincere desire to follow His standards

and leading (Luke 6:46; Acts 26:20; Matt. 7:24-27).

3. Ask Him to give us of this Spirit according to the promise He made us in His Word (Luke 11:13; Rev. 3:20).

Becoming a Christian means receiving a Person—not seeking an experience. The process of making contact, and receiving into ourselves the presence of the Almighty God is an awesome, fearful experience. Not many people can approach marriage, or adoption, or change in career without some hint of fear. To have cold feet is common even in the bravest person. The difference between a coward and a hero is that the hero feels fear and continues to press forward, while a coward feels fear and runs for a hiding place.

The usual reason we meet fear and defeat it is because we want what is on the other side enough to face the obstacles. How many young bridegrooms have cleared their throats, wiped the sweat from their hands, and asked themselves, "Am I sure I want to go through with this?" Then the girl he loves enters the room. His heart jumps and he mentally answers his own question. "Yep, I am sure . . . I think." When the young man finally stands before the preacher and says, "Yes, I do accept her as my wife" he is legally, morally, and publicly joined to her. He says openly that he is willing to fulfill his obligations to her and is accepting on faith that she will keep the promises she has made to him. Everything he has and is belongs to his wife and everything she has and is belongs to him.

A Spiritual Touch

When we make our decision for Jesus, we take our stand and say both by word and action, "Yes, I do accept Him to be my Saviour" and are legally, morally, and publicly joined to Him. We say openly that we are willing to fulfill our obligations to Him and accept on faith that He will keep the promises He has made us in His Word. Everything we have and are belongs to Him and everything He has and is belongs to us. And frankly, we get the best of the bargain!

A spiritual touch like this is hard to forget about, just as a real marriage ceremony is hard to be uncertain about. Either you are married or you aren't. Either you have made such a contract as this one with the Lord or you haven't.

One month after the marriage ceremony you may still find yourself saying, "But I don't *feel* married!" Yet, you know beyond doubt that you *are* because it happened. You remember the moment you said, "I do." After you make a commitment to Jesus, after you are saved or born again, you may see times when you are tempted to complain, "But I don't *feel* like a child of God." But you *are* a child of God just the same. You know this because you were present when it happened. You remember the moment you said, "I do."

Spiritual touches from God's own hand do not stop with a commitment to Jesus—they begin there. I have heard pastors say they would not ask people in the congregation to stand and tell what Jesus has done for them because they all tell about when they were saved 20 or 25 years ago. "I don't want to hear about what God did for them years ago! What has He done this week?" How sad that so many Christians seem to have nothing to tell about their personal relationships with Christ beyond what happened when they were saved years ago!

Just as love between two people gives birth to an emotional response to one another, love between us and our God gives birth to emotional responses. Just as two people in love want to meet each other's needs, so love between us and God should result in our obedience and His provision of our needs.

People in love with God can testify to a touch from Him daily. They feel inclined to pray about pressing burdens and feel them lift as the Lord takes them. They can tell Him about needs (even the need for a parking space when town is crowded, or about a complicated situation that looked hopeless when they first talked to Him about it six months ago). If we don't sense His loving touch we are missing something we could have.

Encouragement as an Emotion

Just as we feel defeat and depression inside, so we often feel courage and hope. When we seek to encourage others, we touch their emotions, and, within the Christian fellowship, encouraging one another is something we are prompted, even commanded to do. "Encourage one another daily" (Heb. 3:13). "Let the word of Christ dwell in you richly as you teach and counsel one another with all wisdom, and as you sing psalms, hymns, and spiritual songs with gratitude in your hearts to God" (Col. 3:16, NIV).

Our individuality is a gift granted us by God. Like snowflakes, no two of us are exactly the same. Yet, down deep inside, when we consider the basic needs, the reasoning power, and emotions, there is a vast similarity. It is possible for us to look beyond the differences of mankind and touch similar feelings and emotions even though they may seem to be expressed differently in other cultures.

On TV the other day I saw a news story about films on foreign television. There were Adam, Hoss, and Little Joe Cartwright galloping across the Nevada range yelling in perfect Japanese. Almond-eyed children with olive skin who didn't know what a "Nevada" was, still giggled when Hoss got a bucket of water dumped on his head and shivered when Little Joe faced the bad guy in a shoot-out.

Ideas from books translated from one language to another can cross the lines of cultural background and stir others living half a world away.

The Bible was divinely inspired, yet written by man, and it explores the depths of man better than any other book. It exposes man's needs without God and shows the possibilities of man rightly related with God. We open up its pages and truly meet ourselves. We open the Bible and read of people of a different environment, different color, different *everything*, living eight or ten thousand years ago. Yet, we can in reading it say, "That's me, Lord. That's just like me!" We see reflected in them the same weaknesses, failures, and misunderstandings that we find in ourselves.

We may never write a great musical score that endures through time, or be a philosopher whose writings alter the path of the thinking world, but God has endowed each of His children with a capacity to touch one another emotionally. Because emotional and spiritual responses are so intertwined, it is possible to produce eternal results.

The touch of encouragement must always be based on the truth of God's Word. We could tell another, "Don't worry, there is no such place as 'hell' " but our comforting words wouldn't do that person much good when the gates of death are slammed shut behind him and he is sealed in prison with the damned. The sound doctrine of truth is the only real encouragement. Paul wrote, "He must hold firmly to the trustworthy message as it has been taught, so that he can encourage others by sound doctrine and refute those who oppose it" (Titus 1:9, NIV).

Physical touch is worthless if it is not the response of true love. It can become one of the vilest tools of the devil when its foundations are not rooted in holy love. Likewise, emotional touches of encouragement and instruction are worthless if they are not backed by love and truth. If we encourage others to follow a trail we ourselves are unwilling to pursue, or instruct them with a holier-than-thou attitude, such hypocrisy is a terrible evil before God.

Few things do as much harm to other Christians as false doctrine and hypocritical people. And few things can do so much good as the personal witness of people who have tested the promises of God and found them trustworthy.

Christians need touches of truth and encouragement from those who are wiser in the faith than themselves! How much it means to us to see God's hand alive and working in the lives of flesh-and-blood people like ourselves!

The way of love is hard and often perplexing. When you have found a smooth path leading around a boulder, mark the trail so someone else can follow. When you fall into a hole, stick up a warning sign before you press on. When you have reached a mountain peak and breathe the cool, clean air, recognize that this is not the end of the trail since many peaks rise ahead. Enjoy your well-earned rest and taste the freshness all around you. But don't forget others who are struggling on the trail below, where you were not long ago. Take time to remember how hard it was and call down a word of encouragement. The one traveling behind you just might be me and I need all the help I can get!

5

LOVE
and Saying So

Kay* had been divorced for less than a year and, being the breadwinner for herself and two teenage children, it was all she could do to make ends meet. Often she and the children did without things they really needed. Kay worked eight hours a day. Driving to her job and back took another two hours, and she was still responsible for housework, cooking, shopping, school and church activities just as she had been before the divorce. She was terribly lonely. But the hardest trial she faced was the poor relationship between herself and her 15-year-old daughter we'll call Tracy. Violent quarrels went on almost daily and sometimes the two would even strike each other.

Tracy worked after school and on weekends in a local drugstore. Pouring soft drinks and dusting merchandise brought her at that time only 50 cents an hour, yet, by Christmas of her first year she had saved $25. Tracy used all her savings as a down payment on a $49.95 coat for her mother and signed a contract to pay the balance at the rate of $5 a week.

When Kay opened her fine present Christmas morning she felt crushed and guilty. She knew how many long hard hours Tracy must have worked to pay for such a nice coat. She knew there was no gift she had given her daughter that was nearly so expensive. Because of her love for Tracy, Kay refused to accept the present and insisted the coat be returned to the store.

Tracy, in return, was crushed by her mother's refusal to take the present. She desperately needed her mother's love and approval. She had poured all she had into that one sacrificial gift because she wanted to please and comfort her mother after the loss of her husband, and when her mother refused to accept the gift, Tracy felt she was refusing to accept her. Hurt and bitter she stormed, "I won't take it back and you can't make me!" Another violent quarrel followed.

Both Kay and Tracy were Christians. Both loved and desperately needed to be loved by the other. Both shared the same problem: they could not understand the way the other person was trying to say "I love you." It is tragic when others are trying to say they love us by using deeds rather than words and we fail to understand what their actions really mean.

When love is present in the heart, it tries to find a way to express itself, just as surely as a stream tries to find its way to the sea. A stream, however, cannot always take the most direct course to its destination and love does not always express itself in ways we find easy to understand. Due to differences in personality and background, the words,

"I love you," may be difficult to hear in the deeds of another.

Susan* was an unrealistic, romantic young woman. She had married Jerry five years before and, though she loved him very much, it seemed the romance had gone from their marriage and she longed to have it back. One evening when Jerry returned from work, he found the children being cared for by a neighbor and a candlelight dinner for two spread on the table. Jerry was tired and wanted to relax with the paper before eating. He did not like candlelight because he couldn't see his food and told Susan how foolish it was for them to pay a baby-sitter while they were home eating supper.

Within a year, Jerry and Susan were on the brink of a divorce. Jerry could not understand his wife's bitterness. To his mind he had always been a faithful husband and good provider. What more could she have wanted from him? Jerry did not realize that in her perhaps foolish, romantic way, Susan had tried many times to say, "I love you" and each time when he thwarted her efforts he was being understood to say, "I don't love you, neither do I want what you have to offer me."

A large stream can be blocked by a small beaver, who can dam it up. Before the stream can flow on, it must bend a little or change its form. Our ability to express love to those around us can also be blocked. Satan has been capitalizing on our hang-ups ever since we were born and he can use our natural temperaments or unpleasant childhood experiences to keep us from communicating our love to others in ways they want to hear it. A person who is shy by nature may find it more difficult to express his love in words than someone who is a natural extrovert, and those who have been trained to keep their feelings on a tight rein can find it almost impossible to express their feelings verbally. So we express these feelings in other ways.

Suppose someone had grown up in a home where boys were expected to be "little men" and never cry or express emotion. He may never once have heard his parents tell each other, "I love you" and when he marries, words of love to his wife come hard to his own tongue. Soon they may vanish from his vocabulary and instead of words, he may give his wife money, "for no reason." But his wife may grow tired of his money. She may have a job of her own and some months bring home more than he does. She longs to hear words of love and wonders if her husband cares for her at all. Judging that her husband has stopped loving her when he stopped saying so with words, she may become defensive and distant. She may not know that every time he gives her money he is, in fact, trying very hard to say, "I love you."

Choosing the Right Language

The language of love has as many dialects as there are people to express it. It hurts us when we say, "I love you" with a deed or a look, and our beloved ignores what we say. Yet we often neglect to learn the language our beloved is using to reach out to us in his native tongue.

For years it puzzled and irritated me that every time my husband and I hit a domestic snag, he would come around shortly after and say, "Let's go check cows."

I don't like cows and invariably have more important things to do than bounce around the pasture in a truck. Cows were not my language. When we were first married and I wanted to say, "I love you," after a rough spot, I tried to look warm and tender, and dress up nicely when he came in from work. But my efforts usually brought no results at all. Almost always, it seemed to make the situation worse instead of better.

Then one day it dawned on me that while I was condemning him for not understanding my language, I had made no effort at all to understand his. Bill's cattle were his lifework and chief interest. An invitation to come with him to count the cows was an invitation to come join his life; it was his own special way of saying, "I still love you." So, I started accepting his invitations. I have never learned to like cattle, but I have learned that when the one you are married to is trying to say the words of love (regardless of what form they take) you won't turn a deaf ear if you care anything about your marriage.

We are supposed to get smarter as we go along, and in time even I figured out that the language people understand best is usually their own native tongue. Perhaps I should not only listen to Bill's cow language, I should try speaking a little of it myself. Now I know that when nerves get tense and the words of love seem dry, I can always get through to Bill with the message that I indeed still care by offering, "Come on, honey, let's go count the cows." Then my husband, the man who would not respond at all to my make-up-and-clothes language, responds to his native tongue with a smile, hug, and passionate kiss.

Learning to recognize, accept, and even speak

another's love language may not be all there is to learning love, but it sure helps!

The Spoken Word of Love

Barbara* told me about the time she and her husband had reached what seemed to be a dead end in their marriage. They lived in the same house and performed the same duties they always had, but due to the infidelity of one partner the feelings of love had been drained from their relationship. There had been no dramatic fights to end the marriage. Rather, like an undernourished child, it weakened and expired with nothing more than a pitiful whimper. There seemed only two paths open to them: either stay married for the children's sake or admit that their love was gone and get a divorce. Both paths looked ugly and cold to Barbara, but what else was there?

Late one night her husband, John,* unable to sleep, got up and rattled aimlessly around the kitchen, then returned and sat on the edge of the bed in the moonlight. Barbara wanted once more to feel love for this man stir inside her, but the feelings would not come. Neither of them spoke for a long time, then with tears in his voice John asked, "Just tell me one thing, do you love me at all anymore?" Barbara did not answer right away. She wanted to say, "yes." But wouldn't those words be a lie? she wondered. She thought back to the definition of love given in 1 Corinthians 13 and reminded herself that love was not as much what she felt as it was what she was willing to do. She did not at that moment feel either forgiven or forgiveness toward her husband, but she was willing to learn how to make these things true. She did not at that moment feel love inside herself but she was *willing* to love.

On that basis she answered in honesty, "Yes, John, I love you." There were no lightning flashes nor rushes of tenderness, but Barbara believes that those five words marked the turning point for their relationship. During the weeks to come, Barbara earnestly prayed that the Lord would restore to them the feelings of love they had lost through sin and neglect, and over and over again she said the words "I love you" to her mate. Sometimes she had the feelings to back up those words; sometimes she didn't, but the words were always true for they did not depend on her feelings but on her willingness.

Piece by piece, God answered her prayers, and stroke by stroke He painted the living portrait of a happy, love-filled home. Today Barbara and John are more in love than they were six months after the wedding.

It is difficult to find anything more powerful or sweeter than the actual spoken words of love. The writer of Proverbs said, "Pleasant words are as sweet as honeycomb, sweet to the soul, and health to the bones" (Prov. 16:24). Love words are sweet; they are something we delight in that gives us pleasure and joy. They are like frosting on a cake or ice cream to a child. Love words bring health deep inside us when our spirit is broken and our heart is bruised. Words of love are vital to the mental health of us all and no child can grow as God meant for him to without words of love and commendation.

There is power in words of love—power to encourage, and lift, and build. Who can guess how many lives have been snatched from destruction, how many tears have been dried, and how many people on the edge of despair have been given a glimmer of hope by a word of love spoken at the proper moment? I have seen people's moods change from gloom and confusion to joy and certainty as they realized for the first time that Jesus really loved them. I have seen tears of gratitude flow when for the first time in years people faced each other and said words that meant, "I love you." Words of love can break down walls and build up foundations. They can turn off bitterness and make sympathy flow like a river. They can bind up wounds and comfort the lonely. Beyond doubt, there is power in the spoken word of love.

One way this power is seen is in the fact that *words* of love actually encourage *feelings* of love to grow. Even when our heart is cold and the emotions of love seem dead, pouring on spoken words of love can be the water that revives them. Spoken words create an atmosphere in which feelings can do to our hearts what a spark plug does to an engine. The next time you are involved with a marriage that has grown stale or a strained relationship between a parent and child, try applying the power of open, honest, spoken words of love.

Spend time thinking up new ways to say, "I love you" when the old ways seem to lose their impact. Say it verbally and repeatedly. Say it physically with an embrace. Say it with a kind deed. Say it with a prayer. When you have presented the Gospel to someone and that person fails to respond, when the church fellowship breaks apart into separate armed camps, when personal relationships are not what they ought to be, apply the power of open, expressed love and pour it on in generous supply.

This power is effective not only in our relationships with others, but with God as well. If your love affair with Jesus has become a religion (and that is about the worst thing that could happen to it!) put out an effort to find new ways to say, "I love You, Lord." Write it down, speak it out loud, breathe it in silent prayer, meditate on the words, "Jesus, I love You" and you may find new life being breathed into a relationship you suspected had expired.

The Power Block of Unbelief

Beyond doubt there is much power in expressed love. But this power can be blocked, it can be made completely ineffective by our stubbornness. Gunpowder is a powerful substance that can blow up stumps standing in the way of progress. It can blast out yards of earth to change the course of a river. But this powerful material can be made as impotent as ashes by simply soaking it in water. Likewise, all the good and powerful forces of expressed love can be rendered totally ineffective by the dampening effects of unbelief. Love, the most powerful force in the world, can be made void by the most dangerous thing in the world, unbelief.

A man could love his wife deeply and tell her so by every means available to him. He could speak his love and act his love, but if his wife fails to believe him, all his efforts are in vain. His love could never provide her with the comfort or courage that it might have provided because she won't accept it. Just as half a pair of scissors can never do the task it was designed for unless the other blade is in cooperation, so love cannot perform the task it was designed to do unless it is both offered by someone and accepted by someone. It takes someone to love and someone to be loved just as surely as it takes two halves of the scissors to cut. Even the pure and powerful love of God does not change us when we refuse to accept that it is real, and refuse to believe.

Since love is such a powerful thing and so desperately needed it would seem unthinkable for a person to be offered love and yet refuse to accept it. However, it happens both in families and between Creator and creature. "Why," we wonder. Why would anyone ever hear words of love and refuse to believe that it is real? What is in us that steps between our ears and our hearts so that our need to be loved goes on unsatisfied even though love is available?

There are probably many answers, but here are at least three:

1. *Unbelief frees us from responsibility.* Everyone senses a responsibility to respond to love freely offered. We often soothe our gnawing guilt by convincing ourselves that the love we were offered was not real and therefore we are not guilty when we fail to respond.

It is easier for a man to divorce his wife if he insists on believing she doesn't love him. One partner may plead, "I love you, don't go," but the other walks out the door saying, "No you don't." If he is able to convince himself, it will greatly ease his feelings of guilt.

Failure to believe can release us from responsibility and set us free to pursue our own lust. More than one affair has been justified in the eyes of the guilty person by reasoning that his mate doesn't love him anymore.

Likewise, if a sinner can convince himself that the love of God is a myth, it is an easy matter to believe that he is not responsible to God for his actions. Unbelief can be an open door that frees us to chase our own selfish ends and to cut us loose from the responsibility of fulfilling our obligations.

2. *Sometimes we don't believe others love us because we can't love ourselves.* In some pursuits the devil is glad to give us a helping hand. One such pursuit is the search for imperfections within ourselves. As long as Satan can blow these faults out of proportion and use them to bind or grieve us, he will joy in giving us a guided tour through all the dark corners of our hearts to see our past sins and present faults. He knows that if he can keep us looking at and concentrating on our sin and not the Saviour, he will have the battle nearly won. He will remind us of every sin, every physical defect, and every flaw of character until we become so full of self-hate that we can never accept the fact that anyone could love us.

Satan is on a constant lookout to find any handle in our lives he can grab or any hole in which he can stick a claw. Once he gets a grip he will hang on for dear life. It may be some scar on your soul by a bad experience from years gone by. Or he may find a personality that is naturally shy or that naturally desires a lot of physical affection and use this as a handle to pry his way into the mind. But whatever he finds, he is sure to make that one sore spot swell and hurt until it fills our lives completely and we are convinced that we will never amount to anything and never know anything but failure.

For example, if someone studies himself in a

mirror and notices that he has attractive eyes, Satan will immediately counter, "Yes, but look at your nose! It is so wide and flat! No one could ever love a face with a nose like that sticking in the middle of it." And should he begin to wonder if the grace of God is enough to cover his sins and use him despite his faults, all hell will be stirred as if an alarm has gone off and many demons will be sent out to bring before that person everything he has ever done that even remotely resembles sin. They all seem to shout, "No, not you. God doesn't want the likes of you! And besides, remember that ugly nose."

If the victim should be a Christian and consider doing something for the Lord, hell's forces will call, "You know what a big ego you have. Remember when you tried to serve the Lord last year? It was nothing more than your ego then, and remember how you failed? Better leave the serving to those who are more noble than yourself."

Nowhere in the Bible does God look down on a man or call him a worm to be crushed under God's heel. He created man and placed him in a position of honor. A realistic view of ourselves and an ability to be as kind to our own soul as we ought to be to others is one of the first steps in learning how to love, and learning to believe that others can love us too.

3. *Sometimes we don't believe love is real because someone has failed us in the past.* True love never fails (1 Cor. 13:8) but the feelings some people *call* "love" do fail, and it is this failure that can hurt us so badly that we become bitter and doubt love the next time it is expressed to us.

When someone whose love we have every right

to expect turns away or when he says he loves us and his works show differently, we can become disillusioned. Perhaps it was our parents or our marriage partner, someone who has taken our love and then failed to return to us the things we thought we had a right to receive. Such an experience can make all other offers of love seem like a mirage in the desert to a thirsty man—a vision he wishes with all his heart were true but a vision experience has taught him not to trust.

It can be a fearful thing to trust in the love of another and lay ourselves open to the possibility of being hurt. It is risky to accept and respond to the fact that someone loves us. It takes faith in others, and if through past experience our faith has been taken advantage of, our fear can be a high, difficult mountain to overcome.

Expressing Love to the Lord

Regardless of how it is expressed, regardless of possible problems in accepting the love of another as being real, open expressions of love are both powerful and sweet. It is good to express our love toward one another and the same is true of our love for God. In fact, His people are commanded to express love to Him. Such a command should not be difficult to accomplish for, as stated before, when love is present in the heart it will try to find expression and if we truly love God, we will try to find ways to say so.

By song (Isa. 42:10); by poetry (Ps. 145); by dance (Ex. 15:20; Ps. 149:3); by musical instruments (Ps. 150); by every means and in all situations, God's people praise their Creator. "Let the redeemed of the Lord say so!" encouraged the writer of Psalm 107:2, because celebrating and shouting our love for our Lord until the hills echo with our rejoicing is a privilege reserved in a special way for those children He has redeemed. No other creature God created can feel the joy of praise quite like man. No angel can sing His praises, no cherubim can feel the greatness of God like a man, because none of them has been created in His image, then fallen, and once again experienced His grace. Only those with the capacity to grieve have the capacity to rejoice. Only those who have been lost will fully know the goodness of being redeemed.

Expressing our love for God in both word and deed is a vital part of the Christian experience. It is giving back to God our gratitude for all He has given us.

Much of this expressed love comes in the form of verbal praise; words that we speak to glorify and magnify God while we tell of His love. We can praise God standing up (2 Chron. 20:19). We can praise Him with singing (Ezra 3:11). We can praise Him in a congregation (Ps. 22:22); in a mixed multitude of people (Ps. 109:30); or with a select group of leaders (Ps. 107:32).

No matter how much we offer praise with others or approve of the beautiful praise of a choir or gifted poet, it can never take the place of our own personal praise to our own personal God. Our hearts must praise, not just listen to or approve of others praising Him. David had an orchestra of 4,000 members whose sole duty was to continually offer praise to the Lord (1 Chron. 23:5), yet David did not use this as a substitute for his personal involvement with his own praise of God. He sought to offer praise personally seven times a day (Ps. 119:164).

We are taught to praise our God in all situations, both when we are full and satisfied (Ps. 63:5) and when we are poor and needy (Ps. 74:21). We praise Him *in* our difficult situations because we know that He is able to see us through them, not *for* situations as though we were glad to be in pain or to blame God for our problem.

God commands us to love Him. Jesus said the greatest of all commandments was, "Hear, O Israel; The Lord our God is one Lord: And thou shalt love the Lord thy God with all thy heart, and with all thy soul, and with all thy mind, and with all thy strength" (Mark 12:29-30). He expects us to show that love in praise (Ps. 150). God does not command these things because His ego needs a boost, or because He is primarily interested in building Himself up, but because these things are good and profitable for a man. His love is centered on our benefit and even His request for our love and praise is engineered for our good.

Praising God reminds us of His ability and power. When we praise the Lord for victories of the past, our assurance that He can handle the future grows stronger. Repeatedly throughout the Bible rings the call to *remember* what the Lord has done. This is not limited to what He has done for us alone, but for what He has done for others as well.

One of the sweetest experiences I ever had with praise was when I realized I could join in the song of Miriam and praise my own God for delivering the Children of Israel from Egyptian slavery. I had read the Exodus story probably a hundred times. I had known about it all my life and believed it. I had seen it through the medium of a motion picture and watched the sea parting to let God's people through. But the story became real to me in a new and vital way when I began to realize it was *my* God who had done this and I could personally praise Him for it.

We are told to publish far and wide the wonderful works of God and tell to the world what He has done for us (Ps. 26:7). We are to let our children know what the Lord has done for us personally (Josh. 4:21-22) so that they might remember and praise Him too. As our children become fully convinced that God has indeed come to our aid when we called on Him, they will find hope for their own lives as well. Remembering God's might is a vital part of real praise.

Praising God also helps to keep our trials and problems in their proper perspective. My children learned a little song from television which says, "That's about the size, where you put your eyes, that's about the size of it. / Oh, the big becomes the little when you move it back a bit; / the large becomes the small which is just the opposite, / of the huge that is the dinky when you move on back a bit, / and that's about the size of it."

How true! A $5 bill may seem like small change when times are good but if sickness comes or the union goes on strike that same $5 can look like a fortune. A petty problem, when it belongs to someone else, becomes a giant when it sits in our own lap.

One thing makes the difference between a problem looking like a dragon or a lizard—our attitude. The size of our troubles depends more on where we put our eyes than on the problems themselves, and when we are engaged in praising the Lord our eyes are focused on His ability and away from whatever is hurting us at the moment. Looking at Jesus can make our trials shrink like a deflated balloon. Keeping a proper perspective on life is helped by keeping our hearts full of praise for our God.

We know from the prophecy of Scripture that love will become increasingly rare as the coming of Jesus grows nearer. People will be harder and less concerned with the welfare of others. Self-gratification will be all that matters and because *self* can never be satisfied, loneliness, confusion, and emptiness will be all many people ever know.

In days like these, how important it is for us to express actively what love we have inside us and to use the power He has placed in our hands! In the church family, in the home, between husband and wife, between man and God, let us tell others how much we love them.

---

*True stories, fictitious names

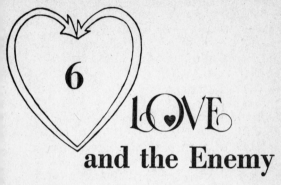

6

LOVE

and the Enemy

About 1666, a long-haired fellow named Isaac Newton discovered some of the principles God uses to run the universe. His discovery ranks him as one of the greatest scientists that ever lived. One of his principles states, "For every action there is an equal and opposite reaction."

While that may not sound too profound on the surface, any fellow who could get knocked on the head by a falling apple, and use the incident to figure out the law of gravity in relation to the movement of the stars and planets is bound to go a long way.

Action and reaction is what makes cars go, keeps airplanes up and bruises our toes when we stub them. One force pushes one way and a different force pushes back the other way. This physical principle is a dependable law. I believe there is a similar principle or law of action and reaction in force in the spiritual world and that it is clearly seen in the realm of love. Love expressed is an active force and every demonstration causes a reaction from the evil one as sure as the laws of gravity and motion.

Let a local church become involved in real revival where people start caring about others in the community and start to rob hell of a few would-be residents and the devil will waste no time sending one of his servants to stir up trouble. He will find some old grudge in a shallow heart and try to use it to crack the fellowship of the family of believers, or he will stir up pride in a leader, or he will try to substitute man's logic and good intentions for God's leading.

Let a Christian rededicate his life to the Master and begin to seek the Spirit for leadership and strength, and it will not be long before his way is hindered by some kind of trouble.

Let a wife decide that she is going to lay aside wounded pride and self-will in order to give love to her husband to win him to her Lord, or let neighbors decide they will learn the art of spreading love and Christian concern among those with whom they come in contact, or let a businessman decide that he will seek the best for those who work for him and deal in the honesty Christian love demands, and in each case something usually goes wrong to make all the firm decisions and good intentions twice as hard to keep as each of these people thought it would be. Because the devil is real, he can be depended on to move against our acts of love.

Some people scoff at the idea of the existence of a real, live devil. Others fear and cringe at the thought. Still others observe with mild curiosity and pass by, thinking if they ignore the thought of him, the possibility of his existence will go away. Even if I were not a firm believer in the Bible, I think I would still believe there is a devil. I feel like the fellow who said, "I know there is a devil because I've done business with him!" I believe two of the most urgent needs of modern Christians is first, to have an adequate concept of the holiness and power of God and, second, to have an adequate concept of our enemy, Satan.

A pastor I know gives this illustration from an experience in his ministry. He had been asked to counsel a young wife whose husband was mentally unbalanced. The man would seem to get along fairly well for a while. Then suddenly he would start slapping his wife, breaking up furniture, threatening to kill everyone in sight. He was unable to hold a job because of his violent temper and was becoming physically ill. His wife was afraid for her own life and her children's lives.

The pastor told the woman if she would only go to her husband, put her arms around him and say, "Honey, I love you and forgive you" that it would be the first step to recovery for the family. But in desperation the woman pleaded, "He may come home and kill us all tonight but I can't say, 'I love you.' I just can't!"

Next, he went to the husband and told him the same thing, "Go to your wife and tell her you love her." Again the reply was, "I can't."

In an effort to break the impasse, the pastor began to question the man about his past life and learned that his father had been a drunk who repeatedly beat and shamed him as a child. "Even though he is long dead," said the man, "the thought of him comes to my mind and I can't stand it. I hate him and everyone else. I want to destroy and tear things apart. I hate him. I hate him!"

Through counseling, the pastor encouraged this man to consider the devil as being at the source of the problem. "Everytime thoughts of your father trouble your mind," he said, "I want you to think of your father, but behind him I want you to try to imagine a shadowy figure who is bigger and stronger than he is. This shadow will be pulling strings like a puppeteer, and the strings will be attached to your father. It was this shadowy figure, Satan, who made your father beat you and do the bad things he did. Blame all your hate and all your hurt on him."

In time the man began to realize that his father was not fully to blame for what he had done to him as a child. I suppose a psychologist would explain the man's healing in other terms. Probably the father was unloving because he himself had not been loved as a child and he was only passing on the poison to another generation. The devil's purposes are accomplished anytime we, for whatever reason, don't or can't love one another. In the final analysis, since Adam and Eve's sin, all our emotional and psychological defects are indirectly a result of Satan's work.

In such cases as the pastor dealt with, psychologists might try to accomplish the same goal on strictly a physical and emotional level by trying to get the victim to stop hating his father and get him to turn the feeling of hate into something else —perhaps pity, by showing that the father himself was a victim. When the pastor placed the blame on the evil one, and ultimately he *was* to blame, the man found both emotional and spiritual release.

Whether or not the pastor used the best emotional healing technique, the shadowy figure behind the father was real.

God does not ask His children to view life as if it were all cream and roses. He wants us to see the truth. The Word of God is very clear in showing that evil, pain, and wrong are part of our experience in this world. God does not expect us to close our eyes to the reality of evil any more than we are to close our eyes to the reality of God Himself. As I have allowed the belief in the existence of God to become stronger in my mind, the existence of Satan becomes clearer too. If I ever forget for a moment that my enemy is real, I have only to look at saints of God saved for a life of joy, service, and satisfaction who experience all kinds of unnecessary grief, sorrow, and loneliness. I see Christians whose talent and influence have all been siphoned off by sin, and their reputations lost in a world that returns to them nothing but emptiness and scorn. We all know Christians who have become nothing more than dry, dusty holes when people around them are longing for the water of life. Christian mothers don't know enough about the Bible to lead their own children to Jesus. Christian businessmen have compromised their morals and lost the powerful influence they could have had. Bitterness exists where joy should be, self-centeredness where love should have grown, and helpless confusion where seeds of faith should have been planted. We see these things and know that our enemy is real.

The Real Christians Need to Stand Up

Many today seem to have divorced Christian principles from their daily living. Many who attend church regularly live as though they have taken God, the devil, miracles, prayer, and anything else that cannot be measured with a ruler and put them in the same category as Santa Claus and the good fairy. But God is not calling us to narrow-minded stupidity. He did not ask us to forsake reality and live in a dream world. Christianity is not a fairy tale concocted from old wives' tales and superstitions. It is not a cop-out for minds that are too weak to face the problems of life. On the contrary! The Bible uses words like wrestle (Eph. 6:12), war (1 Tim. 1:18), and fight (1 Cor. 9:26), to describe the Christian life. It is a life designed for the strong-hearted who fight in God's strength, under His command, and who use His promises as their weapons.

I don't know when mankind first began to think of Christianity as something for old ladies, children and fools, but somewhere between the time bold and rugged men turned the world upside down and the present time, the tears, blood, and sweat of the beginning church has been thought of as weakness, red water, and the meager effort it would take to lift a silver communion cup. Art work of the past, picturing religious themes, may be partly responsible for this warped view. To my mind there is something false about soft men with halos about their heads and saints with upturned eyes, downturned mouths and folded hands. The paintings that illustrate many of our Bibles and hang in some of our churches have a decided note of the unreal and in my opinion should be put back in the art museum where they belong.

The first saints had no halos, nor did they walk around with upturned eyes and far-gone expressions. They did have sore feet, children, in-laws, taxes, and problems. And they did have a vital relationship with God that gave them logical and workable answers to the ups and downs. They had something that was worth living and dying for, and they had then a real enemy who was just as powerful as he is today.

We see Satan in action through nearly every book in the Bible. He is called our enemy (1 Peter 5:8-9). He is a liar and he deceives people with lying wonders (2 Thes. 2:9). Satan is powerful. He snatches the Gospel and the hope of finding God from the minds of men (Matt. 13:18) and blinds their minds so they cannot understand the truth (1 Cor. 4:4). He perverts and twists Scripture (Matt. 4:5-7), and appears as an angel of light but has death and hell in his purpose (2 Cor. 11:14). He stands before God continually accusing Christians (Rev. 12:10). He always resists the work of the Lord in the world (Zech. 3:11). He hindered the Apostle Paul in his work (1 Thes. 2:18) and he will hinder you. He can bind people with illness (Luke 13:16) and is called a murderer (John 8:44) and a snake (Rev. 20:2).

Satan gave Eve trouble at the beginning of time, found Job and slammed him around a bit, tempted Christ Jesus, and sent trouble to every saint that has ever lived. He has plotted against the Church for 2,000 years and if you think he is going to let you love people without throwing an obstacle in your path, you need to think again. The moment you get serious about loving others, an alarm goes off in hell. As surely as the physical laws that keep the planets and stars moving in order, the laws of hell against love will move.

God's Reaction

In the realm of physical science the forces of action and reaction are always equal, but in the spiritual realm they are not. We have assurance from God's Word that the action from heaven is stronger than the forces of hell. "You, dear children, are of God and have overcome them, because the One who is in you is greater than the one who is in the world" (1 John 4:4, NIV).

The Word of God abounds with encouragement as we stand and fight our enemy. We are not alone. Heaven's bank is full, its armies are powerful, its ammunition is effective, and its Captain is experienced and ready and on our side!

Just a few Scriptures to consider on this subject are:

"Where sin increased, grace increased all the more" (Rom. 5:20, NIV).

"Finally, be strong in the Lord and in His mighty power. Put on the full armor of God so that you can take your stand against the devil's schemes" (Eph. 6:10-11, NIV).

"My [God's] Word shall not return unto Me void, but it shall accomplish that which I please" (Isa. 55:11).

"I have told you these things, so that in Me you may have peace. In this world you will have trouble. But take heart! I have overcome the world" (John 16:33, NIV).

"Is anything too hard for the Lord?" (Gen. 18:14)

"All things are possible with God" (Mark 10:27, NIV).

"It is God who works in you" (Phil. 2:13, NIV).

God and His love are greater than any of the

forces of hell. He is greater than our situation. He is greater than our weakness. He is greater than our past sins. Paul encouraged the Ephesians with the words, "Now to Him who is able to do immeasurably more than all we ask or imagine, according to His power that is at work within us, to Him be glory in the church and in Christ Jesus throughout all generations, for ever and ever!" (Eph. 3:20-21, NIV)

When a marriage has nothing left but a meaningless shell and love seems to be an impossible dream, God is able for those who will yield to Him.

When a church is cold and the words, "Brother and sister in Christ" are a mockery, when the family of God is acting toward one another like uncaring strangers and fresh Christian love seems like an ancient corpse no power could resurrect, God is still able to work in those who will yield to Him.

When our love has been rejected as we pour all we have to give on another loveless human and that person absorbs it but gives nothing in return, and everything seems to fail and we wonder if loving is really worth it after all, God is still able to work in those who will yield to Him.

Those early Christians with their in-laws, children, and taxes, found that learning to love was a real thing that could be accomplished in their own lives. They were noted for their outstanding ability to love and it seemed to be the most famous aspect of their reputation. Jesus said that love would be the mark of Christians, identifying them as God's children in the eyes of the world (John 13:36).

We have the same Jesus they had and the same source who supplies all our needs, yet, could it be said that we are famous for our love? Why not?

Could part of the answer be that love is a learning process and, like all learning, it takes time and applied effort to progress? Could it also be that this education is available only to those who remain His willing students?

God's great love is always sufficient, but man sometimes is not. Sometimes we are unwilling to be used where we could turn the tide of hell. Often we are unfaithful and will not stand in the gap and fight. Often we just give up, tired of the struggle. It is a wonder that God ever manages to get anywhere at all considering He is working through such a disorganized army of misfits as we often appear to be.

Learning to love is not easy. Heavenly things are foreign to our fallen nature, and Satan is there to trip up our thinking and sneak in false teaching. No wonder we are so easily blown off course! The only things we have going for us are the continual working of the Holy Ghost within us, the prayers of Jesus on our behalf, the ministry of angels, the support of the Christian brotherhood, and the never-failng love of our Father. But that is more than enough to make us conquerors.

For anyone who is willing to stand and be used in the war of love and hate, it will be a continual uphill struggle. One of the first things we will have to learn is how to tap His strength. To fight for our own strength is useless against such a foe as the evil one. But rest is provided along the path and there are occasional fresh breezes of God's refreshing love when we are weary. And there is a goal at the top—the goal of experiencing divine, super-human love as a part of our own personality. It is a goal well worth the struggle.

7

LOVE
and Sharing

I once had a landlord who was a millionaire. He owned a huge ranch, a showcase home, banks, and oil wells. But he had a loveless family who were tearing at each other constantly. Their quarrels were fuel for the fires of country gossip and it seemed that all his money was of little value when there was no place he could go to find peace.

When someone's home is a place of constant argument what does it matter if it looks like a palace? When someone has no place he can take off his shoes and say to himself, "In this place they do not condemn me, here they care and try to understand," then what good is money?

Finally, this family sought out a counselor. Part of the advice given them by the counselor was that they select a family project, something they could all work at together. The project they chose was the breeding, showing, and selling of expensive pinto horses. I never knew how the family made out after that for we shortly moved from there, but

I sometimes see advertisements for their stock in ranch magazines and wonder. This little incident seems almost humorous to me, for when all the frills of the counselor's office are taken away and all his degrees wiped off the wall, what his advice to this troubled millionaire boiled down to was that the family needed to practice sharing with each other. It is the same instructions I give my screaming, squabbling little boys when they fight over who gets to play with the baseball bat.

The simple act of sharing is sometimes thought to be kid stuff. We instruct little children in the basics of sharing and pat Johnnie on the head and tell him he is a big boy when he lets a visiting cousin take turns with his much-loved bike. Many adults would be insulted if we sat them down and, with motherly tones, told them they were selfish and needed to learn how to share. We often consider sharing to be something children must be taught and adults already know, much like the ABCs or counting to 10. Yet, I believe that the ability to share is precisely what many of us modern, sophisticated adults lack. We may not be like a two-year-old who resents having to share his toy, but we may resent having to share our time. We may not scream because we have to share a toy fire engine but we might squall inwardly when we have to share our place of honor with someone we feel does not deserve as much credit as we.

Sharing is part of loving. When love begins to wax cold, sharing becomes a strained, unnatural thing. A young couple who started out their married life, willing to give each other anything and everything they owned, may find three years later they are very irritated because one mate wants to watch channel 3 while the other wants to watch channel 12, and great arguments can start over who gets to read the front page of the paper first.

I know some people who have been married three or more times—and always to the same person they started out with! It seems they can "love" each other dearly just so long as they don't have to live in the same house. They do well as long as they only see the sweet, nice things about each other and nothing is demanded of them. But when they live together and have to share the bathroom mirror, the bank account, and the television, fury and tears are unleashed.

For the growing Christian it is not usually hard to find a broken or at least cracked relationship lying in some corner of our lives. Perhaps it is a husband or wife who has grown distant to us through the years and we no longer enjoy that feeling of oneness we used to know. Or maybe it is a child we can no longer communicate with, or a neighbor who rubs us the wrong way. Whatever it is, sharing can be a glue that helps stick things together if we enter into it willingly. If we will purposely, deliberately look for ways to share not only our material possessions but abstract things, such as time and patience, with the one we are trying to love, we will have gone a long way toward our goal. It does not matter so much that we have a feeling inside telling us we want to share as that we are *willing* to share regardless of feelings. The very word *share* implies a free giving.

The Receiving End of Sharing

Last summer it seemed as though Little League baseball practice would never end. Several times a week we mothers would gather on hard bleachers in the hot sun and slap at the flies while our boys sat in the dugout and cried because the coach wouldn't let them play first base, or the umpire called them out, or someone called them a name. Every week it was the same story. Yet the boys could hardly wait for the next game and thought the whole affair, crying and all, was exciting fun.

One particularly hot afternoon a mother spoke up bitterly. "All I hear is baseball, *baseball*, BASE-BALL!" she lamented. "I'm sick of it! I told those kids on the way here that if they didn't shut up I was going to scream and beat them every one!"

I thought it sad. Here was a mother who was taking time to share the family car by taking the boys to practice and sharing her time as she sat on the bench while they played. Yet, she was doing neither with a sweet spirit and was completely rejecting a special part of their lives that her young sons were trying to share with her, namely baseball.

I could sympathize with this mother, even though I knew her attitude was wrong, because baseball is not exactly one of my passions either and I know from experience that it is not easy to work up enthusiasm for something we feel the world would be just as well off without. Whether it is a teenager's cloud-nine thrill over a letter from a member of the opposite sex, or a young boy's depression over the home run he barely missed, or a husband's delight over the way his new fishing lure works, or a wife's concern over the color of the living room drapes, there are many things people around us value that don't stir a ripple of emotion in our soul. And when they try to share what they value with us we may find ourselves uninterested and irritated. Learning to humble ourselves and accept what another is offering to share can be a very difficult thing to do because the first thing we have to lay aside is self and make room for the opinions, likes, and personalities of others. It took 17 years for me to get humble enough to share my husband's love of farm animals and even now the Lord has to give me a refresher course once in a while, especially about the pigs.

Family Sharing

One of the best places for sharing to be taught and practiced is within the family unit, but finding a time and place for this in our hurry-hurry world can be very difficult. I have struggled with this problem for years. Bill works shifts and his schedule changes from week to week. The children each seem to have their own interests in sports and school. Meanwhile I am constantly involved with first one project, then another. Even in church our family looks fragmented as I sit in the choir and the children are with their respective friends. It worried me for a long time and I felt cheated by a society that would rob me of precious moments of family togetherness. I thought for a long time, but there seemed to be no way to draw all the loose ends together. Vacations were impractical. There was no time. And too many ranch chores. Family projects were out because no two people had the same interest and there was no money. What then? I finally found the answer when I stopped looking at expensive things "out yonder" and started looking at what was near at hand.

A shopping trip could be a sharing experience

if I were willing to take all the children and lean on the Lord for patience. So could a Little League ball game or berry-picking. Dozens of small experiences could be turned into sharing times with a little patience and prayer. It takes a lot more effort to spend an hour and a half sharing the baking of a batch of cookies with a group of children than to spend 45 minutes making them alone.

One of the best sharing experiences I can remember was last winter when our family shared making a snowman. Every member of the family went outside that beautiful, cold afternoon—even me—and we built a six foot Mr. and Mrs. Snowman on the front lawn. Each of us contributed something to the final product and shared that moment in each other's lives. The snow long ago melted and summer is here but the other day my little girl pulled an apron from the drawer and exclaimed, "Mama, this is the same apron we put on Mrs. Snowman! Didn't we have fun that day?" She talked on and on about that day in the snow. It is a memory of sharing love that will last her a lifetime and did not cost one cent.

Sharing Dreams

Few things draw people closer or stick them together more firmly than sharing a common dream or goal. Whether within a marriage or among church members, or between a parent and a child, or between ourselves and the Lord, sharing a dream can create a bond that is stronger than legal documents or more binding than the biological tie of shared blood.

Love thrives in shared dreams and can shrivel and almost die without it. Marriages can break apart for lack of a mutual dream. "We have nothing in common anymore" the partners plead and a legal document is set aside and the divorce is granted on the grounds of incompatibility. The tie of shared blood between a parent and child should be strong but it can seem almost nonexistent as the two drift off each into his own separate world because there is no common sharing ground remaining between them.

When a man comes home from work, tired, and looking forward to rest and finds his only son sitting on the floor crying because he cannot fit his train track together, it is an act of love for the father to lay aside his tiredness and help the little boy make his dream to see the train run a reality. A woman, who would work side-by-side with her husband through long hours and lean years until his dream of an insurance business becomes a success, is showing her love by sharing in his dreams. Even if our only part in another's dream is to listen to him and hold back critical judgment, we have taken a step toward loving.

The foolish ramblings of a five-year-old who says he wants to fly to Mars may sound like foolish ramblings to a busy mother, but to his mind it is important and real. One of my sons wants to be a fisherman though he has never set foot in an ocean. Another has decided to get a jump on everyone and be the man who makes all the laws. Neither of these boys regards these dreams as foolish and they are both extremely serious. Dreams, even little, foolish ones, need to be shared with people we love.

Someone has to be special to us before we are willing to share our inmost desires with him. We have to respect someone before we will share our dreams with him. When we invite someone to participate in the fulfillment of our dreams we are taking him very close to our heart. Even God seems to have dreams, if we can call His desires that.

One of God's hopes is that each one of His children will be conformed to the image of Christ (Rom. 8:29). We know this has not yet happened entirely, for indeed, some of God's children are not yet born. Another of God's desires involves His entire creation which is now fragmented as one piece wars against another. God's purpose in sending Jesus Christ into the world was that He might gather together all the universe, both spiritual and physical, into one harmonious paradise (Eph. 1:10; 2 Peter 3:13; Rom. 8:19-22), and that He might live in peace and holiness among His people (Rev. 21). This paradise has not yet occurred so it must still be one of God's hopes—one of His dreams.

God is all-knowing and can see the end of history as well as the beginning and the present. The things He desires and plans will come to pass as surely as if they were already history, yet, while they remain future on the line of time, as long as they are destiny and not reality, I think we do the Scripture no harm calling these things our Father's dreams.

There is one dream of God in which we are especially involved because we are a key factor in its fulfillment. He has a dream of world evangelism.

God has opened His arms wide to the whole world. He is not willing that any should perish but that all men should be brought to repentance and learn of His love (2 Peter 3:9). God is in the business of redemption; He is saving the world one soul at a time; He is touching each individual life with His power and love; and He has extended to us the opportunity to take an active part in His business. The door of opportunity was opened when Jesus said, "All authority in heaven and on earth has been given Me. Therefore go and make disciples of all nations, baptizing them in the name of the Father, the Son and the Holy Spirit, and teaching them to obey everything I have commanded you. And surely I will be with you always, to the very end of the age" (Matt. 28:18-20, NIV). He told His followers, "You will be my witnesses" (Acts 1:8) and this call included us present-day followers as surely as it included those who heard Him speak those words nearly 2,000 years ago. We are still His witnesses in this world testifying to the power and love of our Lord. But God didn't give us this responsibility as a grim task to perform. He did it partly to share His heart's desire, His hopes, His dreams with us. He did it as an act of love.

Jesus looked on the thronging masses of mankind and had compassion on them because they were like lost, hungry, aimless sheep with no one to care for them (Matt. 9:36). Because true love longs to pour itself into the needs of others, Jesus longed to guide the lost, give food to the hungry, and purpose to the aimless. His great love is still seeking to do this and as we see a glimpse of His heart we too can feel that longing. As we move through this world and by His power reach out to meet these needs we become a partner in His work, we share in His dream and the bond between His heart and ours grows as strong as the cord of life itself.

When through His Word, God shares His dreams with us, He is opening His very heart to us. He is showing us that we are special to Him. He is demonstrating His respect for us, His creation, and honors us with trust by offering us an opportunity to take part in the fulfilling of His great dream.

8
LOVE
and Illusion

Men have died in the desert, stumbling along following a distant mirage that looked like cool, life-giving water but always just out of reach. One could struggle on and on, following the illusion and pass right by a real spring of water somewhere nearby.

Sometimes we are like the dying man on the desert when it comes to our love relationships. Sometimes we are so involved with what we *think* people are that we walk right past the real person, just as a man dying of thirst perishes within a short distance of a spring.

We all live with certain illusions. For example, pastors often complain about parishioners regarding them as spiritual supermen who are somehow separated and different from the rest of the world. Their children are supposed to behave like angels and everything from the pastor's tone of voice to the clothes he wears must conform to the image the congregation has determined for him no matter

99

what his true feelings and personality may be. The moment he or his family deviate from that image the congregation is restless or even shocked. In this case, the congregation has created an illusion of the pastor and his family.

Pastors are not the only ones who get blocked in by illusions. The other day I was cleaning house in a long, cotton skirt, bare feet, and rollers in my hair when a young man from the church knocked on the door. He had been in my classes and seen me singing with a microphone in my hand but had never seen me in any other situation. He had evidently formed some mental picture of what I should be and somehow the hardware in my hair just did not fit that image. All during our conversation his eyes kept roving back to those pink and blue rollers. Finally he laughed. "You washed your hair!" he said incredulously.

"Sure did," I answered back. "I've got bare feet too," I said, and hoisted one foot and wiggled my toes to prove the point. The young man seemed to get the idea. His mental illusion of what he thought I was had been one-sided and I was glad the rollers and bare toes helped give him a more realistic picture.

False images that get in the way of building real relationships are not uncommon. Parents often have a mental image of what they want their child to be and become disappointed when the real child God sends them doesn't fit the mold. Susie may not want to be a beauty queen and Tommy may be much more at home in the library than on the football field. Married people may have an image of what they think their mate should be and never learn how to stay in love with the real and sometimes faulty person they vowed to stand by forever.

Illusions and images get in the way of our loving and add to our disappointment with life as people can't conform to the molds we have built for them. Trying to build a love relationship with an illusion rather than the real person is like trying to hang your coat on an imaginary hanger. It just won't work.

The One that Got Away

My boys went fishing the other day and said that they "almost caught a bass" in the creek. Every time they tell the story that fish gets bigger and closer to being caught. I don't really think my little boys know the difference between a bass and a mud-sucker but because the fish didn't come home with them to bind them to reality, their mental image grows and grows. It is not that they are lying but in the absence of hard fact, their minds are free to contrive what they like best and ignore what they find to be unpleasant.

This exaggeration process probably will not do the boys any real harm, but it can be disastrous if it continues on in life. We can build up illusions about a person whose characteristics are more fancied than real and even fall in love with them. I have met many women who have been married for years, yet still have tucked away in their hearts a knight-in-shining-armor image of the man they didn't marry. Everything their husbands do is mentally compared with that wonderful young man they once knew, who is now more mythical than historical, and hubby always comes out on the short end of the comparison. Men also treasure illusions, and sometimes carry around in their hearts a memory of someone they once knew. It might even be an image of what they only wished they had, but it is an illusion just the same. These misty shapes can interfere with building real relationships.

It takes no effort at all to have a dream and then to fall madly in love with it. It is much easier to dream about the beauty and promise of the baby we want than to meet the thousand small demands of a newborn and listen to him cry at night. It is easier to love the girl that got away and imagine all her charms than to live peaceably with the one who sits across the breakfast table each morning. It is easier to dream of what we would be if we had been given the chance than to be faithful to the small opportunities we already have.

Much of the marriage hopping going on these days is due to people chasing dreams that don't exist. It is easy to love someone who is not there. We don't have to share our paycheck with illusions, they never belch at the table, or have an itch in public. They don't contradict our opinions, or have moods that are different from ours, or develop physical defects. Real people can do all these things and usually do.

It is easy to love imaginary people. For example, look at the way we often think more highly of a person when he is dead than when he is alive. His faults don't bother us nearly as much when he can't repeat the offense. When he is gone, our minds are free to pick out the good points which oddly seem to grow more evident after the demise. This phenomenon of change in heart can be astounding.

I heard of one man who never said anything

more flattering to his wife than to call her, "that old battle-ax." They lived all their married life rocking on the edge of divorce but, six weeks after she died, he was calling her "the most sainted woman on earth" and longing with tears and great mourning to have her back. I suspect that as more time passes, her memory will become sweeter and even more holy.

"The grass is always greener on the other side of the fence" is more than an old proverb. It is a basic fact of human nature—a fact we need to guard against if we want to build real love with living people. If we are to practice accepting the real, we must be willing to discard the false and let go of the illusions we have held for so long. Old illusions don't like to be buried and they may kick and scream as they go. But don't let it bother you. They are only mannequins that have been given animation by the many years of thought we have lent them.

Rainbows and Ashes

Illusions have a way of turning to ashes when we get a chance to taste them in reality. We have all seen things we just knew would make us happy if we could only have them. But when we got them, the colors faded and that which was supposed to satisfy leaves us uncomfortably hungry again. I knew a pastor who for years asked the Lord to give him a certain church. He was sure that if he were only that church's pastor he could do great things for the Lord and be very happy. The Lord granted his petition and the pastor spent the next three years sitting on a situation as explosive as a powder keg and looking for a way to get out of the mess.

Satan has had thousands of years of practice learning what makes us tick and how he can best turn our natural inclinations to his own advantage. So it is not too suprising that he should be involved in building illusions for us to chase. He never stands before us empty-handed but always has sparkling toys and pretty dreams for us. He offers a way that appears to lead to satisfaction. His words are as smooth as honey, "See what I've got? If you had this thing you could be happy and proud. If you had this everyone would admire you and love you. All your wishes would be fulfilled, if you only had *this*." He leads us on with a dream and as soon as one thing proves disappointing he immediately rushes in a substitute. He keeps us off balance chasing one dream after another. In the process, our attention is drawn away from the Lord, the Source of true love and satisfaction.

Some of us never catch on to what the devil is doing. We chase our rainbows to the very end of our lives saying, "If only God would give me this thing, or put me in that situation, then I would be happy." I have a dog that has been run over three times but he still chases cars. Sometimes I think the way we chase illusions is just as futile and dangerous.

An example of the devil's tactics would be to convince a young girl to begin thinking, "If only I were popular like Susan. I could be so happy if I were like her." By age 16 the girl's dream has changed to, "If only I had a car . . . ." and soon "If only my parents weren't so strict. I can never be happy as long as I am under their thumb." This young girl becomes a young woman and graduates from school with her head full of visions of herself as an independent, sophisticated, career girl and she works very hard to make her dream come true. But when that dream becomes a reality she still finds a vague dissatisfaction inside herself and trades her past visions for another dream, "If only I had a loving husband. I would be so happy and contented with a man who loves me, and little children." After 10 years of marriage, budgets and diapers, this same dissatisfied woman is saying, "Oh, I wish I were single again. I was happy alone. If only I were unmarried and free again!"

The problem may not be so much with this woman's marriage as with her own heart. Dream after dream has been fulfilled and they all proved they can't satisfy. Yet she will reach out for another, thinking, "If only I had this, if only I were in that circumstance, then I would be happy." But she probably wouldn't.

Two of the most useless words in the English language are bound to be "if only." We hear them all the time and seldom do we see a sad or lonely person who does not have an "if only" dream that he believes could cure all his ills if only it would become reality. "If only I had a baby . . ." "If only I could be beautiful . . ." "If only I had a different job . . ." "If only I had married Jane instead of Carol . . ." "If only I had more money . . ." The list goes on and on—as endless as man's mind.

It amazes me that all of us as Adam's children are so slow to learn! We work very hard and obtain something we desire, but six months later, if that long, we decide that what we really wanted was something else so we begin to chase another dream.

The devil knows that if he can keep us chasing misty illusions, an object or a person, he will almost have the battle won. We will be continually trying to satisfy our self-centered wants, we become too preoccupied to try to satisfy the needs of another, which is what love really is. Everything in our lives will be working the exact opposite of the way God intended and happiness will be as elusive as trying to steer a car with a transmission that only goes in reverse!

The Lord doesn't ignore our desires and ambitions: nor does He expect us to live aimless lives that reach for nothing. He desires that we find our satisfaction and source of happiness in Him and in fulfilling His desires toward others. God has a reason for this and it is not because He has a huge ego that all mankind is feeding, but that He knows everyone and everything else will fail us in the end.

The Bible abounds with God's invitation to reach, to desire, to dream. God invited the psalmist, "Open thy mouth wide, and I will fill it" (Ps. 18:10). Jesus repeatedly told His disciples to ask the Father for what they wanted. Again and again He used such words as "knock," "ask," and "seek" as He encouraged them to give a specific name to their desire and watch their Father make that desire a reality. Hannah asked for a baby (1 Sam. 1:26-27); Jabez asked for a larger piece of land (1 Chron. 4:10); Hezekiah asked for a longer life (2 Kings 21:1-5), and God granted each request according to His will.

But when we look to temporary things as the source and goal of happiness, we are headed for trouble. Under the inspiration of the Holy Spirit, James wrote: "Look here, you people who say,

'Today and tomorrow we're going to such and such a town, stay there a year, and open up a profitable business.' How do you know what is going to happen tomorrow? for the length of your lives is as uncertain as the morning fog—now you see it, soon it is gone. What you ought to say is, 'If the Lord wants us to, we shall live and do this or that'" (James 4:13-15). We can seek. We are encouraged to do so. But our first goal and consideration must be the Lord's will.

Knowing and Accepting Reality

There seems to be an appetite today for knowing what is real and exposing it to the light. From what goes on in politics to what those chemicals in our breakfast cereal really do to us, the nation seems to be struggling to get to the bottom of everything. We want truth in our relationships, our religion, and our automobile tires. Madison Avenue has cashed in on this appetite and tells us that Coca-Cola is the real thing. Some of the ugliest movies, books, and television programs have been put on in the name of reality and because they claim to "tell it like it is" they have a tendency to be accepted no matter how degrading they may be.

The cry on every hand seems to be that we "lay it on the line." But values, people, styles, opinions, and our own hearts change at such a rapid pace we can't even find the "line," much less a reality to lay on it. Grabbing hold of reality is not always an easy thing to do.

Everything shifts and changes in this world, including our minds and feelings. At times we can feel that the disjointed, out-of-place thing in life is not the world but us. We can feel like actors in a play who wear the proper clothes, smile the proper smiles, but somehow we seem not to be connected to reality. I have read that one of the first signs of serious depression is a feeling of detachment from reality. I try not to accept blindly everything I read, but my own experience has proven this true.

As a child we are aware of the smells, tastes, and sounds around us but our senses dull with time and trouble until we sometimes feel that life is flowing past us as if we were standing on the shore alone, disconnected from the mainstream. I have watched people trying to capture again the feeling of being alive, trying to move out of the mist and find something or someone who could make them feel alive again. A researcher once asked a woman why she committed adultery. The woman replied that she thought if she took a lover she would once more be aware that the sheets were smooth and made of cotton and that the blanket was soft. She would be able to feel and know that she was alive.

All depression is characterized by a mind that sees only the dark side of life and a heart that feels alone and separated. When depression comes sneaking into my life, covering over my spirit inch by inch like a fog creeping through a valley, there are a few practical steps I usually take to sharpen my senses to life and love.

For me the first step is to *be aware of the good things about my body*. Ignore any spot that hurts (you can take that up with God some other time) and look for something about yourself that pleases you. I often think of how good it feels to be able to breathe deeply and exhale freely. Then I do so several times just to prove the point. The same goes for muscles. Arms and legs are marvelous tools. Not everyone has full use of his body and there will probably come a day when I will no longer have trouble-free use of mine.

Choose something good about yourself—maybe the color of your eyes or the fact that you are tall. Then take a moment to thank your Maker for it. It could be the start of refreshing your spirit in Him.

Next, I *notice the color and texture of things around me*. Too easily we become dull to the richness about us. We pass by the familiar things and forget how much they pleased us when they were new. If I am sitting at the desk, I feel the texture of the wood with my hands and observe the variations of color and tone. I notice—really notice—the colors in the picture above the calendar and the books on the corner of the bookshelf. The same feeling, observing process goes for the water and soap suds if I am doing dishes, or the smell and feel of the soil when I'm gardening.

Third, I *widen my awareness* by letting my mind expand to wherever the Lord would lead it. Things that please me I name one by one. I try to be specific—not merely grateful for my children.

A few moments of this exercise has been an aid to me in restoring a feeling of hope and reality in being alive. It is no cure-all, but in this rush, rush world, it helps.

An NBC news report recently stated that Americans spent $40 million in 1977 on sleeping pills and nerve-calming drugs and this figure did *not* include prescription drugs. I wonder how many of these people were born-again children of God, who should have been able to rest in their Saviour. Much of this kind of pill popping could be eliminated if those who know the Lord would take moments during the day to be truly aware of the things that surround them and find something real that they could sincerely thank God for.

When we can accept the reality about ourselves —our responsibility, our aliveness, our connection with God, our faults, our talents—and respond with gratitude toward the One who made us, we are in a position to accept the reality about other people. Our illusions melt and we have taken one giant step toward learning to love the way He does.

9
LOVE
and a Sad Song

I sometimes wonder why things which started out as a commonplace slice of time carved from an ordinary day will stay on through the years to become warm and precious memories. Some of the moments that stick with me most firmly and warm me most dearly are memories of rocking my children to sleep. I find a solace in rocking babies, so I rocked each one of mine until the next one was born and took his place. There was such a long time between my first child and the last three that my oldest daughter was rocked until she grew quite large. With those sweet hours of rocking came songs—lullabies, folk songs, spirituals, hymns, dozens and dozens of them. Of all the songs I recall most vividly, the one that stands foremost is:

A song of love is a sad song;
   Hi-lilly, hi-lilly, hi-lo;
A tale of love is a tale of woe;
   Don't ask me how I know.
A song of love is a sad song;

For I have loved and it's so.
I sit at the window and watch the rain;
I think that I never may love again;
Hi-lilly, hi-lilly, hi-lo.

From Shakespeare's *Romeo and Juliet*, to a sad love song on the radio; from the make-believe world of books and movies to the very real world of personal experience, the fact that love can have a painful side is a well-publicized truth.

Love can be expensive. It can cost us hurt feelings, bitter disappointments, money, and a hundred times of stooping over to pick up the broken pieces and begin again.

Love is not only expensive, it can be risky as well because not everyone will love us back. It is not at all out of order to consider whether or not we want to run the risk of learning to love.

Love-shy

A big German shepherd dog rules our yard like a king over his court. He is very gentle with the children and obedient to command, most of the time, but he himself decides who will and will not be allowed close to our house. More than one stranger has sat in his car and honked rather than risk walking to the front door if Prince growls and bares his teeth. Yet, for all his bravery, our dog has an Achilles heel that defeats him every time. If the car should backfire, or someone would make a loud bang, Prince would race for the nearest hiding place, whining all the way.

Two years ago Prince was shot with a rifle and though the bullet only grazed his spine, he has never forgotten the horrifying sound of a gun blast. Any sharp loud crack that remotely resembles gun fire—the pop of a whip, or a firecracker exploding—will turn all his bravery into gelatine. Because he remembers the pain, Prince is gun-shy.

No one should be too hard on the poor dog. He has a lot of kindred spirits among us supposedly more intelligent creatures. People are sometimes injured in a wreck and become car-shy, or are thrown by a horse and become saddle-shy. And it is not unusual for someone to try to give or receive love and become love-shy when things don't work out as smoothly or as quickly as we thought.

Perhaps it happened to one of us when we, with an abandonment of self-consideration, offered our all to God. We reached out and gave willingly to another. It felt good. Then somehow our adventure didn't turn out the way we expected. God did not respond as quickly as we thought He should have. The appreciation we thought belonged to us was snatched away and we were hurt. Really hurt! Like the sad notes of the song we moan, "I think that I never may love again" and pull our heads into our shells like a turtle or lick our wounds and whimper like a wounded animal.

Or we may have been hurt when we tried to give love to another person. We swallow our pride and offer an olive branch to John Doe; then immediately good ol' Johnny sets fire to it. Angry with John for hurting us and angry with God for allowing such injustice, we withdraw into our shells and peek out at the world with cynical eyes.

Withdrawing into one's shell might seem the safe and pleasant thing to do when we first consider it. Inside we are consoled by our own self-pity, thinking, *Nobody will ever hurt me!* But the shell has one big problem—you have to live with yourself inside. You become your only succor, only comfort. You are your only occupation, your only center of thought. You become your own worst enemy. And worse yet, you may get so wrapped up in yourself that you forget how to get out of the shell and may have to live that way from then on. Who wants to go through life with only a bitter cynic like you for company?

For anyone who has indeed forgotten where he sealed up the exit, and wants to give life another try, as one who has been there, I give you this advice. A sure cure for that kind of self-centeredness is to love until it hurts and keep on loving until it stops hurting.

It is natural to avoid places, people, and circumstances that have hurt us. But one look at the example God's love has given us and we know that never to love again is not His way. Nor should it be ours.

When we have been wronged and our love has truly been bruised or rejected, we should find consolation in the fact that Jesus walked this trail before us and knows our pain. We can also turn our hurt over to Him and let Him stop our bitterness before it takes root and becomes a permanent part of our personality.

His Example
Jesus knew the way of loving was a hard and painful road (loving us would cost Him Calvary). He was honest with His followers, warning them to count the cost before they begin following in His steps that would lead them to touch the highest experience of love (John 15:13).

He asked His disciples, "Suppose one of you

wants to build a tower. Will he not first sit down and estimate the cost to see if he has enough money to complete it? For if he lays the foundation and is not able to finish it, everyone who sees it will ridicule him, saying, 'This fellow began to build and was not able to finish'" (Luke 14:28-30, NIV).

Jesus knew that before we set our hearts to do something we would be wise to consider the cost. The more deeply something will dip into our resources the more we need to consider seriously the value of that in which we are investing.

Jesus did not take up the cross unthinkingly, but considered the situation before the foundations of the earth were laid and decided with purpose and reason that the agony was worth what lay on the other side. Scripture is clear as to what cost was involved and what benefit He hoped to accomplish. "Let us fix our eyes on Jesus, the Pioneer and Protector of our faith, who for the joy that was set before Him endured the cross, scorning its shame, and sat down at the right hand of the throne of God. Consider Him who endured such opposition from sinful men, so that you will not grow weary and lose heart" (Heb. 12:2-3, NIV). Jesus set a high example of what loving really means.

The reason Jesus endured the cross was because of the joy He knew lay beyond it. This was not a self-indulgent, self-centered joy that He was seeking but *our* joy that He was reaching for. It was His joy to take us out of the blinded, lost state in which we were mired and set us free in the liberty of His love. It was His joy to expose to the mind and heart of man what loving really was. Because of His free and open loving, Jesus has and is receiving new glories and honor (Rev. 5:9; Phil. 2:6-11).

Jesus considered the price of loving us and deemed it was worth it.

The Self-Proclaimed Martyr

Because there can be a sacrificial, painful element in loving, it is not surprising that Satan has been quick to slip in his own counterfeit. The devil is a great imitator. I can think of no single truth of God that Satan has not attempted to counterfeit, and the suffering side of love is no exception.

There are few things more gloomy than a full-time martyr—someone who thinks misery is a godly virtue and he has cornered the market. Such people are determined to be miserable and determined to let you know it. People who are full of self-imposed misery are as different from those who suffer as a result of their love as circles are different from triangles. We can easily identify these people for they will use their "suffering" as a tool to force others into a certain response. They try to bend and shape those around them into a form that pleases them better than the original—by hammering on them with their pain and tales of trouble. Sometimes God is the One these people are trying to rearrange or impress. They try to make themselves worthy of His consideration or grace by inflicting pain and difficulty on themselves.

These people are much to be pitied for they have never learned that love cannot be bought. Real love is never sold, bought, or earned. Not with tears. Not with effort. Not with suffering. Not with good works. Nor with bribery. The only way love can be transmitted is by freely giving and receiving it.

As long as our hearts are set on earning something for ourselves, even love or pity, all our giving and sacrifice become useless. Any sacrifice we make to get love, rather than because we already do love, will gain us nothing. Paul put it this way: "If I give all I possess to the poor and surrender my body to the flames, but have not love, I gain nothing" (1 Cor. 13:3, NIV).

We could give away everything we own. We could walk the streets dressed in rags, mourning and weeping our lives away. But as long as we are doing these things so someone would give us love, as long as our goal is to gain honor for ourselves or somehow make God obligated to us, all our giving and pain are useless.

It would be vain to beat ourselves with sticks and crawl on our knees until we were broken and bleeding, then look up at God and say, "See how miserable I am making myself? Now, You owe me Your love."

Love for others can cause us to give sacrificially, and at certain moments in history has even required that people give their lives in martyrdom. Many have, in love, laid aside personal hopes, dreams, and ambitions to make room for loving another person. But martyrdom is something that comes about as a result of love—not in order to make ourselves worthy or to manipulate.

I fear that some women who let their husbands lead in all things are secretly trying to manipulate them with their femininity, bribe them with their sexuality, and use "obedience" to get their way.

Can This Be Love?

Philip* belonged to a congregation that was putting up a new church building. He gave $100 to plant trees around the church, saying how much they would be needed for recreation by the children who attended outdoor Bible clubs each summer. Philip really believed that the only reason he gave the money was because he loved his Lord, his church, and the children. If anyone had told him he also had selfish motives in his heart he would have been most offended.

At the end of the building program a list was published of all those who had given large amounts and certificates of appreciation were mailed to all who had given $100. Philip's name was accidentally left off the list and he received no certificate. Deeply upset over the situation, he reminded the building committee, the preacher, his Sunday School class, and several friends that he had been the one who presented the trees. A certificate of appreciation arrived the next week. But when the church letter came out there was no mention of the oversight and his name was never announced as a major contributor. Philip felt that he had not been given the honor due him. He allowed his hurt feelings to grow and before a year had passed, he changed his membership to another church.

Philip thought his motive for giving was love. But was it?

It is not easy to know our own hearts or clearly see our motives. The heart is deep and complicated. Solomon compared the heart to water hidden in a deep well (Prov. 20:5). Asaph made it a practice to communicate with his own heart and search out the things he found there (Ps. 77:6). David also made this a practice and advised us to do the same (4:4). If we honestly want to know the motives of our hearts, we must be still long enough to examine ourselves. We may have to put the kids to bed, turn off the television, and shut our mouths long enough to consider our own hearts. Answers don't usually come at once or in flashes, but as we practice communicating with ourselves and with God, we learn some surprising things about ourselves. We may find a few knots being untied in both our stomachs and our spirits. God knows the secrets of our hearts (44:21) and our inmost thoughts (94:11). He knows what we are made of (103:14) and is willing to share His knowledge with us (James 1:5-7).

As we search our hearts to find the real motive behind our giving, we can easily be fooled. We often have the added complication of pride and emotional ties. And of course, our enemy Satan is always lurking close by waiting to trip us up if he can. But our search can be well rewarded, for some of the problems and pain of loving can be eliminated by knowing what is really in our hearts and what is most important to us, giving to aid the beloved, or getting something to aid ourselves?

Love may at times be a sad song, but it *is* a song. A lovely song with melody that adds a delightful richness to life.

---

*Fictional story.

10
LOVE
and Tragedy

The dark wood paneling of our small living room combined with the rustic gold and orange color scheme creates a relaxed, warm atmosphere. The Bible reading for the night was over and four assorted-sized children were quiet for the first time since dawn.

My red-headed, eight-year-old theologian wrinkled his brow and asked, "Why did He do that?"

"Do what?" I responded.

"How come God didn't fix the famine instead of just telling the Christians what was going to happen?"

I scanned the last few verses of Acts 11, "Some prophets came down . . . to Antioch. One of them . . . stood up and through the Spirit predicted that a severe famine would spread over the entire Roman world (NIV)."

"Well. . . ." I paused to buy time. "God was warning Christians so they could get ready and not be hungry when there wasn't any food." I was pleased with that answer and considered the subject closed but my theologian had other ideas.

"How come?" he asked again. "If God had just fixed the famine then nobody would have had to go hungry. Couldn't God fix a famine?" He looked puzzled a moment, and then his face brightened. "Oh, I get it!" he exclaimed. "God was trying to trick 'em and test 'em to see if they would do what He told them to. Isn't that right, Mama?"

Mama was still studying the first "how come" and was not yet ready for a second.

"Billy," I said at last, "I don't believe God tries to trick people, nor does He make them go hungry just to see what they will do. When wars come, it is not that God wanted the war but that people wanted to fight. When famines come, it is because of sin. . . ." I tried to think of something else to say but could not.

Four pairs of trusting eyes were fixed on my face. They were so young, so open. They asked questions that wiser minds than mine had struggled with for centuries and expected an understandable answer in 10 easy words or less. I studied their eyes —then blurted, "Look, God doesn't always fix this world so it treats us Christians right; He fixes us Christians instead." Thoroughly satisfied with that answer they scurried off to bed.

I made night rounds, putting away dishes and toys with my usual absent-mindedness. I could not lay aside the thoughts little Bill had brought to mind. Children have a way of reducing the most complex problems to a simple question, why *didn't* God fix the famine? Come to think of it, why didn't He fix a lot of things, like earthquakes, premature death, car wrecks, drought, and more? If God is all-powerful, if God is love, and if His primary desire is to give good things to His children, why does trouble ever strike a child of His? Especially the kind that jumps up suddenly out of nowhere and gouges a gaping, painful hole in our lives. How can a loving God and a pain-filled world coexist?

It was the same question I had successfully avoided for years. I had not wanted to examine God's motives too closely nor allow my mind too much freedom in questioning His power. Was I afraid of what I might find hidden in heaven's closets? If God was not all love and all powerful, where did that leave me? During those turbulent months of searching to know and understand love, I knew this question would have to be answered with a logic and truth that I could understand. If my Source of love were selfish or weak, then I was left to depend on what I could find within my own heart—and I knew that would never supply my need.

Tragedy. Like a lion, it stalks us. Hidden in the shadows it shows its ugly face in the most unexpected places. Tornados twist whole blocks of homes into rubble. Floods and earthquakes strip away whole towns taking children, the aged, the good and the bad, all in a mighty sweep and we bewildered, grieving humans wonder why.

A few weeks ago I was talking to a young neighbor about the God of love that I serve. She flipped her long, dark hair behind her slender shoulders and said, "I would like to believe as you do but I just can't. If God is love as you say, how can He just let this world go on as it has? Why doesn't He stop all these bad things?" Her brown eyes were piercing as they demanded a logical, believable answer. "What about the dam that broke and killed all those people the other day? Why didn't He stop that if He really loved those people?"

We Christians talk about the power and strength of God. We tell people how He is all-wise, all-knowing, present everywhere and mightier than any human mind can imagine. We say that nothing can happen outside of His will and that He is in control of everything. While all these things are true, it is easy to see how an unsaved person can look at all the misery and injustice and say, "If this is God's will, He is cruel and I want no part of Him."

The Bible firmly claims that God is love. When we look at Him, especially in the form of Jesus, we see all of the best of love in action. Yet, when we turn our faces and see the world and all the heartache He allows to exist there, we question, "Can this be part of love?"

I have searched Scripture and listened to others who are wiser than myself and prayed. Three reasons have presented themselves to me and although they may not give a full explanation, they are logical and reasonable—and until He redeems me fully and I "know even as also I am known" (1 Cor. 13:12)—they will be enough.

Allowed Will of God
Often I have heard the phrase, "allowed will" or "permissive will" of God as opposed to His "perfect will" and usually I walk away from the one who is offering this instruction more confused than when I came. The problem remained one of shuffling around fancy, theological words without much

bearing on my daily life until a few months ago when I received a letter from mother in the morning mail. "You know as I do that this is no accident," she had stated, and referred to the mishap as "the allowed will of God."

My sister's husband, Steve, had been working on an oil derrick when 3,000 pounds of metal hit him in the face. Fully conscious, he was given emergency medical treatment at a nearby hospital, then rushed to Fort Worth, 50 miles away, where a team of surgeons was waiting to repair what the doctor had called, "extensive head damage." On the trip to the hospital, with his nose smashed into his face, sinuses crushed and a chunk knocked from the back of his skull, Steve witnessed to the ambulance driver about the goodness and grace of the Lord. His surgeon, amazed to find his patient conscious, told him what a lucky young man he was to still have a head. Steve replied that it wasn't luck, it was the Lord. During the surgery doctors found that his nose, though pushed back into his face, could be repaired surgically. Within three days Steve was home again with nothing more permanent than a few small scars.

Mother claimed what happened to Steve was not an accident but was the "allowed will of God." But what did that mean? Had God been using a whip of pain on our family to drive us to prayer? Or did He perhaps that morning say, "Well, I think I'll prove to these people that I can still work miracles by knocking ol' Steve's nose off, and after they pray, I'll show 'em it can be repaired"? That reasoning did not sound like the God I had been serving all through the years. What was His purpose then? Had God dropped an oil derrick on

Steve and mutilated his face for the purpose of exposing one ambulance driver to the Gospel? Wouldn't it have been simpler to have the driver tune his radio to the nearest Christian station?

Allowed will of God—were the words Christians used to explain away what they could not understand. Did people want God to be good and wise so badly that they invented these excuses for Him? A screech of tires, a grinding crash, a dead young man on the pavement and the preacher trying to comfort grieving parents by telling them it was the allowed will of God for Johnny to die with all of his promise yet unlived. Were these words useless utterings thrown in the air in hopes of covering up for a God who either couldn't help or didn't care?

When hard, unexplainable times strike close, it suddenly becomes important to know what these high sounding words mean. Through time and trial, I have come to believe that God's allowed will is not at all opposed to the love of God. Despite the troubles and seeming injustice all around us, His allowed will had its origin in the inmost part of His love.

Gratitude can sometimes be bought for the price of fine gifts. Obedience can sometimes be forced by threats of punishment. Lip service can be extracted with promise of reward. But love must be given of one's own free will. There was only one way for God to allow us the freedom to really experience love. That was to voluntarily limit Himself and allow us room to do as we pleased even if we pleased to do wrong. This is the basis of the allowed will of God. We are in error when we assume that because God is all-powerful this world must operate the way He likes it best. God doesn't cause what is bad and painful; it is not that He cannot help, but, more accurately, that He has allowed room for us to love or not love as we will. God has given this freedom of will not only to good people but to evil people as well. We may not get drunk and crawl behind the wheel of a car but someone else may use his free will to do exactly that and we may both end up on the same road at the same time.

The simplest chemical formula can be thrown completely out of balance when one small ingredient is omitted. The most sophisticated computer will come out with the wrong answer if you leave out one pertinent bit of information. If a missing element can make a fancy computer come out with a wrong answer, how much easier is it for a man to flounder without correct answers when he fails to consider all the facts as he tries to sift reason and logic. The fact we most often leave out of our calculating is that mankind is in rebellion against God.

Sometimes our pain is brought about by another person using his free will to sin. But if we are honest with ourselves, we know that our pain is often caused by our own wrong choices or rebellion. A grieving widow might sit, wringing her hands, wondering why God was so cruel as to allow her husband to be killed in a car wreck. She could grow bitter toward God and never once consider the fact that her husband had drunk several beers before he left and was driving over the speed limit. I have seen people abuse their bodies for years and then be angry with God because He allowed illness to touch them.

We don't want to pin the reason for our pain

on the people we love and we surely don't want to blame ourselves! It hurts to admit those we love are partly responsible for the trouble we are facing. And it is embarassingly painful to know our present unhappiness is of our own making as we reap the unholy crop we have sown.

When God questioned Adam about his sin, Adam said, "Eve made me do it." Eve said, "The snake made me do it" and we have been blaming someone else ever since. When an unhappy experience is small we blame it on some person who is small, like John Doe or Henry Poe. And if our unhappiness is big we usually blame somebody who is big, like God or the devil. How often we have heard people say, "the devil made me do it." Our attitude seems to be, blame it on anyone but don't blame it on me or anyone I love. When wondering about the "why" of the pain of life we dare not leave ourselves out of our calculations because our free wills are a part of the problem.

The world is not what God wants it to be. He does not greet everything that is done with approval and a smile, but neither is He sitting by idly while His children struggle as best they can. Just because God has given us the freedom of not loving and obeying Him is no proof that those who do choose to follow Him are left at the mercy of the world.

The writers of our Bible knew God intimately and they called Him, "A very present help in trouble" (Ps. 46:1); "My rock and my fortress" (Ps. 71:3) and David prayed, "Lead me to the rock that is higher than I. For Thou hast been a shelter for me and a strong tower from the enemy" (Ps. 61:2-3). While God leaves us in the world we are subject to many of the same troubles as the rest of mankind. We grow old, have accidents, and sometimes illness catches us, but our strong tower is dependable.

In Our Troubles or From Our Troubles?

God rules supreme above any trouble we will ever face. He is all-sufficient in every situation and well able to make any problem we face melt like dewdrops before sunshine. He can make disease vanish instantly. He can cure a drug addict without the usual pain of withdrawal. He can miraculously cure financial problems overnight. And truly He sometimes works in just such dynamic ways. I like nothing better than to hear of an out-and-out miracle story from a Christian whom I know I can trust. Few things give me more hope and courage than to read of some awesome work of God as He snatches up a hopeless person and changes him in an instant, or takes some impossible situation and straightens it out as easily as I can uncurl a paper clip. These things are beautiful but they present a problem—they are usually happening to other people—seldom do they happen to me. Other people walk up to a problem and He zaps it out of their way. I walk up to a problem and He hands me a sword and says, "Okay, Baker, I'm going to teach you to fight." God can instantly and miraculously do anything He wants to do, but more often than not, what He wants to do is teach us how to be saved *in* our troubles now and *from* our troubles later.

Most every growing Christian has come to the time when he must face problems as if he were valiantly brandishing a sword at some two-headed monster. Our hearts gain strength by the presence of the Lord, as we realize His control over the situation. Then suddenly we don't feel the Lord's presence anymore and we begin to doubt His control. At times like these we turn around and say, "Hey, Lord! Where'd You go? I thought You loved me!"

When dry, lonely times are upon us we need to know beyond doubt that God is love. We need to refresh ourselves in the fact that love *always* has at its heart the good and advancement of the beloved. But that is hard to accept when our pain is real and all our prayers seem to fall on deaf ears and the two-headed monster of a problem seems to grin at our helplessness. Probably all of us have faced the time when we did not feel the presence of God and found ourselves pleading, "Why, Lord?" Even Jesus knew the moment when He prayed, "My God, My God, why have You forsaken Me?" (Matt. 27:46, NIV) and heaven was silent. As far as we can determine from the Bible account, Jesus got no answer to that question this side of death. And this brings us back to the original question, "If He loves us why does He allow these times?" Why do we ever know sorrow if He saved us to share His joy? Why are we ever buffeted by Satan if He saved us to know victory? Why does God ever answer, "Wait" or "No"?

Part of the answer as to why He lets the feeling of His presence leave us at times is because we stand in danger of letting our genuine love for Him change to selfish-love as we become so involved in *receiving* feelings we can no longer *give* service without them. The following story illustrates another reason.

Dr. Elizabeth Kubler Ross did research for her book, *On Death and Dying,* in hospital wards among terminally ill patients. She spent many, many hours among the dying studying how best they could be helped. She watched children and old people die and sought through it all to learn from the experience of death the most basic needs of the dying. She was armed with a brilliant mind, a good education, and plenty of subject material, but one of her greatest insights to the subject, I once heard her explain in a television interview, came not from all these fine assets but from a maid.

Dr. Ross explained how she could not understand why every time this particular maid went to clean a patient's room the atmosphere of the room was somehow changed. This woman seemed to leave some indefinable something in the room when she left and often the patients would need less pain medication after she had been there.

Dr. Ross became curious and began to question the maid about what she did while she was alone with the patients but the woman was most apprehensive about such questions and fearfully insisted that she did nothing to the people but "just do my business and get out."

It took some time before Dr. Ross could win the woman's trust enough to open up once again the delicate subject of how one uneducated maid could do something beautiful for dying people that medical science and psychology could not. One day over a cup of coffee the woman began to tell Dr. Ross about her life.

She told of how she had grown up in the ghetto and all the things she had suffered. Then at last she told of her three-year-old child who had died in her arms as she waited in line at a charity clinic because she could not afford a doctor.

She summed up her uncanny ability to aid the dying by saying, "You see, ma'am, I know death and trouble. I have faced them and made my peace with them and in a way they are my friends. I told you the truth. I don't do anything to the patients but clean their rooms and sometimes I go over to the bed and touch their hands. I have made my peace with death and they know it and it helps them to make peace with it too."

So it was that Dr. Ross learned that a very important factor in ministering to the dying was not education or psychological know-how but that you, yourself, have personally met the terror they are facing and have made peace with it.

This is a fear-ridden world. We watch our dollar shrink smaller and smaller and we are only half joking when we ask if it will vanish altogether. We see natural disasters both small and great around the world. An earthquake in South America and thousands upon thousands of people are suddenly homeless. A flood in Asia and tons of what were once breathing, living people are carried away with the debris. A drought and England can no longer grow enough food to feed her people. These places have ceased to sound far away and, as rational people, we know *our* home, *our* life, *our* food might be next. There are troubles close to us. A friend, just our age, is stricken with cancer and spends years wasting away slowly, painfully. A home on the other side of town is robbed and the occupants brutally killed. There are the unseen fears: a noise outside our bedroom window in the deep of the night. A siren on the street when one we love has not yet come home. There are the inside fears of humiliation, old age, rejection. And there is the ultimate fear—death. On every hand, in every way, Adam's children are creatures riddled through and through with fear.

It might seem logical at first thought, that if God really loved us, He would place a shield around each of us and we would not have to face fear and trouble like the rest of the world. Would not placing us in a protective bubble be a way to demonstrate His love? A nice soft bubble where we could close our eyes and never see the results of evil, close our ears and never hear the anguished cries of evil, close our hearts and never feel the pain of evil.

But the will of our loving Father was not to spin us inside a warm cocoon where we would be unaware of the dangers of this world, but rather that we would walk hand in hand with Him and approach each dangerous, fearful thing head on. By doing this we prove to ourselves and then to others that God is bigger than any evil this world has to offer. It is the will of our Father that we make our peace with each of the troubles and tragedies of life, that we be able to walk up to financial disaster and say, "I don't fear you, for my Father owns the cattle on a thousand hills." That we could touch illness and say, "I don't fear you, for the source of my peace and happiness is God—not physical existence." That we could face death, the ultimate fear, and confidently say, "I will fear no evil for God is with me."

This is no task to be accomplished overnight! It is a lifetime of learning to trust God. It is getting so close to the fire we can smell the charred wood and feel the heat on our skin. It is knowing the flood so well we can describe to another how it feels to be swept away by the tide and rushed along by a power we cannot control. It is watching Him give us peace when any logical human would panic, and it is marveling as He opens a door at the last moment. It is a forever accelerating adventure in faith and learning.

As we face adverse circumstances, doubts, and fears like the rest of the world and make our peace with them and overcome them, we prove to troubled people that the hope we tell them about is real and that the help of God is practical and available to them also.

Jesus never asks us to go where He does not lead the way (John 10:4). Jesus came to earth to experience the same trouble, fear, and temptation that each one of us faces. He lived in an age of violence and political corruption as the Roman government subjected His people to total rule. He saw illness close enough to smell it, and injustice close enough to touch it. He knew the power of nature as storms squalled over the Sea of Galilee. He was taxed and He paid the tithe and more than likely was for some time the financial support of His earthly family. He did all this to help us learn how to suffer and not be overcome.

The writer of the Book of Hebrews spoke of the reason Jesus chose to live like one of us in the world when he wrote, "Since the children have flesh and blood, He too shared in their humanity so that by His death He might destroy him who holds the power of death—that is, the devil—and free those who all their lives were held in slavery by their fear of death. For surely it is not angels He helps, but Abraham's descendants. For this reason He had to be made like His brothers in every way, in order that He might become a merciful and faithful high priest in service to God, and that He might make atonement for the sins of the people. Because He Himself suffered when He was tempted, He is able to help those who are being tempted" (Heb. 2:14-18, NIV).

Jesus never sinned, though He was tempted, and He never gave in to fear. Yet, by facing what we face, and feeling what we feel, He put Himself in a position to help us when we face these things because He has overcome them—made personal peace with them—by trusting in His Father's control of all things and by yielding to His will.

The Forever Side of Man

Tragedies touch God's children because of the free will God has given each of us. Experiencing these tragedies puts us in a position to minister to a lost world. Tragedies also give God's child, along with the pain, something precious and permanent that can be his very own.

We will take only one thing from this earth when we die—one thing that is all our own. It is the only thing God ever asked us to lend Him because it was the only thing we ever really had charge of in the first place—ourselves and our memories.

I have moved many, many times but one thing I could never leave behind was myself. I could leave behind friends, personal belongings, and pets, and once when a teen I even tried to leave behind my name, but I could never leave myself. Self has tagged along wherever I went. Even when I moved out of the kingdom of Satan and by the power of the blood of Christ became a child of God, self made the move with me. At that moment I was indeed a new creature in Christ (2 Cor. 5:17) but it was also true that I had the same intelligence, same will, and same basic personality I always had. I was still me. When I make the move from this earth to my heavenly home I will take me along. I won't be a mindless blob or cease to exist as an individual personality; God's plan is not to destroy me but to develop me.

Jesus asked a group of people, "What good will it be for a man if he gains the world, yet forfeits his soul?" (Matt. 16:26) Would we be any better off to gain every dream we ever desired if in the process we ceased to exist as individuals? If God gave us health, wealth, and shelter from all adverse circumstances of life, yet in the process let us keep our selfishness, pride, and shrunken hearts, are we really better off? The circumstances of life are temporary, but our personhood is for eternity. I will live with me a lot longer than I will live with a circumstance. Therefore, I need to be able to live with myself.

When God produces inside us a greater ability to love, or show patience, or understanding, or goodness, He has given us a gift that will last through eternity. Even if He allows pain to touch us in order to produce these fine things it can still be said that He has given us a good and perfect gift (James 1:7).

The man who wrote Psalm 66 had walked with God through trouble and trial and after he had come through it all he said, "Sing to the Lord, all

the earth! Sing of His glorious name! Tell the
world how wonderful He is. . . . Let everyone bless
God and sing His praises, for He holds our lives
in His hands: And He holds our feet to the path.
You have purified us with fire, O Lord, like silver
in a crucible. You captured us in Your net and laid
great burdens on our backs. . . . We went through
fire and flood. But in the end, You brought us into
wealth and great abundance. . . . Come and hear,
all of you who reverence the Lord, and I will tell
you what He did for me: For I cried to Him for
help, with praises ready on my tongue . . . He
heard my prayer! Blessed be God who didn't turn
away when I was praying, and didn't refuse me
His kindness and love" (LB).

11

LOVE
and Rejection

The sign said "Taylor VA Hospital." The large complex of buildings, gardens, and parking lots looked pleasant enough to the eye but the sight of them left me cold inside. I had traveled 400 miles to get here and now that I had arrived, I wasn't sure I could go through with it. I passed the first gate and the second. There was a coffee shop across from the third and largest gate and I pulled in there instead. Maybe a soft drink or cup of tea would untie the knots in my stomach.

The entire front of the little shop was glass and as I sat at the counter and ordered a cold drink, I felt as if the huge buildings across the street were staring down the back of my neck. A shiver went through me. In an effort to be brave, I turned sideways on the stool and looked right back at them. But I knew it was not the buildings that bothered me. It was the man somewhere inside them.

How long had it been since I last saw him? I began to count the years. Thirteen. It seemed like so much longer. What would our meeting be like? What would I call him? Daddy? The words didn't seem to fit my mouth.

I had been so surprised when someone from the hospital phoned me and took a tape recording of my voice giving them permission to do the surgery. Why me? I turned around and glanced aimlessly at my drink. Indeed, it was the uncanny timing that assured me God's hand was in this situation regardless of how many knots were in my stomach.

The last time I had seen my father face to face was in a cheap hotel room in my hometown. I had threatened to kill him and slammed the door behind me, vowing never to lay eyes on him again. Eight years passed. I next heard about him in a tearful telephone conversation I had with my younger sister. She said he was living on the streets in a nearby town. Winter was approaching and she feared he would not survive another winter. I had mailed a coat, gloves, and hat for him to her address but I made no effort to contact him. Five more years had passed.

I began to write a book on love and the Spirit began to deal strongly with my heart saying, "You can't write about love when you still avoid this situation with your father." I tried to avoid what must have been the urging of the Spirit. I did not want to go back and open up old wounds. "Go back and face him" the Spirit seemed to say and I knew that I must once more open communication with the man who had hurt me so badly.

At last I contacted my sister to see if she still knew where our father was. She did. Having received legal custody of him from the government, she had placed him in a home for veterans where he had been drying out from his alcoholism for several months. I wrote him a simple, short letter telling him where I lived, how many children I had, and encouraged him to write if he wanted to. I never really expected to hear from him again.

In the meantime, my father had become ill and the lady who managed the home had taken him to the VA Hospital for a checkup. They had phoned her a few days later and asked the name of the next of kin so they could obtain permission to operate. Since my sister was in the process of moving, her phone was disconnected, so the lady gave them the name and address on a letter that had arrived only the day before—which was my letter, the first one in 13 years. The hospital was not even sure I was related to the man in question but they called just in case.

Because I had felt so strongly that the hand of the Lord was actively involved with these events, I knew He wanted me to see my father. It seemed impossible. There were many mountains to be moved, including one stubborn husband. But one by one the mountains melted and I had traveled these 400 miles.

I finished my soft drink and turned around once more to face the hospital. The years had worn away. I was no longer that bitter, frightened girl storming out of a hotel room. I was now a woman, a Christian writer studying the subject of love.

In the corner of my eye I noticed an elderly gentleman looking at me with curiosity and I wondered if the anxiety inside me was as obvious as I felt it was. It was hard to cross that street but I knew I had to.

Half aloud I quoted, "I can do everything

through Him who gives me strength" (Phil. 4:13, NIV) and got up and walked out the door to meet my father. His mind was dulled by alcohol and his face was aged beyond his years. I played a few games of checkers with him and left saying, "Good-bye . . . Daddy."

Someone has said, "The saddest words on tongue or pen are simply these, it might have been." As I pulled out of the parking lot that day and headed toward home, all those "it might have been" possibilities ran through my mind and I saw the words in a new light. What would life have been like without the liquor and illness and lean times? Would I have become a different woman? I considered the possibility and decided that I was in God's hand and there was no need for either the present or the past to do me permanent harm. We can be hurt from the outside—hurt deeply—but in His hand we mend and are stronger and better for the wear. Even the deepest scars can fade into insignificance when time and the Master work together.

All those years I had thought my father rejected me and scorned my love. But as the miles of highway slipped past and sun moved steadily across the sky, I began to wonder if I hadn't perhaps been rejecting him because he did not live up to my standards.

Years ago, I thought it was my privilege and duty to tell everyone about what a hard life I had had, but when I stopped talking long enough to listen, I discovered that everyone has had a hard life one way or another. Divorce, disappointments, alcohol, rebellious teenagers, shiftless parents, drugs, faithless friends, crooked business partners

—the list is endless! All of us on occasion are slammed against situations we can't help and don't understand. Often these situations are caused by someone who failed to show genuine love to others.

It hurts to have someone deny us the love that we felt was rightfully ours, or when others fail to respond to the love we offer them. Such hurts can scar our personalities with bitterness. Sometimes we try our best to establish a good relationship with someone and all our efforts seem as effective as a person trying to swim his way out of quick sand.

Our difficulty might be caused by long-standing ill feelings between us and someone else, so we decide to take the first step to set things right. We go to the person and apologize. He treats our apology as hypocrisy and refuses to forgive us.

Or, maybe, the problem is a poverty-stricken family we may know. We or our church group may want to help them, so we bring in clothes, help the children with school supplies, and show other acts of kindness. Then, much to our surprise, the family abuses and throws away things as fast as we bring them in!

I once knew a woman who lived in poverty and filth. Her husband had died, so the ladies from a local church brought in food and cleaned the filthy house as well. For three weeks they came to help the poor woman. But when they failed to show up on the fourth week, she called the preacher and demanded to know why. When told that she could not expect others to help when she showed such little effort on her own part, the woman told the preacher off in very colorful terms.

What are Christians expected to do with people who refuse to respond to love? How do we deal with someone who refuses to forgive and forget? What about those who take for granted all our kind acts of love, and fail to respond? These people are not always extreme examples way across town. They can be our own blood relatives.

The Legal Right To Be Loved

There is such a thing as having the legal right to be loved. When God gave man the law, "Thou shalt not steal" (Deut. 5:19), He was in principle giving me the right to keep and control what I lawfully earned. Likewise, when God gave the commandment for a man to love his wife (Eph. 5:25), He was in principle saying that wives have the right to expect to be loved by their husbands. The teaching that states that neighbors are to be loved (Luke 10:25-37) implies that neighbors have the right to expect to be accepted by those who live around them. A child has the right to expect to be loved by his parents simply because he is their child (see Luke 17:1-2). To give that child, that neighbor, that mate less than his right is sin (1 John 3:4).

When someone steals from us, we are not the sinner. He is, because he has deprived us of what God said was rightfully ours. At times, it can be a very needed thing to learn that when someone deprives us of the love that is rightfully ours, we are not guilty—he is.

Many a child has faced life feeling guilty because his parents failed to love him. He feels there is something wrong with him and somehow it is his fault that they don't treat him as they should.

This child needs to know that he is not guilty for someone else's sin.

Pastors can be crushed by guilt that rightfully belongs to their congregations.

Marriages can become a living hell as one partner tries to shoulder all the blame when feelings of love die. We cannot force others to love. God did not put in our hands the responsibility of making others act right, and if they fail to meet their obligation of love we should not let Satan convince us that we are guilty of their sins.

There is a large degree to which we can encourage others to love and create an atmosphere in which love can grow. There is a degree to which we are responsible to show them love by our example. But we should not bear the weight of sins for which we are not responsible. We were never designed to carry such burdens. In fact, we can't even bear our own guilt, which is why we need a Saviour. How complicated and burdensome we make our way when we try to shoulder guilt that is not rightfully ours.

Jesus knew what it was like to have His rights denied, including His right to be loved (John 1:11) and, just as Jesus always does, He has shown us the proper way to handle the situation. He has been in that circumstance before us and understands.

One sure way *not* to handle the situation is to cut ourselves down to worm size and begin to think we are not worthy of other people's love. Jesus never cut Himself down or claimed that He was not worth the love of others. He did not seek favors and complain when He was denied. Jesus knew His own value. He was Messiah, the King, and He indicated that He knew He had a right to the love and respect of His people. Yet, when they denied Him this right, Jesus treated the situation just as He did when they denied Him other rights, such as His right to justice, His right to the throne of David, and His right to life. **He allowed others the freedom to do wrong.**

When they stole the clothes off His back (Matt. 27:35) He did not call down fire from heaven or demand that angels come with flaming swords to grab back what was rightfully His. Neither did He meekly say, "Well, soldiers, I guess you are right. My back is not really worth covering." But He did recognize that what they were doing was sin and He committed His cause to God and asked that He forgive those who wronged Him (Luke 23:34). This demonstrated His trust that God was in charge of judging sin and showed His love for the thieves despite their wrongdoing.

Are we not expected to follow His example? Aren't we supposed to allow someone the freedom to do us wrong? Yes. The only exception is when God has divinely delegated some of His authority to man. For instance, civil authority has the God-given right to exercise judgment and punishment over its citizens (Gen. 9:5-6; Rom. 13:1-7). The local church has this same responsibility over its congregation (Heb. 13:17; Acts 5:1-11) and a father has this right in his home (1 Tim. 3:4-5; Eph. 5:22). But in our everyday, adult relationships we are not given the responsibility to sit as judge and jury over others. This does not mean that we must never call wrong things sin, but it does mean that we leave the judgment and punishment of that sin to God.

We cause ourselves immeasurable trouble by trying to run God's business for Him while the small tasks He has given us to do are ignored! It is not my business to be the vanguard and first defense of my reputation, feelings, or physical self. That is His business—mine is to cooperate with Him by doing what He asks and to take the opportunities He provides. I don't have to worry over next month's house payment—that is His business. Mine is to take the opportunity for work that He has provided and be a good steward of what He gives. If someone hurts me because he does not exercise toward me the love and respect God would have him give, it is not my responsibility to charge or condemn him. That is God's business. Mine is to make sure my own motives are as pure as my self-knowledge and my prayers can make them, and leave the rest to the Lord.

The Stewardship of Love

We are to be responsible stewards of all God has given us. This responsibility includes physical things like money, but it also includes intangible things like prayer and love. There will be times when others will not respond to the acts of love we invest in them. There are people to whom you could give and give and give again, yet they would remain shriveled, self-centered drones. There are those whom no amount of love would warm or change. Judas was a good example.

One person can offer love but it doesn't guarantee that it won't be rejected. Even God's great and perfect love was ineffective until we accepted and responded to it.

There are people for whom we are not encouraged to pray (1 John 5:16) and times when acts of charity are to be withheld (1 Tim. 5:3-4; 2 Thes. 3:10-11). It is not because we no longer love and want to aid them but, because of their self-centeredness, our acts of kindness are useless. They simply absorb our generosity and become dependent leeches.

It is not pleasant to realize that by their own choice people are sometimes ruthless, but at times it is a very necessary fact to admit. We must simply recognize that some people will not respond to the love we want to show them. And we must be prepared and willing to suffer the pain it may cause us.

Love relations can be broken both by ourselves and by others. But God often seems to do His best work on broken pieces! We only need to let Him do as He chooses with the results of our efforts.

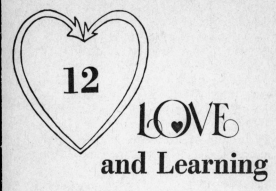

12

LOVE

and Learning

They had all gone. The mighty fire had departed and now there was no heat except the warmth of the sun on his shoulders. He stood alone. The sound of the rushing whirlwind and the beating of the horses' hooves had faded in the distance. The sound of the nearby river and the rustle of leaves were all that broke the silence.

He stood alone. Never again would his friend offer him counsel. Never again would his teacher walk beside him and talk about the things of God. Elijah was gone.

He bent over and gently picked up the mantle that lay crumpled on the ground and slowly walked back toward the river. They were all gone. The mighty fire. The mighty sounds. The mighty teacher. They were gone. Had God left him too?

He reached the edge of the river and, holding the mantle above his head he shouted, "Where is the Lord God of Elijah?" He slapped the coat against the water and it parted. Elisha walked on the bottom of the riverbed because Elijah's God *was* still there.

Many Christians have probably felt as Elisha did that day. In loneliness, they want to slap the river and cry out, "Where is the God of Elijah?"

Bill and Gloria Gaither wrote a song that says, "You have knelt beside the rubble of an aching, broken heart / When the things you gave your life to fell apart."* Every time I stand before an audience and sing those lines, I invariably see someone's eyes light up with recognition and heads begin to nod as if to say, "Yes, Lord, I have been there."

I remember the last time I stood in that place. Though it was a long time ago, it is as clear as yesterday, for severe trials are not forgotten quickly. I remember the impossible path that lay before me and the terrible loneliness I felt—the confusion, the pain. And I remember the reason was love.

Probably every growing Christian will someday face a moment of crisis when what we gave our life to seemingly falls apart. I have been there. Probably you have too. You have told others about the happy life in Christ and then had a tragedy creep up and knock an aching hole in your own life. You firmly believe in the power of prayer and yet have seen your most earnest request go unanswered. You have told others about the power of love and the Source of love only to find your own heart grow stone cold. You may have been by the edge of that river and chances are you wanted to slap the water and question, "Where is the God I have been telling others about? Where is the Lord God of Elijah?"

Many of our problems are caused by a lack of

love in others and our own inability to love as God would have us. It is easy to say that God can heal loveless situations by replacing our cold hearts with warm and tender ones, but to experience this in daily living is a challenge. Sometimes we wonder if we will ever learn to love as we should. Sometimes we feel like asking with the psalmist, "Where is thy God?" (Ps. 42:3)

Love is the theme of Christianity. We preach it from our pulpits, sing love from our hymnbooks, and it is the central message we carry to others. It would seem that anyone so thoroughly saturated with the teaching and philosophy of love would have no trouble laying hold on love in our daily relationships. It is one thing to teach a class of children the story of Ruth's sweet and strong love for her mother-in-law, Naomi, but quite another thing to love our own mother-in-law. It is one thing to listen while a teacher speaks of the beautiful, balanced relationship between husband and wife as outlined in the Bible, but quite another to work out that relationship in our homes. *Talking* of love is one thing, but *loving* is another. We talk about love and believe that God is love and know God lives inside us, yet we may still be unable to exercise a consistent, patient, growing love to those most dear to us. And then we start feeling uncomfortably like a hypocrite.

A friend called the other day and asked if I thought it was possible for real love ever to die. The question has puzzled me ever since. I would like to say that love never dies but my experience has been otherwise. I think people often wake up and discover that their marriages have grown cold. Someone may find his feelings toward God have become routine or may have trouble with a child he no longer understands and discover that what he had been calling "love" is gone. Perhaps such love has been overshadowed by stronger emotions or more pressing problems, or perhaps such love never really existed in the first place, but regardless of what made it vanish, love can be relearned.

Jesus encouraged His followers to "learn" of Him (Matt. 11:29). To learn of Him is to learn love, for He is the reflection of God and God is love. Whether we are trying to love a brother who irritates us, a neighbor who needs Jesus, a child who has wandered from the principles of the faith, or a church congregation that is acting like a bunch of ill-mannered horses, or a mate who has become distant to us through the years, love can be learned. It can be made new and fresh once more.

The Disciple of Love

In his poem, "Death in the Desert," Browning writes what he imagined to be the last words of John as the old and seasoned saint lay dying:

For life with all it yields of joy and woe
   And hope and pain—believe the aged friend—
Is just our charge o' the price of learning love.
How love might be, hath been indeed, and is.
And that, we hold to the uttermost.

Imagine! All the experiences of life: tears, joys, laughter, pain, *all* of it being our price of learning real love!

A study of John's life and his letters are adequate proof to me that, although he did not pen the above words, John would probably have agreed

with them. As a young man, John burned with
ambition. He longed for a choice seat in the cabinet
when Jesus became king of Israel and, to the disciples' way of thinking, that time was not far off.
He and his brother James tried to squeeze a promise from the Lord that these high positions would
be theirs. They wanted to be one cut above the
other disciples and thought themselves well qualified for these positions (Matt. 20:17-23). John was
a hot-tempered man in his youth. To him right
was right and wrong was wrong and he was ready
to spit in the eye of anyone who said different!
Once a Samarian village refused to welcome Jesus,
so John and his brother sought permission from the
Lord to call fire from heaven and burn the place
to the ground (Luke 9:51-56). Jesus even nick-
named the two young fire-eaters, "Sons of Thunder"
(Mark 3:17). Though John possessed an excellent
mind and a poetic nature, the strong but gentle
ways of love seemed foreign to his personality. But
the teachings and reprimands of the Master had
their effect. John learned what real love was by
watching his Lord put it into practice. Later, in a
letter to the church he wrote, "This is how we
know what love is: Jesus Christ laid down His
life for us. And we ought to lay down our lives
for our brothers" (1 John 3:16, NIV). John has more
to say about love than any other writer in the
New Testament. He studied the subject both by
watching Jesus and by personal experience. He
knew love's pain and its cost and he had found
that love was a very learnable subject.

An old tradition of the early church has been
that John went back to Ephesus after his time in
exile on the isle of Patmos and spent the last few

years of his life there. He was supposedly so old and feeble that he had to be carried to the meetings of the church. At the end of each service the pastor would ask John if he had any word for the brethren and each time John would say the same words, "Little children, love one another." Once a fiery youth became a bit impatient with the old gentleman and asked, "But don't you want to say something else?" To which the old sage replied, "My son, there is nothing else."

How Do We Learn Love?

At times we are required to love people we normally wouldn't even like. For instance, a new member of our Bible class "rubs us the wrong way," or we need to minister to a neighbor whose manner of living, race, physical appearance, or social status repels us. Sometimes it is those who are closest to us that we have trouble loving. Love is not necessarily a natural reaction of the heart simply because two people have been married 10 or 20 years. It is not automatically assured that parents will love a child just because they gave him birth. Often relationships between friends or relatives are broken by divorce, gossip, misunderstandings, differences of opinion, or simply that two people have grown away from each other with the passing of time. We know we ought to love ol' so-and-so but aren't sure how to go about changing the things our hearts feel.

I don't know all the answers about how to love, but I have struggled with the problem enough to discover a few tools that work on my own cold heart. Perhaps you will find them helpful too.

1. A *healthy attitude about oneself* is necessary

before we can build love for others. We must recognize our own needs and abilities and limitations. I personally don't believe we can love and appreciate others until we have learned to love and appreciate ourselves. I have heard it said that a friend is someone who knows our faults and loves us anyway. There are times when we need to be our own friend. If we are filled with feelings of guilt or fear or inferiority we will find loving someone else a difficult if not impossible task. Being our own friend is not an excuse to allow us to live any way we want, or commit any sin we happen to desire at the moment. It is simply an admission of our humanity. We accept ourselves with our frailties, trusting Him to correct and improve us. We accept ourselves with our talents and are happy for them, recognizing that every child of God has his own proper place in His plan. When we have a healthy attitude about ourselves, we are in a better position to tap the resources of God.

2. *Freedom for the beloved* is necessary before love can grow. We must set other individuals free from our picky attitudes, criticism, and condemnation before love can grow and bloom. We must turn others loose to be themselves and not try to make them extensions of us. Too much of what we frequently call "love" is nothing more than an all-out effort to make others think as we think, feel as we feel, and do as we do. Often we are not truly seeking to aid and build up those we claim to love but are seeking to bend them into a shape that is more pleasing to us.

Paul asked, "Who are you to judge someone else's servant?" (Rom. 14:4) What right do we have to say how others should comb their hair, shape their political views, and how they should dress? If what others are doing is not contrary to God's Word, it is not our business to speak unless asked. It is not a wife's business to correct her husband's table manners; it is not a mother-in-law's responsibility to say how her son's kitchen should be run. Other people are not our servants—they are God's servants and must be free from our picky condemnation.

3. *Fasting* is another tool I sometimes use when trying to build love. Fasting is taught in both New and Old Testaments. Jesus gave His followers instructions on how to fast just as He gave them instruction on how to pray (Matt. 6:10-19; Luke 11:1-4). Many people have forsaken this custom, but I believe in it. Fasting does not help because God likes to see us go hungry, neither is it some magic club with which we beat God to make Him give us what we want. I believe it works because it is a practical exercise in laying aside immediate self-wants for a larger purpose. That to me is a basic element of loving and a hallmark of Christian growth. Even if practiced for only one meal or on certain types of food, fasting can help teach self-discipline—and self-respect also.

4. *Follow an active investment program.* If we are serious about learning to love someone we must be willing to make investments in their lives. We should look for ways to aid, comfort, and lift our beloved and then do them. This investment in them is not a license for meddling into their affairs or making ourselves a nuisance, but an encouragement to lay aside self-interest to show love to others. Often the most valuable things we can invest are small things such as a birthday card, the

cheerful loan of a garden tool, an invitation to supper. Some of our investment could be intangible things like prayer, consideration, and courtesy. Often we need to invest an open ear and a shut mouth. While we are investing we need to keep our eyes on how we hope to benefit the beloved and not on what we hope to receive for our investment.

5. *Abide in Jesus lest your love go dry.* Jesus is our path to God and God is the source of every good thing, including love (James 1:17). When we sin we are clogging the pipeline between ourselves and God; we are cutting ourselves off from our supply of love, and what could have been a river of living water flowing from us is choked off to a trickle. It can happen without our being aware of it, as tiny sins stick here and there to obstruct God's love. We grow cold and sleepy as bit by bit we drift from Him. Jesus said that we would produce much fruit if we would abide in Him (John 15:5) and one of these fruits is love (Gal. 5:22). We cannot abide in Him and ignore sin in our lives. If we would build love, we must be willing to wage a war against personal sin.

Sinning seems such a simple, natural thing. But God has made the solution for it simple too! All we need do is confess (1 John 1:9). One of the best exercises to engage in while building love is to pause for a moment each night and think back over the day, identify any sin found there, and confess it. Perhaps it was a sin of thought or neglect or perhaps it was what we would think of as a big, ugly, mean sin. But the solution for all sin is basically the same; when the Spirit brings it to light we must confess each sin to our Father and be willing to forsake it. When the path is cleared between us and God, the way is open for His love to fill us.

Investment in Action

Last summer Bill ignored our anniversary. It wasn't that he forgot what date it was—he knew all right, but he chose to ignore it except for a passing reference at the breakfast table. My old self rose up and was as mad as a hornet all day. *This man claims to love me, yet he has failed to give me something my love had a right to receive,* I thought. I had given to him and he had not given back and I felt I had every right to be angry.

When Bill came home that evening and asked about my surly disposition I wasted no time telling him in very blunt terms what I thought about his forgetting our anniversary. His only response was to smile, firmly slap my back side and say, "Now, mama, don't get hostile."

But mama *was* hostile and growing more so by the minute. About sundown he suggested that we ride across the pasture and check the cows. Again, this was his way of showing his love. I was strongly tempted to pick up the words God had made me stop using and tell him that if he wanted those cows checked he could check them by himself. That was what I wanted to do but like a hundred times before, I knew that how I *wanted* to react and how I *should* react were two different things.

It is not a sin to be angry or hurt. But it becomes sin when we let those feelings hang on (Eph. 4:26). We are told to be careful lest any root of bitterness spring up in us (Heb. 12:15) and anger can be fertile soil for the roots of bitterness or self-pity. There is a time to lay anger and hurt aside. I was married to this man and claimed to love him. I had expressed my feelings and told him my thoughts about what he had done. Now it was time to lay aside anger and I knew it.

But exactly how does one do that? Do we just say, "OK heart, do an about-face. Throw out the feelings of anger and replace them with love and you have five minutes to accomplish it." I don't know about your heart but mine does not always obey such instructions on command. What then?

First of all, I used my tool of freedom for the beloved. I thoroughly believed Bill had been wrong but I needed to allow him the freedom to be wrong if that was the way he chose. I needed to set him free from my condemnation. I did not have to lie to myself and say his inconsideration was right but I had to stop being judge, and jury, and hangman; I needed to set him free to be himself even if I did not approve of his actions. This was not an act of the emotions or commanding my heart to feel a certain way, but an act of the will and intelligence—a decision I made without any help from my feelings.

I still felt angry.

The second tool I picked up was yielding myself to make an investment. He wanted to bounce around the pasture in a truck, so I climbed into the truck. I invested in our relationship; I laid aside personal wants (and stubbornness) and yielded myself to do something that I knew would please the one I was trying to love. I got in on the passenger side and snuggled hard against the door because my anger had only cooled enough to make a little investment, not a large one. Bill tried to open the conversation but my only response was an occasional grunt.

The next tool was used to open the path of communication between myself and my God. My feelings had been bruised because someone had failed to return to me the things I felt my love had a right to receive. I began to think about God being all love—pure love—and of how many, many times I failed to give back to Him the things His great love had a right to receive. The Bible says that we can grieve God (Eph. 4:30) by our actions. When I mistreated Him He did not swell up and refuse to speak to me. Realizing that this small picture of His patience, grace, and love had to be multiplied by the total number of God's children, the idea astounded me. When He was so gracious to me what right did I have to nurse my anger and refuse to be gracious to the man I had pledged to love for life? "God," I asked, "are You *always* laying aside self-consideration and giving to Your beloved instead?" I could feel the Holy Spirit laugh. Of course! Because God is the highest measure of love.

Although he was still fighting for a toehold, anger was slowly being forced out.

It was time for another investment installment. What could I invest? I studied the profile of my man for a moment then asked, "Do you want me to wash your hair when we get back?" Bill knew the storm was almost over and his eyes held a tenderness as he reached across the truck seat and took my hand. "That's all right," he said, "I can do it." By the time we reached home, the feelings of love were once more inside me.

Although this is a simple illustration using a

minor problem, the principles it teaches have proved beyond value to me and have worked repeatedly in large problems as well as small. These teachings, especially the art of laying self aside and investing in the one we hope to love, have saved my marriage, retained my usefulness to the Lord, and made love for my children a reality.

It is never easy to learn the art of love. Like the work of any artist, lasting, giving, Godlike love does not spring up by itself. It takes devotion, effort, and a lifetime of practice to perfect. We are continually bumping into knots in our lives—times when our love-ability is sorely tried. At times every ounce of self will be in rebellion against the idea of being laid aside while an act of investment is performed for another, but if, in the process, we are able to learn to love and spread love and enjoy love, then all our trouble will be well worth the effort.

Our families need our love, our church and community need our love, a dying world needs our love. These are the last days and the love of many is growing cold, the warmth and stability of being loved by another is being denied to lonely people all around us. The last commandment Jesus gave His followers before He faced the cross was that they love others.

People are searching for genuine love. Their hearts are hungry for it. On a papyrus fragment preserved in the Berlin Museum, an unknown author bemoans the lack of love in his days of 2,000 B.C. Yet only a few years ago, one of the top songs in the U.S.A. was "What the World Needs Now is Love, Sweet Love." Four thousand years have passed between one poet and the next, but people are still searching, still trying to find the rainbow of love they have been chasing for so long.

Elisha slapped the water in despair and called on God to show Himself real and alive and active in the affairs of men. We, too, face those moments when we need the reality of His presence and the assurance that He can supply us with joy and the ability to love in this world of rush hour traffic and strained relationships.

We have told the world that our God is sufficient. Now we need to step out in faith and prove it. Even though we still face the problems of budgets, marriage relationships, peer pressure, emotional ups and downs, and all the other trials of living, we must prove that our Source is able to teach us peace and love. We must show a thirsty world that the Lord God of Elijah still lives.

We who know the Lord know the Source of perfect love. Let's learn to love and then give it to the people we touch each day.

---

*"Joy Comes in the Morning," Gaither Music, P. O. Box 300, Alexandria, IN, Copyright 1974.

"Grace..." Something urgent was overtaking him, almost shaking him.

"Do you really think I don't know you want me, too?"

They were so close, the rain pounding down all around them, stranding them beneath a noisy umbrella. Wolfe Manor, with all of its howling ghosts and terrible memories, faded away until there was nothing but the weather, this umbrella and this overly polite, overdressed woman who had somehow wedged herself under his skin.

And she was dismissing him.

"I want a great many things that are no good for me," she told him. "No one should get everything they want. What kind of person would they be?"

"Me," Lucas said, an odd note in his own voice. "They would be me."

"Well," she said after a moment. "Life is not about *want*, Mr. Wolfe."

Something passed between them, electric and alive, dancing in the breath of space between their bodies and jolting into him. "If I kissed you right now," he said, his eyes trained on hers and the truth he could see there—the truth that resonated in him no matter what words she threw out to deny it, "I could make you forget your own name."

That hung there like smoke for a heartbeat, then another, and then, impossibly, she laughed.

At him.

Caitlin Crews

THE DISGRACED PLAYBOY

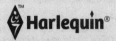

TORONTO NEW YORK LONDON
AMSTERDAM PARIS SYDNEY HAMBURG
STOCKHOLM ATHENS TOKYO MILAN MADRID
PRAGUE WARSAW BUDAPEST AUCKLAND

Recycling programs
for this product may
not exist in your area.

ISBN-13: 978-0-373-23770-8

First published in the UK as 'The Shameless Playboy'

First North American Publication 2011

Copyright © by Harlequin Books S.A. 2011
Special thanks and acknowledgment are given to Caitlin Crews
for her contribution to The Notorious Wolfes series

Printed in U.S.A.

All about the author...
Caitlin Crews

CAITLIN CREWS discovered her first romance novel at the age of twelve, in a bargain bin at the local five-and-dime. It involved swashbuckling pirates, grand adventures, a heroine with rustling skirts and a mind of her own, and a seriously mouthwatering and masterful hero. The book—(the title of which remains lost in the mists of time)—made a serious impression. Caitlin was immediately smitten with romances and romance heroes, to the detriment of her middle-school social life. And so began her lifelong love affair with romance novels, many of which she insists on keeping near her at all times, thus creating a fire hazard of love wherever she lives.

Caitlin has made her home in places as far-flung as York, England, and Atlanta, Georgia. She was raised near New York City, and fell in love with London on her first visit when she was a teenager. She has backpacked in Zimbabwe, been on safari in Botswana and visited tiny villages in Namibia. She has, while visiting the place in question, declared her intention to live in Prague, Dublin, Paris, Athens, Nice, the Greek Islands, Rome, Venice and/or any of the Hawaiian islands. Writing about exotic places seems like the next best thing to moving there.

She currently lives in California with her animator/comic book artist husband and their menagerie of ridiculous animals.

CHAPTER ONE

GRACE Carter glanced up from her computer, frowning at the figure that sauntered so confidently into her office high above the cold, wet February streets of central London, without so much as a knock on her door as warning.

And then she went very still in her chair. Something that felt like fire rolled through her, scorching everything in its path. She told herself it was indignation because he had failed to knock as any decent, polite person should—but she knew better.

It was *him*.

"Good morning," he said in a low, richly amused and somehow knowing voice that seemed to echo inside of her. He seemed to smolder there in front of her, like a banked flame. She straightened in her seat in reaction.

"By all means," she said, her voice cool, ironic. "Come right in."

He was dressed in a sharp, sleek Italian suit that

clung to the hard planes of his celebrated body and looked far too fashion-forward for the staid and storied halls of Hartington's, one of Britain's oldest luxury department stores, where *conservative* was the watchword in word, deed and staff apparel. His too-long dark chocolate hair was tousled and unkempt—rather deliberately so, Grace thought uncharitably—and fell toward his remarkable green eyes, one of which was ringed by a darkening bruise. It matched the split lip that failed, somehow, to dampen the impact of his shockingly carnal mouth. His cuts and bruises gave him a faintly roguish air and added to the man's already outrageous appeal.

And well he knew it.

"Thank you," he said, those famous green eyes bright with amusement, quite as if her invitation was sincere. His decadent mouth crooked to the side. "Is that an invitation into your office or, one can only hope, somewhere infinitely more exciting?"

Grace wished she did not recognize him, but she did—and this was not the first time she'd seen him in person. Not that anyone alive could fail to identify him on sight, with a face that was usually plastered across at least one or two tabloids weekly, in every country in the world. Showcasing exactly this kind of inappropriate behavior.

She was not impressed.

"Lucas Wolfe," she said, as a gesture toward good manners, though her voice was flat.

He was *Lucas Wolfe,* second son of the late, notoriously flamboyant William Wolfe, darling of the paparazzi, famously faithless lover to hordes of equally rich and supernaturally beautiful women—and Grace could not think of a single reason why this creature of tabloids and lore should be standing in her office on a regular Thursday morning, gazing at her in a manner that could only be called *expectant.*

"All six resplendent feet and then some," he drawled, his dark brows arching high above his wicked green eyes. "At your service."

"You are Lucas Wolfe," she said, ignoring the innuendo that seemed to infuse his voice, his expression, like some kind of molten chocolate. "And I'm afraid I am busy. Can I direct you to someone who can help you?"

"Too busy for my charm and beauty?" he asked, that wicked grin making his eyes gleam, his expression somewhere between suggestive and irrepressible—and surprisingly infectious. Grace had to fight to keep from smiling automatically in return. "Surely not. That would require hell to freeze over, for a start."

She ignored him, rising to her feet to regain the appropriate balance of power.

"I would invite you make yourself comfortable,"

she said with a tight smile, close enough to courteous, knowing her voice would make the words sound sweeter than they were, "except that seems rather redundant, doesn't it?"

Every instinct she had screamed at her to let this man know exactly what she thought of his kind. Womanizing, useless, parasitic, just like all the men her poor mother had paraded in and out of their trailer when Grace was a child. Just like the father she'd never met, who from all accounts was yet one more pretty, irresponsible wastrel in a long line of the same. Just like every other idiot she'd had to slap down over the years.

But as a member of the Wolfe family Lucas was considered royalty at Hartington's, given that his family had once owned the company. The Wolfes might not own Hartington's any longer, but Hartington's board of directors loved to play up the connection—and as the events manager who was in charge of Hartington's centenary relaunch in a matter of weeks, Grace was expected to act in Hartington's best interests at all times no matter the cost to herself.

"I am always comfortable," he assured her, his voice a symphony of innuendo, his green eyes wicked and amused. "Making myself so at every opportunity is, I confess, very nearly my life's work."

She had a huge project to manage, which meant

she had better things to do with her time than waste it on this useless, if shockingly attractive, man. Grace hated wasting time. *That* was the feeling that expanded within her, she told herself, threatening her ability to breathe.

"I'm sorry," she began, the polite smile she was known for curving her lips, though she knew her gaze remained cool on his. "I'm afraid I'm quite busy today. May I help—?"

"Why do I recognize you?" he interrupted her, languidly, because of course *he* had all the time in the world.

Grace was horrified to feel that rich voice of his wash through her, sending tendrils of flame licking all over her skin, coiling low in her belly. She *felt* it, and it panicked her. Surely she should be immune to this man's brand of practiced, cynical charm—she, who prided herself on being absolutely unflappable!

"I can't imagine," she said, which was a lie, but it was not as if she and Lucas Wolfe would ever speak again, would they? She could not fathom why they were speaking *now*—and why the cynical boredom she'd sensed in him in a chic and crowded hotel bar the night before had changed to something else, something dangerous and edgy. As if a dark fury lurked within him, just out of sight, hidden beneath his well-known and deliberately polished exterior.

But surely not. She was being fanciful.

"I know I've seen you before," he continued, his green eyes narrowing slightly as he looked at her, then warming as he let his all-too-practiced gaze drop from her face to skate over the figure she'd dressed in Carolina Herrera and other exclusive labels no doubt down-market to a man of his tastes. His lips moved, sensual and inviting for all they were cut, seeming to…*suggest* things. "You have the most extraordinary mouth. But where?"

Heat danced through her, simmering in every place his green gaze touched her: her breasts, the indentation at her waist, her hips, her legs. Grace was forced to remind herself that a man like Lucas Wolfe more than likely looked at every single person he encountered in that very same way— that the promise of sex and intrigue that seemed to heat his expression meant about as much to him as a handshake meant to anyone else. Less.

She felt a strange sort of echo sound through her, a deep alarm, reminding her of that naive girl she'd been so long ago and had sworn she would never be again. Not with another man like this one, who would render her just as pathetic and deceived as her poor, trusting mother. Who would destroy her whole life if she let him.

That was what men like this did. Simply because they could.

Grace knew that better than anyone.

"He's more than a bit of all right, isn't he?" the fashion buyer from Hartington's had cooed to Grace last night, when she'd first seen Lucas—much drunker and far more disreputable than he appeared now, if that was possible—at an extraordinarily glamorous fashion show thrown by Samantha Cartwright, one of London's most beloved and avant-garde designers.

Mona had sighed lustily, gazing at Lucas from across the trendy bar as he'd flirted with Samantha Cartwright herself, oblivious to all the watching, judging eyes around them, Grace's among them. "And, of course, we're to treat him like a king should he so much as glance our way. Boss's orders."

Grace had nodded, as if she'd had the slightest expectation of interacting with the famous playboy, known as much for his devil-may-care attitude as for his long and illustrious string of lovers. Not to mention his much-discussed allergy to anything resembling work, particularly for Hartington's, who had been after him for years to take a figurehead position with the company as his equally disreputable late father had once done.

She'd felt a potent mix of awareness and disgust as she'd watched him. How could a man like Lucas, who was unabashedly making a play for the much older, and very much married, Samantha Cartwright right there in full view of half the city, also manage to seem so…*alive* and *vibrant,* in the midst of London's crème de la crème, as if he were the real thing and they were nothing but fluff and misdirection?

However, all his sexiness and charm had not prevented Samantha Cartwright's husband from expressing his displeasure at finding Lucas secluded with his wife sometime later—all over Lucas's pretty face.

The fact that she, personally, had had a strange moment, a near-interaction with this man, did not signify. He clearly could not recall it and she—well, if her sleep had been disrupted last night, what did that matter? It could as easily have been the espresso she should have known better than to order after dinner. It had to have been.

"I believe I saw you last night at the Cartwright show," she said now, and felt gratified when he blinked, as if not expecting that response. Grace smiled, razor sharp, and let her dislike for him—for all men like him, so careless and callous—flood through her. "Though I cannot imagine you remember it."

"I have an excellent memory," Lucas replied, his voice silky, and she had to admit that it got to her. It should not have affected her at all, the lazy caress of it, like bourbon and sin, but it did. The man was lethal, and she wanted nothing to do with him.

"As do I, Mr. Wolfe," she said crisply. "Which is how I know that we do not have an appointment today. Perhaps I can direct you…?"

She let her words trail off, and waved her hand in the general direction of the door and the offices beyond. But Lucas Wolfe did not move. He only watched her for a moment. His battered, sexy mouth curved slightly.

"You knew who I was the moment you saw me." He looked amused. Triumphant. She could not have said why that seemed to claw at her.

"I imagine every single person in England knows who you are," she replied briskly. She let her brows arch, hinting at disdain. "One assumes that must be your intention, after so many scandals, all of which are dutifully reported in the papers."

"And yet, you are not English," he said, shifting his body, making Grace suddenly, foolishly glad that her desk stood between them.

She was abruptly aware of how powerful he was, how well-tuned and whipcord tough his body was, for all he kept it concealed behind a lazy smile, calculating eyes and sophisticated clothes. Leashed and hidden, though the truth of it lurked beneath the surface. As if his playboy persona was a mask he wore…but that was ridiculous.

"You are American, are you not?" His head tilted slightly to one side, though his gaze never left hers. "Southern, if I am not mistaken."

"I cannot imagine why it should be relevant, but I am originally from Texas," Grace said, in quelling tones. She did not speak about her past. She did not speak about her private life at all, come to that—never at work, and certainly not with perfect strangers. The origin of the accent she'd worked so hard to minimize was about as far as she was willing to take this conversation. "But if you will tell me why you are here, I can find a more appropriate—"

"Exactly what did you see me doing last night?" he asked, interrupting her again, his gaze amused, his grin widening. "Did I do it to you?" His gaze warmed, became more suggestive. "Do you wish that I had?"

"I hardly think you would have had the time," Grace said with a short laugh, but then his eyes gleamed and she recollected herself.

She had not worked as hard as she had, nor overcome so much, to ruin it all over someone like this. She didn't know why Lucas Wolfe, of all people, should get under her skin in the first place. Grace had been working in events management since college, and she had seen her fair share of huge personalities, the very rich and the wished-to-be-famous, and everything in between. Why was this man the first to threaten her renowned calm?

Lucas only gazed at her, his green eyes mild,

though Grace could not quite believe what she saw there. She had the sense, again, that it was all a mask—the shocking masculine beauty, the roguish appeal, the sexy swagger—and that beneath it lurked something far shrewder. But where did such an idea come from? She dismissed it, impatient with herself.

"If you will excuse me," she said, her voice perfectly calm, betraying none of her strange internal struggle, "I really must return to my work."

"But that's why I'm here," he said, an unholy glee lighting up those marvelous green eyes. His mouth pulled into a smirk, and he shifted again, as if bracing himself for a blow—a blow he was fully prepared to handle, his body language assured her.

A prickle ran through the fine hairs at the back of her neck, making her hands itch to smooth her sleek, understated chignon and make sure it continued to tame her wild blond hair into something appropriate for her position. Making her want to remove herself until she had reverted to the ice queen norm that had saved her time and again, and until she'd gotten the best of this baffling heat he seemed to generate in her.

"What do you mean?" she asked, hoping she sounded cold instead of anxious. Stern instead of thrown.

She was resolved to fire whichever member of

her staff had let this man in here to unsettle her like this when all of her focus needed to be on the relaunch. Yet even as she thought it, she knew that no one who worked at Hartington's could possibly deny this man anything—he was a Wolfe. More than that, he was *Lucas Wolfe*, the most irresistible of his whole compelling, colorful family.

Even she could feel that pull, that attraction— she who had long considered herself terminally allergic to men of his ilk.

"I am the new public face of Hartington's, like my dearly departed father before me," he drawled, his green eyes sharp and mocking, as if he knew exactly what she was thinking. "Just in time for the centenary relaunch."

He smiled then, that famous, devastating smile that Grace discovered could light a fire within her even when she knew he must practice it in his own mirror.

"I beg your pardon?" she asked, desperately, though she already knew. She could not seem to believe it, to accept it, and her stomach twisted in protest, but she knew.

That smile of his deepened, showing off the indentation in his jaw that had been known to cause hysteria when he flashed it about like the deadly weapon it was. The smile that had catapulted him into the hearts and fantasies of so many people the world over. The smile that drove so many women to distraction and regrettable decisions.

But not me, she told herself desperately. *Never me!*

"I believe we'll be working together," he confirmed, smiling as if he knew better. As if he knew *her* better than she could ever hope to know herself. As if he had that power already, had claimed it and who knew what else along with it. "I do so hope you're the hands-on sort of colleague," he continued, in a voice that should have infuriated her and instead made her feel weak. Susceptible. His smile deepened like he knew that, too. "I know I am."

CHAPTER TWO

SHE looked appalled, which was not a reaction Lucas often inspired in women. Not even in starchy, standoffish females like this one, not that he met a great many of that breed in the course of his usual pursuits.

"Working together?" she echoed, sounding as if he'd suggested something unduly perverse. *"Here?"*

"That's the idea," he said, smiling wider. "Unless, of course, you can think of a better way to pass the time in this dreary office."

Normally, even the most constitutionally un-impressed—librarians and nuns and the like—melted at the very hint of his smile. He had been wielding it as the foremost weapon in his arsenal since he was still a child. It had felled entire battalions of females across the globe. It was, in his practiced opinion, even more devastating than that of his younger brother Nathaniel, who was currently up for a Best Actor Sapphire Screen Award and whose inferior smile could be seen via every press outlet on the planet. Lucas was not entirely certain why Grace Carter, prim events manager for bloody Hartington's, should be immune when legions before her had dissolved at the merest sight of it.

In point of fact, she scowled.

"I certainly cannot," she said, judgmental and starched stiff and horrified. "And I'll thank you to keep your suggestive comments to yourself, Mr. Wolfe."

"How?" he asked with idle curiosity, shifting toward her and watching her tense in reaction.

"How...?" she repeated icily. "By exercising restraint, assuming you are capable of such a thing."

"How will you thank me?" he asked, enjoying the flash of something darker than temper in her eyes, despite himself. "I am quite easily bored, you understand, and therefore only accept the most shocking and ingenious displays of gratitude these days. It's my personal policy. One must have standards."

"How interesting," she said smoothly. Too politely. "I was under the distinct impression that your standards were significantly more lax."

"A common misconception," Lucas replied easily. "I am not so much lax as laissez-faire."

"If by that you mean *licentious,*" she retorted.

Her gaze flicked over his battered face. Her distracting Southern drawl went suspiciously sweet. "I certainly hope you won't be left with any unsightly scars."

"On my famously beautiful face?" Lucas asked, affecting astonishment with a small tinge of horror. "Certainly not. And there are always surgeons should nature prove unequal to the task."

Not that a surgeon would be much help with his other, less visible scars, he thought darkly. Lucas had not been particularly bothered by the appearance of Samantha Cartwright's movie-producer husband at a delicate moment the night before. It took more than a few punches to impress him, and in any case, it was only sporting to let a wronged husband express his ill will. There was nothing about the situation that should have distinguished the night from any other night, bruises included.

Except that, upon leaving the hotel, Lucas had not ordered the waiting car to take him to his soulless flat high above the Thames in South Bank. Instead, responding to an urge he had no interest at all in naming, he had ordered it to take him out into the wilds of Buckinghamshire to Wolfe Manor, the abandoned familial pile of stone and bad memories he had assiduously avoided since he'd left the place at eighteen.

He'd heard a rumor that his prodigal older brother, Jacob, had returned after disappearing some twenty years before and Lucas, with the typical measure of cockiness brought on by the liberal application of too many spirits, had decided this particular drunken dawn was high time to test the truth of that story.

But Lucas did not want to think about that. Not about Jacob himself, not about why Jacob had disappeared, nor why he had returned and certainly not about what Jacob had said to him that had spurred Lucas into a series of unlikely actions culminating in his arrival in this office. And so, as he had done with great determination and skill since he was young, he focused on the woman in front of him instead.

The one who was still scowling at him.

"If I was someone else," he said, letting his gaze drift to that expressive mouth she held so tightly, "I might begin to think that scowl meant you disliked me. Which is, of course, impossible."

"Never say never," she replied, so very sweetly.

"I rarely do," he assured her in a low voice, lifting his gaze to hers and letting them both feel the heat of it. "As I'd be happy to demonstrate."

There was a brief, searing pause.

"Did you just suggest what I think you suggested?" she demanded, her dark eyes promising fire and brimstone and other such irritants. Her full mouth firmed into a disapproving line.

He couldn't have said why he was so entertained.

"I can't say that I remember what I suggested," he replied, smiling again. "But one gathers you're opposed."

"The word is *insulted,* Mr. Wolfe," she retorted. "Not *opposed.*"

But he knew what that spark in her gaze meant, and it wasn't insult. "If you say so," he said, and let his gaze move over her body.

She was tall and slim, with rich curves in all the right places, bright blond hair and soulfully deep brown eyes, making her the perfect, long-legged distraction. Unfortunately, she was also wearing entirely too many severely cut articles of clothing, all of them designed to force a man's eye from the very places it was naturally drawn.

Add to that her scraped-back, no-nonsense hairstyle and it was abundantly clear that *this* woman was one of those stuffy, deeply boring career women who Lucas found tedious in the extreme. The only kind of distraction this woman would be likely to provide, he knew from painful experience, would come in the form of a blistering lecture concerning his many moral failings rather than a few hot moments with her long legs wrapped around his hips while he thrust deep and true.

A great pity, Lucas thought, grudgingly.

"I beg your pardon?" It was not the first time she had said it, he realized. She was still staring at him in a horror he found overdone and on the verge of insulting, her honey-and-cream voice laced with shock. "I don't mean to be rude, Mr. Wolfe, but are you by any chance still drunk?"

She might have gone out of her way to hide her many charms, but he happened to be a connoisseur of women. He could see exactly what her full lower lip promised and could imagine the precise, delicious weight of her full breasts in his palms. Why a woman would hide her own beauty so deliberately was a mystery to Lucas—and one he had no interest at all in solving.

Not today, when there were mysteries to go around. Not ever.

He moved to one of the chairs in front of her desk and lowered himself into it, watching the way her huge brown eyes tracked his every movement as he sprawled into a much more comfortable position. Not with the shell-shocked, often lascivious awe to which he was accustomed, but with a certain, unexpected wariness instead. He was interested despite himself.

"Not at all," he said, smiling at her, knowing that one of his legendary dimples was even now appearing in his lean jaw. "Though a drink would certainly not go amiss. Thank you. I find I am partial to bourbon this week."

"I am not offering you a drink, or anything else," she said, a snap in her voice, though her smile remained nailed in place. "From what I observed last night, I can't imagine you would ever require another one."

"I'm sorry," he replied easily, still smiling, propping up his jaw with one hand. "Did we meet last night—or were you simply one of the many onlookers? Part of the inevitable crowd? Perfect strangers do so love to watch my every move and make up stories to suit their own opinions of my character."

It was meant to embarrass her, as Lucas knew well that even the most prurient gossipmonger hated to be called out as such, but she did not balk. Instead, she waved a hand at his black eye, his split lip, her eyes steady on his. Bold, even.

"Is a story required?" she asked from behind that veneer of politeness that he noted and knew better than to believe. "The truth seems sordid enough, surely."

He forced himself to sink even farther into the chair, every inch of him decadent and debauched, exactly as vile as she believed him to be. He knew more about veneers, about masks and misdirection, than anyone ought to know. It had always been his first and best defense. He thrust aside the dark cloud of memory that hovered far too close today, another offense to lay at Jacob's prodigal feet, and forced a smile.

"The wages of sin," he murmured, his voice suggestive, smoky.

She would see what he wanted her to see, he knew. The useless parasite, the indolent playboy. They always did.

"Sin is your area of expertise, Mr. Wolfe," she said briskly. "Mine is events management."

"And never the twain shall meet," Lucas said with an exaggerated, theatrical sigh. "My heart breaks."

"I rather think you operate from a different part of your anatomy," she said, those dark eyes gleaming.

"I'm delighted you think about that part of my anatomy," he replied smoothly. "Feel free to indulge yourself. At length." He smiled. "No pun intended."

He was fascinated by the color that showed against her high cheekbones, the way her full mouth firmed. She was dressed to exude a particular message—competence and elegance—and Lucas could see she hit those notes perfectly. But only a blind man could miss the fact that she was perfectly formed—which made him wonder about the rest of her, the trim body buttoned up tight beneath her layers of black and gray.

She held herself under such tight control. How could he not imagine what she would be like without it?

"I should tell you," he said idly, flicking an imaginary piece of dust from his lapel as if he was not watching her closely, "I have never laid eyes upon something buttoned-up that I was not drawn to unbutton, whether I choose to indulge that urge or not." He smiled as her hand crept toward the buttons on her suit jacket and then dropped sharply to her side as if she'd reprimanded herself. "It is one among my great many personal failings."

She crossed to the front of her desk and leaned back against it, folding her arms over her chest. In that position, as she was clearly well aware, she could look down her fine, delicate nose at him as he sprawled below her in the visitor's chair. He was no doubt meant to feel his inferiority keenly. But Lucas had grown up subject to the uncertain temper and intermittent cruelty of the late, unlamented bully William Wolfe, also known as his deeply despised and little-mourned father, and he knew power games when people were unwise enough to play them in his vicinity. He also knew how to win them. After all, he was Lucas Wolfe. He was not a legend by accident.

Something moved inside of him, rolled over and shook itself to life.

"Let me be frank, Mr. Wolfe," she said, smiling at him again, that bland, placid smile that he knew, with sudden certainty, was meant to manage and soothe him even as it hid her own feelings. Unfortunately, it only drew his attention to her mouth.

"If you have so far been less than candid, I cannot imagine the difference," he drawled as those brown eyes narrowed. "Will I require full body armor?"

That sweet, fake smile sharpened. "Not at all," she said, and her honey-and-cream voice seemed to pool in his groin, making him uncomfortably hard. Surprising him. Intriguing him. "I do apologize if I seem anything less than thrilled about what will be, I'm sure, a long and productive relationship between you and Hartington's. As you know, Hartington's greatly values its relationship with your family."

His family. Lucas refused to think about them, the great damaged mess of them, much less the cavern of guilt that always yawned open when he considered his own epic failures where they were concerned. He shoved the thoughts, the memories, aside—cursing Jacob's name, his sudden reappearance. And then, as ever, himself. He needed to sleep, he thought; he needed to regain his usual equilibrium, to reaccess his sense of humor, at the very least.

"Do you always speak in press releases?" he asked mildly, allowing no hint of his inner turmoil to color his voice. "Or is this for my benefit? Because there are far more interesting ways to secure my undivided attention."

"My focus is the centenary relaunch of the

Hartington's brand," she continued, only the faintest flash in her milk–chocolate brown eyes to show him she'd even heard him. "You may not be aware that we will be throwing a gala event in just over three weeks to celebrate our hundredth year as we reintroduce Hartington's to the modern age."

"As a matter fact, I do know that," he said, his gaze captured by the front of her stern jacket, where her crossed arms drew attention to the tempting valley between the breasts he saw only the barest hints of behind the gray silk of her blouse. He dragged his eyes north and bit back a laugh when he saw her eyes were narrowed even further in outrage. A different woman might have preened, but she didn't, and Lucas found he was less disappointed by the fact she was not that woman than he should have been.

"Then you must also know that this is an exciting time for Hartington's," she said. Lucas did not think she sounded at all excited—rather, she sounded as if she would like to have him forcibly removed from her office. He was well acquainted with that tone, having heard it so often in his lifetime, even if, in her case, it was drenched in all that Texas honey. "I'm sure that a man of your stature will have a great deal to contribute."

"And by 'stature,'" he murmured silkily, unable, somehow, to look away from her narrowed chocolate gaze, and just as unable to rationalize his own behavior—why should he care what she thought or meant?—"am I to assume you, in fact, mean 'notoriety'?"

"Yours is a face with which the whole of Britain, and indeed the world, is intimately familiar," she said, her cool gaze at odds with her soft, velvety voice. "Your headline-grabbing antics are, truly, a gift to the public relations department. No publicity is bad publicity, after all."

"I will have to schedule further antics at once," he said, with bite, though she neither quailed nor colored as she gazed back at him, as she should have done. "I am certain there is no limit to the number of headlines I can grab, all for the greater glory of Hartington's."

"You are too kind," she said sweetly, as if she had not picked up on his sardonic tone, when he was more than certain she had. He could see that she had. She nodded at his battered face. "Though perhaps you might let those bruises heal a little bit first."

Lucas realized, belatedly, what a powerful asset she had in that voice of hers, so soft and sugary and deadly all at once. A rapier-sharp blade sheathed in honey and cream. It was impressive.

But he did not wish to be impressed.

"In any case," she continued, "I am truly delighted to have had this opportunity to meet with you, Mr. Wolfe—"

"By all means, call me Lucas," he said quietly, weighing that soft, sweet voice against the steel he could sense beneath, and could even see in her gaze. "I insist that all character assassinations be made on a first-name basis."

"—and I am certain," she continued, that smile remaining firmly in place, "that I will have the pleasure of working with you sometime in the future, after we've had the relaunch. I'll be sure to schedule a meeting with the PR team in the next few weeks, once you've had time to settle in and get your bearings...."

This time she trailed off as he shook his head, her brows rising in inquiry. Lucas found he enjoyed that far more than he should.

"You are Grace Carter, are you not?" He enjoyed saying her name—because he could see that she did not like the way he said it. As if he could taste the flavor of it with his tongue. It was his turn to smile. "Charlie assured me you were the person I needed to find."

There was a slight, humming sort of pause. She blinked, and he felt it like a victory.

"Charlie?" she asked, an odd, slightly strangled note in her voice.

"Charlie Winthrop," Lucas supplied helpfully, and was delighted when her cheeks reddened again—this time, he had no doubt, with temper.

It made him wonder what she would look like if it was passion that heated her. If it was him. "I am to be at your disposal," he said, making his voice as suggestive as possible. "Completely."

He was intrigued when the expression that flashed across her face was anger. Most women were not angry when flirted with, especially not when the flirt in question was as accomplished as Lucas, without a shred of immodesty, knew himself to be. He had once made the queen smile while enjoying the races at Ascot. What was one embittered executive next to Her Royal Majesty?

"Of course," she said through her smile, even as she glared at him as if she'd like to incinerate him on the spot with the force of her gaze.

"Perhaps you've heard of him," he said, unable to keep the amusement from his voice. The hint of triumph.

Lucas found himself fascinated by the way she visibly wrested control of herself, wrapping her show of temper behind another wide smile and an extra helping of that sweet, sweet Texas honey with its swift, sure kick beneath.

"If, as the CEO of Hartington's, Mr. Winthrop feels your contributions to the company are best utilized through my office," she said, her voice smooth while her eyes burned, "then I am delighted to have you aboard."

If he had not known better, he might have believed her. If he had not seen her mask slip, and the way she put it back on so skillfully. If he had not been as accomplished a master of disguise himself, he might not even have recognized hers when he saw it.

But, God help them both, he was.

And, worse—she intrigued him.

He shifted in his chair, deliberately emphasizing his idle bonelessness because he knew, somehow, it would infuriate her. He stretched his long legs out in front of him, nearly brushing her feet with his, and watched her spine stiffen as she deliberately did not move out of the way, did not cede her ground. More power games, presumably.

Lucas had never encountered a power game he did not feel compelled to win. That was how he was wired, to his own detriment. And, unfortunately for Miss Grace Carter of the too-dark clothes and the obvious disapproval, he never, ever lost.

Not in decades now. Not ever again.

"You are a liar," he continued, letting his voice drop into an insinuating growl that he knew would get to her. "Lucky for you, so am I."

Their eyes met. Held. *Seared.*

"We should get along famously," he said with a deep satisfaction, and then he let loose his smile, like the holstered weapon it was, and let it do its work.

* * *

When Charles Winthrop had confirmed publicly that, indeed, Hartington's was delighted to welcome the famous Wolfe heir aboard—and privately that he expected Grace to personally manage the wild-card playboy with her usual aplomb—Grace had smiled calmly, exuded serenity and comforted herself with visions of smashing every piece of china and shred of pottery she owned. The deep blue bowl from her first trip to Paris, in smithereens. The candlesticks from her holiday on the Amalfi Coast, in a million tiny pieces. *Bliss.*

When she had explained to her awestruck team—in full view of the smirking, flirtatious Lucas, who appeared to bewitch three-quarters of the staff simply by existing, or possibly by lounging across the cabinets so that his magnificent torso was on display—that Lucas was now a crucial component of their strategy for the fast-approaching centenary project, she had kept a suitably straight face and had imagined lighting a small, personal bonfire on her wraparound balcony and setting ablaze the art she'd hung on the walls when she'd moved in a year earlier. The painting she'd bought directly from the hungry-looking painter with the poet's eyes on the Charles Bridge in Prague. The print of the first van Gogh she'd seen in the famous Metropolitan Museum in New York City. All smoke and ashes. It made her smile feel real.

"We are delighted to have you on the team, Mr.

Wolfe," she said as they walked together from the conference room, her smile sweet and her tone razor sharp. "But in future, please do try to contain yourself. The secretaries are not here to serve as your personal dating pool."

"Have you asked them?" he asked lazily, his rangy body moving with a grace that should have seemed out of place in the dim light of the hallway. Instead, he seemed to take it over. "Because I was under the impression that my every wish was their command. I believe one of them told me so."

"I don't need to ask them," Grace replied, smiling more sharply and pretending she was unaffected by his nearness. "I need only consult company policy."

"Hartington's has a Lucas Wolfe clause?" he asked, in that deeply amused drawl that wove spells through her and around her. "I don't know whether to be flattered or insulted." Against her will, hardly aware of it, Grace found herself standing still in the corridor instead of walking briskly toward her office. Standing, gazing up at him, like a moon-faced calf. How could he beguile her without even seeming to do so?

She could not afford it.

"Leave the secretaries alone," she said calmly, as if he had not slipped past her defenses somehow already. As if she had meant to stop there and look up at him.

"Happily," he said. His abused mouth tilted up in the corner. His green gaze was a banked fire that seemed to kick off echoes within her, hot and wild. "But tell me," he continued softly, pointedly, "where else should I direct my attention?"

"Perhaps to your brand-new job," she bit out, ignoring the way he looked at her, his eyes so hooded, so suggestive. "You may find it challenging, after all, having never had one before."

"I am so sorry to shatter your illusions," he said, laughing, though she thought it did not quite reach his eyes, "but despite my well-documented, dissipated, sybaritic existence, I have, in fact, held a job. We all have our deep, dark secrets, do we not?"

She had no intention of discussing secrets with this man.

"You understand, Mr. Wolfe, that when one says 'job,' one is not referring to your rather questionable relationships with somewhat older ladies of excessive means." She smiled. Hard. "There are other words for that."

"Someday you will have to teach me all the ins and outs of your vocabulary," he said, in a voice that seemed to demand she imagine what tutoring him might involve. Something powerful shook through her, stealing her breath. He smiled. "The job I held was somewhat less illicit, I'm afraid."

"You?" she asked, in disbelief. "Who on earth would employ you?"

"Not everyone finds my face as distasteful as you seem to do," he said, challenge and mockery stamped across his expression. He angled his head toward her, too close, and she had to fight to keep herself from jumping back and letting him see how he got to her. "In fact, some people find it addictive."

"Are you referring to yourself?" she asked lightly, and smiled to take the sting away.

His smile then was as sharp, and far more dangerous. "I mean myself most of all," he said quietly, an undercurrent in his voice she did not understand. "I am my own heroin."

It was the ferocity in his voice that lingered with her even hours later, and the fact she could not dismiss the man from her thoughts made her fantasize anew about destroying all of her belongings in a dramatic—if private—show of temper.

But the sad truth, she acknowledged late that evening when she arrived home and looked around the carefully pristine, perfectly decorated penthouse apartment that normally made her feel happy and successful and tonight felt oddly empty, was that she was entirely too practical.

She could not let herself be so reckless, so

careless. No matter how good it would feel. She'd learned that lesson the hard way.

"Women in our family are built to love," her mother had said with a shrug years ago, when Grace had collapsed in a sobbing mess on her bed, trying to handle the fallout of her first, doomed relationship. Back when her mother still spoke to her. "Too much and too long, and always messy. That's how it goes. It's our curse."

"You don't understand—" Grace had moaned.

"You're no different, Gracie," her mother had said, and shaken her head as she'd reached for another cigarette. "I know you want to be, but you're not, and the sooner you get your head around that the happier you'll be."

Now, so many years and miles away from that conversation, and all the betrayal and pain that had followed it, Grace sank down on her smooth, modern couch in the foreign country she called home, and reached back to let her hair fall, heavy and thick, from its place on the back of her head. She shook out the pins, and ran her fingers through the wild mess of it that she only ever dared let down when she was alone. It was too unruly, too untamed—too reminiscent of the girl she had been, who she preferred to pretend had never existed at all.

I am my own heroin, he had said, and she

thought it was an apt description of his lure, his innate danger.

There was never any *something more* with a man like Lucas. There was only heartbreak and loneliness. She needed only to consider her poor mother's endless string of misery and despair, her life lived on the strength of broken promises and late-night tears, as one more man smiled like he meant it and Grace's mother *believed*. She always believed, and they always let her down. Always.

And Mary-Lynn never blamed the men. She always blamed herself, and so lost a little bit more of herself, her battered heart and the light in her eyes every time. Until the day she'd blamed her daughter instead.

Grace kicked off her shoes and curled up on the couch. She could not afford to be fascinated with Lucas Wolfe. She could not allow herself to be intrigued. She had to throw a relaunch party so fabulous that it cemented her reputation for years to come, and she could not permit any deviation from her plan, especially not in the form of a man who was clearly put on the earth to ruin every woman he touched.

It made her heart ache that she was so susceptible, as if it really was a genetic defect passed down from mother to daughter. When all this time, after everything that had happened in high school had changed her so completely, she'd truly believed she was immune. She would be different, no matter what her mother thought—no matter what she'd screamed at Grace when she'd thrown her out like so much trash. *She would.*

But she would start tomorrow, she thought, closing her eyes, succumbing to her weariness and letting all of her heavy armor drop from her for a moment. She felt the helpless fascination creep in and take her over, and then curled up on the couch with the memory of his devastating smile raging through her like a wildfire she could not bring herself to put out.

Not yet. Not tonight.

CHAPTER THREE

"I'VE remembered you," Lucas announced, swaggering into her office like a conquering hero, his smile far too bright and much too wicked as it played over his mouth. "It came to me over the weekend."

It was Monday morning, nearing eleven o'clock, and Grace was not feeling at all charitably inclined toward her new team member. She sat back in her desk chair and regarded him stonily.

It did not matter in the least that he looked even more delicious this morning, in yet another absurd, catwalk-ready sort of suit that made him seem like a sleek, wild, green-eyed jaguar set down among a fleet of tamed and corpulent house cats. His dark hair was still too long for civility—and the office—and stood about in what she imagined were spikes as carefully managed as his wardrobe. His perfect male form was still showcased to mouthwatering effect, his muscled shoulders and lean hips lovingly defined, his torso a work of art in dark wool. His beauty was still far greater, far more masculine and disturbing, than one would suspect from having seen him in photographs.

His bruises had faded considerably, she could not help but notice. His dizzying appeal had not.

Happily, she told herself with some internal rigor, her moment of weakness had passed. There was no genetic defect, no predisposition. Lucas Wolfe was nothing more than the human version of a well-known painting, widely regarded as beautiful in the extreme—even a masterpiece. One could appreciate such a painting the way one appreciated all forms of beauty. Lucas Wolfe was a curiosity to be admired, and then ignored.

"Mr. Wolfe," she said now, smiling perfunctorily. "I understand that this may be a new experience for you, and I'll try to be sensitive to that, but I think you'll find the team is expected to make it into the office at nine o'clock sharp each morning, not at eleven. Even you, I'm afraid."

"At Samantha's party," he continued, unperturbed. Quite as if she had not spoken, much less reprimanded him. "It was when I went to get the drinks, wasn't it? You were standing by the bar." His dark brows rose in challenge, and something else she told herself she did not wish to explore, even as it slid intimately along her skin, kicking up goose bumps. "I knew I recognized you."

"I'm afraid I can't remember," Grace said, lying coolly and without a single shred of remorse.

"Of course you do," he said, with that easy confidence and a knowing gleam in his bright eyes that arrowed directly into Grace's sex, making her knees feel weak even as she felt herself soften. *For him.* Her heart jumped in her chest. She was entirely too grateful that she happened to be sitting down. He was lethal.

And impersonal, she reminded herself sharply, crossing her legs beneath her desk. *You could be a random shopgirl. A bus driver. The bus itself. He has chemistry with the very air around him—he can't help it.*

"Mr. Wolfe, really," she said, frowning at him. "This project is doomed to failure if you cannot respect the most basic rules of the workplace. Allow me to give you a refresher course."

"Less a refresher course, and more an introduction," he amended, with a careless shrug and no visible sign that he was at all embarrassed he'd never worked a single day in his pampered, overprivileged life of sin and excess—whatever he might have claimed the previous week.

He certainly made it easy to dismiss him, Grace thought. She dearly wished that she could—that she had not been ordered to personally handle him. But she had been, and so she waited until she had his full, if amused, attention, and began to tick off her points on her fingers.

"You must knock and receive permission to enter before barging into an office," she said briskly. "You must not ignore your coworkers when they are speaking to you, no matter if you think what you have to say is more interesting—it is unlikely that your coworkers will agree. And it is completely inappropriate to make insinuations regarding the private lives or thoughts of anyone you might work with, under any circumstances. Do you understand me?"

It was as if he lounged against something, though he stood in the center of her office. Such was his natural indolence. He reminded her of the great cats she found so fascinating in the nature programs she often watched—a lazy grace, sleepy-eyed and seemingly harmless, and yet with all that predatory watchfulness and physical prowess hidden just beneath his sleek surface.

"Did I make insinuations?" he asked, not seeming remotely cowed. Only interested. And, if possible, even more amused. "I do beg your pardon. They cannot have been particularly interesting, if I cannot recall them."

"One imagines that you are so used to insinuating inappropriate things about everyone you meet that it is rather like a comment on the weather for anyone else," she replied sweetly. She let her smile widen. "Please do try to remember that this is not a yacht on the Côte d'Azur, brimming with starlets and debauchery—this is Hartington's, a much-beloved and revered British institution."

He thrust his hands into his pockets and regarded her with that cool green gaze that made her wonder, against her will, what else he hid behind all that sexiness and swagger.

"Rather like me," he said after a moment, his mouth curving, *daring* her, somehow. "A bit tattered around the edges, perhaps, the pair of us, but I think somehow the gilt and glamour remain." He smiled. "Don't you agree?"

Grace eyed him, torn between the urge to laugh—or to scream. Or, worse, to give in to the hugely inappropriate and somewhat alarming urgings of her body and the heat he seemed to ignite within her without even trying. She did none of the above. She did not even fidget under his scrutiny, though it cost her.

"The team will be meeting in the conference room in a half hour for our daily status update," she said instead, pointedly glancing at the slim gold watch she wore on her wrist, and then back toward her computer monitor, dismissing him. "If you don't mind…?"

"You were the only woman in the crowd who refused to smile at me," Lucas said, in that silken voice of his that, she reminded herself sternly, had

seduced millions in exactly the same way. No need
to be the next in line in the endless parade. Not
that she was considering it! "At first I thought you
were one of the ones who scowl at me on purpose,
to distinguish themselves from the fawning fans,
but you didn't do that, either."

"Are you sure it was me?" Grace asked, pretending to be bored with the conversation. "I remember
your rather spectacular exit from the party, but
very little else." She gazed at her computer screen
as if she could read a single thing on it. As if
she was not entirely too focused on the man who
stood so close, just on the other side of her desk,
commanding all the air in the room despite his
seemingly languid slouch and his unkempt hair.

"Neither a smile nor a scowl. You simply looked
at me," Lucas said, his voice like a caress, dark
and unfair as it worked its way through her like
fine wine, turning her too warm too quickly. She
could feel him everywhere. Hot. Shivery. "Even
after I said hello."

"Sorry," she said in mild yet clear dismissal,
her attention on the screen in front of her, as if she
could not feel the pull of him, the heat. "You must
have me confused with someone else."

"No," he said, his gaze shrewd, considering.
"No, I don't think so."

Grace would rather die than admit she remembered that moment—because she had been

quite literally struck dumb to turn from the bar and find him so close, so glowing and impossibly compelling, sexy and rumpled and *male*. In painful hindsight, it ranked as one of the single most humiliating moments of her life. She, twenty-eight years old, a fully grown adult woman who oversaw teams of staff and high-level events, had been struck mute at the sight of this man. This waste of space, famous for no particular reason aside from his name, who used his considerable charm like currency. *Yes,* something in her had whispered, deep and sure—as, no doubt, it did in every silly female who laid eyes on him up close. But Grace had never forgiven herself for losing her head so spectacularly over a man back in high school, with so many horrible consequences; she would not compound the error now. She would not do it again.

"Yes, well," she said, proud that her voice remained cool, "perhaps I was simply astounded that you could manage to speak coherently. You do have the reputation of being somewhat consistently drunk, don't you?"

"Which means that I am rarely incoherent," he said, smiling faintly. "It is my finest skill. For all you know, I could be drunk right now."

But his eyes were too clear, too watchful. His voice too deliberately blasé. He was about as drunk as she was.

"I will keep that in mind in future," she replied briskly. She straightened in her seat and let impatience creep into her voice. "I'm sorry I don't remember meeting you at Samantha Cartwright's party, Mr. Wolfe. How embarrassing, when I am usually so good with faces. But then, it was a busy night for everyone, wasn't it?"

She could not seem to keep her own insinuations from creeping in, and she knew why when she saw his green eyes warm with a kind of rueful acknowledgment. With a kind of recognition she knew she should fight. Instead, something about him made her *want* to needle him, to get under his skin.

She could not bring herself to imagine what that might mean.

Meanwhile, he watched her with those cat's eyes, and he *knew*. Her secrets, her darkest corners. Everything. As if he could see right into her.

It should have horrified her. It should not have made her ache and her skin seem to shrink against her bones. It should not have made her breath catch in her throat, her mouth dry. It should not have made her want to show him all her secrets, one by one, even the ones that still made her cringe.

"It's that voice of yours," he said, musingly, as if he'd given the matter a great deal of thought. His head tilted to one side. "It's so surprising. It goes down like a good cream tea, and then a few moments later the sting sets in. It's quite a formidable weapon you have there, Miss Carter."

"I prefer *Ms.* Carter, thank you," she retorted automatically.

"You should be careful how you use it," he replied, and she knew she did not mistake the threat then, the sensual menace. It resonated between her legs, made her breasts feel too heavy, brought her breath too quickly to catch in her throat. He knew that, too—she had no doubt. His wicked, battered lips crooked to the side. "*Ms.* Carter."

"So you do, in fact, listen when others speak," she said as if delighted and smiled sharply at him. "One did hope. Perhaps next week we can graduate to knocking before entering!"

"But where's the fun in that?" he asked, laughing at her. A real laugh—one that made his eyes crinkle in the corners and his head tip back. One that lit him up from the inside. One that seemed to make her chest expand too fast, too hard.

It was a good thing she had resolved to ignore him, Grace thought dimly, captivated against her will—or she might really be in trouble.

The novelty of his brand-new office wore off quickly, Lucas found. It rather made him feel like a caged animal, for all that it gleamed of dark wood and chrome and featured no-doubt-coveted views of London from the floor-to-ceiling windows that dominated the far wall. But while Lucas was many things, most of them damning, covetousness had never been among his flaws. Why should he covet anything? Whatever he wanted, he had. Or took. And yet he stayed in the grand leather chair, behind the immense desk, and pretended he could convey some kind of authority—*become* some kind of authority figure—by doing so.

But then, he was not sitting in his new office to feel good about himself or his life choices. He was doing it to prove a point. A long overdue point that should not have required proof, he thought, tamping down the surge of anger that seared through him.

"Hello, Lucas," Jacob had said that early Thursday morning, freshly risen as if from the dead. He had looked Lucas up and down from the great front door where he'd stood, the restored master of Wolfe Manor, his black eyes flicking from bruise to cut to disheveled shirt and making Lucas feel as close to ashamed as he'd been in years.

The very grounds around them had seemed infested with the malevolent ghost of William Wolfe and all the pain he'd inflicted on his unlucky children and wives—or perhaps that had just been the sleepless night getting to Lucas. Perhaps it was Jacob himself, taller and broader than in Lucas's memory—a grown man now, of substance and wealth, if his fine clothes were any indication.

For a long moment they had both stood there, the early-morning light just beginning to chase away the gray, sizing each other up as if they were adversaries.

On the one hand, Lucas had thought, Jacob had once been his best friend, his partner in crime and his brother. They were only a year apart in age, and had grown up sharing the brunt and burden of their father's temper. If Lucas could have been there that one fateful night to do what Jacob had done for their family, he would have. Happily—and without a shred of the agony he knew Jacob had felt for what Lucas had always viewed as a necessary act, if not long overdue.

On the other hand, Jacob had taken off without a word and stayed gone for well over a decade. He had left Lucas in his place—a disaster for all concerned. They had been boys back then, if much older than they should have been and far too cynical, but they were grown men now and, apparently, strangers.

But Lucas had not wanted to believe that. Not at first. Not after so long.

"It is lovely to see you, dear brother," he'd said when the silence had stretched on too long. "I would have slaughtered a calf in your honor, but the kitchens are in some disrepair."

"I've followed your exploits in the papers," Jacob had said in his familiar yet deeper voice. His black eyes raked Lucas from head to toe again, then back, missing nothing.

Even Jacob, Lucas had thought, something sinking through him like a stone. But he had summoned his most insouciant smile. He had not otherwise reacted.

"I'm touched," Lucas had replied, blandly. "Had I known you were so interested in my adventures, I would have added you to the annual Christmas card list. Of course, that would have required an address."

Jacob had looked away for a moment. Lucas had wanted to reach out, to bridge the gap, but he had not known how. His head had pounded ferociously. He'd wished fervently that he'd just gone home, slept it off and left the ghosts of his past alone. What good had this family ever been to him? Why did he still care?

"It's not as if we don't already know where this lifestyle leads," Jacob had said, so quietly that Lucas almost let it go, almost pretended he hadn't heard. Anything to maintain the fiction of Jacob he'd carried around in his head all these years. Jacob, the hero. Jacob, the savior. Jacob, who knew him.

"My original plan was to prance off into the ether, abandoning family and friends without so much as a backward glance," Lucas had snapped back at him. "But unfortunately, you'd already taken that role. I was forced to improvise."

"You know why I had to leave," Jacob said in a low voice, thick with their shared past and their family's secrets, public and private.

"Of course," Lucas had interrupted him, years of pain and resentment bubbling up from places he'd spent his life denying even existed. He'd laughed, a hollow sound that echoed against the stones of the manor house and inside of him in places he preferred to ignore. "You're nearly twenty years too late, Jacob. I don't need a big brother any longer. I never did."

"Look at yourself, Lucas—don't you see who you've become?" Jacob's voice had been quiet, but had flashed through Lucas as if he'd shouted.

It was not the first time Lucas had been compared to his father, but it was the first time the comparison had been made by someone who shared his bone-deep loathing of the man who had wrecked them both. By someone—the only one—who ought to know better. It was a body blow. It should have killed him. Perhaps it had.

"I thought you were dead," Lucas had said coldly, unable and unwilling to show his brother how deeply those words cut at him. "I'm not sure this is an improvement."

"For God's sake," Jacob had said, shaking his

head, his eyes full of something Lucas refused to name, refused to consider at all. "Don't let him win."

Staring out the windows of his luxurious office now, Lucas let out a hollow sort of sound, too flat to be a laugh. He had turned on his heel and left his prodigal brother behind—and had thought, *To hell with him.* He'd spent the whole long walk down the private lane pretending nothing Jacob had said had gotten to him. Yet when he'd reached the road, he'd flipped open his mobile and rousted Charlie Winthrop from his sleep to announce he'd had a sudden change of heart and would, despite years of claiming otherwise, dearly love to work for Hartington's in any capacity at all.

Careful what you wish for, he mocked himself now. Especially if you were Lucas Wolfe, and had a tendency to get it.

At half past eleven, Lucas dutifully walked into the conference room, expecting to be bored silly by corporate nonsense. Bureaucracy and posturing. It was one of the reasons he managed his own affairs almost entirely via his computer. But instead of a dreary presentation, he found the room in the grips of evident chaos. One did not have to know a single thing about business to know that something had gone wrong. The very fact that none of the events team seemed to notice or care that he had entered the room told him that—it was a rare experience for him and, strangely, felt almost liberating.

He sank into a seat at the oval-shaped table, reveling in the feeling. It was as if he was very nearly normal, for the first time in memory.

Even smooth, efficient Grace looked harried when she strode into the room a few minutes late, a frown taking the place of the competent, soothing smile he already knew was as much a part of her as her ruthlessly controlled blond hair.

"I'm so sorry, Grace," one of the anxious-looking girls said at once, all but wilting against the glossy tabletop, distress evident in her very bones.

"Don't be silly, Sophie," Grace said, but that marvelous voice was tighter than it had been earlier, and tension seemed to reverberate from her in waves as she set down a stack of files in front of her. "You could hardly have foreseen a burst pipe when you found the place six months ago."

Another team member rushed up to whisper something in her ear, making her frown deepen, and as the rest of the staff took their seats, Lucas took the opportunity to simply look at Grace.

He wasn't at all certain why he found the woman so compelling.

There was absolutely nothing about the severe gray suit she was wearing that should have appealed to him. Lucas preferred women in bright colors, preferably showing swathes of tanned, smooth skin. He liked impractically high heels and tousled manes of lustrous hair. Glimpses of toned thighs and full breasts. Not a skirt that showed far too little leg, a jacket he knew she had no intention of unbuttoning and another boring silk blouse in some pale, unremarkable pastel shade that covered her up to her delicate collarbone.

And yet. There was something about Grace Carter that he could not dismiss. That kept him captivated. That had plagued him throughout the long, boring weekend while he had been surrounded, as always, by the kinds of women he usually preferred yet had found unaccountably tedious and insipid this time. That had kept him awake and brooding until he'd placed exactly where he'd seen her before and why he'd noticed her in the first place. He'd thought her a boring prude, of course—but the point was, he'd remembered her.

That in itself was highly unusual.

"All right," Grace said, calling the meeting to order, her brow smoothing and that great calm seeming to exude from her once again. Lucas could feel the room relax slightly all around him. That was her power, he realized. The gift of that smile.

He felt something in him ease, which should have alarmed him—but, oddly, did not. Instead, he watched her take over the room without seeming to do so. It was almost as if he could not bring himself to look away.

"As many of you have already heard," she said briskly, "we've just had word from the centenary venue that their sprinkler system malfunctioned dramatically over the weekend and flooded the grounds. Completely. They expect that the space will be unusable for at least the next two months, which, of course, means we no longer have a location for the gala." She raised her hands when the murmuring from the staff increased in volume and took on the unmistakable edge of panic. "I suggest we all look at this as a challenge," she said. She flashed that smile. "Not a catastrophe."

She seemed so calm, so at ease. As if she expected no less than seven catastrophes before lunch every day, and what was one more? But Lucas could see something in her chocolate-colored eyes, something that seemed to ring in him. Like she was scared and fighting hard not to show it. Like she had as much riding on this as he did, however improbable. Like she might be someone completely different when she was alone, and had nothing to prove, and was not performing for the crowd.

He could not have said why he wanted so much to believe that. Maybe that was why he opened his mouth, surprising himself as much as anyone else. More.

"Exactly what are you looking for?" he heard himself ask, as if from afar. "In terms of a location?"

Her dark eyes seemed to slam into him. She held his gaze for what seemed too long—and yet even as she smiled politely at him, he could see the wariness, the uncertainty, the panic she hid from the rest. It was almost as if he could *feel* it—he, who felt nothing. Deliberately.

"It must be the perfect melding of old and new, to stand as a showcase for Hartington's—an updated classic." She smiled that professional smile, the one that made him want to lick her until he saw the real one she must have hidden away in there somewhere. "Do you know anything that fits the bill?"

"As a matter of fact," Lucas said, far too easily, "I do."

He hadn't known where he was going with this until it fell into his head, exquisitely formed, the perfect solution. Better by far than the miserable pile of stones and nightmares and broken childhood dreams deserved.

"It must also be suitable for a corporate event, Mr. Wolfe," Grace said. Her dark eyes were level on his, her voice perfectly professional. "Not, for example, a den of iniquity."

"Those are the only dens worth inhabiting," he replied at once, aware of all the eyes on him, on them, as if they could see the same sizzle he felt. "I make an excellent guide to all the local dens of iniquity, in fact. Perhaps we should take a company field trip."

There was a small titter from the group around him, but Grace, of course, merely flashed that calm smile.

"Tempting," she said, though it was clear that she was anything but tempted, "and one has no doubt at all of your expertise—

"I should hope not," he said, his lips curving. "I'm Lucas Wolfe."

"—but I think we'll have to decline." Her smile took on that edge. He should not have found it so fascinating.

"Never fear," he said before she could dismiss him entirely. "I have something far more boring in mind for your event."

"Wonderful," Grace said, her brows raised. She did not trust him, of course. Who did? Who could? He had made certain it was impossible—and so he could not imagine why it should bother him now. "By all means, let's hear it."

She thought he was as much of a lost cause as his brother did, he knew. He had gone out of his way to make sure of it—to make sure he lived down to every single low expectation others had of him. The "famous Lucas Wolfe" was his own, best creation, and he'd taken pride in that for years.

So there was no reason at all he should want to alter her impressions.

"What you need is a place that is intimately connected with Hartington's, yet adds a touch of exclusivity, as well. A destination location." He had no idea what he was talking about, or why. And yet he could not seem to stop himself. He held her gaze. Challenge and demand. Mystery. He could not resist it. Her. "How would Wolfe Manor suit?"

The rest of the team exploded into excited noise, but Lucas could only see Grace. It was worth it, he told himself, to see her stunned expression, to watch her swiftly reevaluate him in that single split second. The fact that he might be a touch cocky in proposing this particular solution hardly signified, he told himself. He could *see* the wheels in her head turning, the possibilities occurring to her, a new plan taking shape.

And then she smiled the real smile he'd imagined, and time seemed to still. There was nothing fake or pointed about this smile—it was all that honey and shine, and he knew beyond a shadow of a doubt that, no matter what, he would have this woman.

He had to.

CHAPTER FOUR

RAIN drummed against the roof of the limousine as it made its way out of London toward Wolfe Manor the following day. Water tracked silken, wet paths across the windows in ever-changing patterns as the car slid through mile after mile of the wet and green British countryside—and yet all Grace could concentrate on was the six feet and more of Lucas Wolfe, stretched out with far too much lazy confidence and sheer male appeal next to her in the confines of the car.

"You can look at me directly," he said in that low, insinuating, endlessly amused voice, far too close to her ear. "I can't imagine why you would fight the urge. I am, after all, quite marvelously handsome."

"I believe the word you're looking for is *conceited*," Grace replied, her gaze on the PDA in her hand as if he did not affect her in the slightest. And yet she could only seem to concentrate on the fact that he was much too close to her on the plush seat, his strong shoulders *just* a whisper away, his spicy, expensive scent—male and seductive and *him*—seeming to inflame her, to tease her and taunt her, every time she inhaled.

He laughed, completely unfazed, as ever. "Conceit cannot possibly be the right word," he countered. She was much too aware of how he shifted in his seat, how he inched even closer. "I've had independent confirmation in the press for years. I am a glorious male animal. You may as well simply admit the truth."

"You should probably not believe everything you read, Mr. Wolfe," Grace replied airily. Easily. She wished she could feel the way she sounded. "It can lead to all sorts of issues. A swollen head, for one thing."

She knew the moment she said it that she should not have used that word.

"My head is the not the part of me—" he began, evident delight in his tone and in his bright green eyes when she turned to frown at him.

"I beg you," she said crisply. "Let us preserve the fantasy that you are not, in fact, a twelve-year-old schoolboy. Please do not finish that sentence."

The wicked smile that should have irritated her, but somehow did not, flirted with his mouth even as his eyes darkened with a heat she wished she could not feel.

"I assure you, Ms. Carter," he said softly. "I am a grown man in all the ways that could possibly interest you."

She was all too aware that he was a man. Just a man, she reminded herself. No more and no less, no matter what the fawning press and her own reactions seemed to suggest. And no matter that, yesterday, he had seemed to sense how agitated she was when no one else had. She had no idea what that could mean.

He had discarded his suit jacket the moment he'd entered the vehicle, stripping it from his lean, masculine form in a manner she'd found entirely too disconcerting—and Grace was forced to note that his biceps were more muscular, his shoulders wider and harder, his torso more sculpted than she had imagined when he was covered in more than just a soft bit of linen. She shifted farther, trying to pull herself as far toward the opposite side of the car as possible without looking as if that was what she was doing.

"Tell me about Wolfe Manor," she said, dropping her PDA into her lap and facing head-on the dragon in its lair. An apt comparison for this man, who was all fire and heat and that coiled danger that no one ever seemed to mention, but which Grace found mesmerizing. And alarming.

His green eyes gleamed and his fine mouth crooked into a half smile as he considered her for a moment.

"If we are to pull off a huge party there in a very short period of time," she said mildly, reminding them both why they were there, together, "I really should know everything there is to know about the place."

"I can tell you that it has never flooded," Lucas said in that silken voice, a dark eyebrow arching high. Grace was forced to consider—and not for the first time—the unnerving possibility that he was much quicker and significantly wittier than any pathetic international playboy had a right to be. She did not know why that thought should unsettle her. Why it should make her arms break out in goose bumps.

"Touché," she said, but still gazed at him expectantly.

"What is there to tell?" he asked then, with a careless sort of shrug. "It is a manor house like any other. The country is infested with them. It is the ancestral encumbrance, passed down through generations, a monument to aristocratic greed. I thank the gods every morning for the great gift of primogeniture, which, as I am not the firstborn son, ensures I need never set foot there again unless I wish it."

A moment passed, and then another. The tires

swished along the wet roadway, the rain drummed against the roof, and still, Grace was too aware of the way his eyes met hers, bold and demanding, daring her to look away. To ignore him. To pretend he was not getting to her.

"Thank you," Grace managed to say in her driest tone. "I'm sure that will be very useful information as we prepare to throw a gala there. No thoughts on an appropriate place to pitch the tent? Where to set up the catering? How to craft the perfect delivery system to ensure the guests are properly wowed as they enter the event?"

Lucas only continued to watch her, that wolfish smile and a silvery light in his eyes that made her feel as if she was made of sand, something insubstantial that would blow away at his next breath. Grace felt almost dizzy, and hated it. Hated *him*, she told herself fiercely, that he should be the reason she felt so wildly out of her depth when she was working—the one place Grace had always exerted complete control.

He was a devil, clearly. He was used to this, to using his incredible sexual magnetism to bend all he encountered to his whim. Simply because he could. But he was not the first devil she'd met, and she refused to be seduced. *She refused.*

"I imagined my role was to be rather more decorative than administrative," he said, his eyes laughing at her.

"My mistake," she said, redirecting her attention to her PDA as if dismissing him. "I thought for a moment in yesterday's meeting that you were a creature of substance as well as style." She smiled, to soften her words—to pretend she was still being professional, when she felt so edgy, so raw and unwieldy within. "But you can rest assured, Mr. Wolfe, that your face alone is of great use to Hartington's, however else you choose to help. Or not."

"I know," he agreed, not appearing in the least chastened by her words. Or even particularly offended by them. "This is not the first time I have worked for Hartington's, Ms. Carter. Though it is true that when I did it last, I was still quite young."

She blinked at him, thrown. She could hardly think which was more astonishing—that he had ever been young, or that he had ever actually worked. Neither seemed possible. He was too dissolute to have ever been a child, surely, and far too committedly lazy to ever have worked for his living.

"Define 'worked for Hartington's,'" she suggested, mildly enough, trying to conceal her interest. She should not find him fascinating. She should not care that he was able to fence words with her so easily. She should not let that soften her. "Because, and do forgive me if I've misunderstood, I was under the impression that you took great pride in the fact that you've never worked a day in your charmed life. Aside, that is, from your vague claims last week of once having been employed."

"Perhaps my charmed life is more complicated than you might imagine," he said, a hint of chill in his voice and that uncannily shrewd gaze of his, but only for the barest moment. Grace was convinced she'd imagined both when he blinked, and that self-mocking smile of his returned. "My brothers and sister and I were once the Hartington's window display at Christmas," he said, his tone light and yet, somehow, Grace could hear only the sardonic inflection beneath, the hint of something much darker. "Decked out in matching outfits like the von Trapps, merry and bright. A true Christmas card come to life. The punters adored us, of course. Who could resist a brood of angelic children? They all but emptied their wallets on the spot."

"As a matter of fact, I've seen the pictures," Grace said quietly, uncertain of him, suddenly. Perhaps he was unaware that there were blown-up photographs of his family all over the executive office suite: seven bright-eyed, shockingly good-looking children arrayed around their attractive father, like a series of Norman Rockwell paintings. They all fairly exuded hearth and home and happiness. She was not sure he would welcome that knowledge. The atmosphere inside the car had changed, and he seemed more dangerous, more unpredictable, though he had not moved at all.

She was imagining things, she told herself. But she remained on her guard.

"Such a happy family we looked," Lucas said in a soft voice that Grace did not believe at all. "Beyond that, my brother Jacob and I worked in the store during every school holiday for years. My father felt it was character building, apparently." His smile seemed knife-edged now, deeper somehow, and resonated through her, making her ache in ways she was afraid to examine. "I spent my time talking the shopgirls out of their pants rather than learning how to operate the till. I built my character carefully, and with excessive practice."

Grace had a sudden, flashing vision of the teen-aged Lucas, prowling about the gleaming sales floors of Hartington's with this same lean and feral edge to him. He would have been much less restrained in his youth, she imagined—all green eyes and cocky swagger and far too much self-awareness. She repressed a sudden shiver. There was nothing safe about this man. She doubted very much there ever had been, even when he'd been small. *If.*

"It is difficult to imagine you young," she said, voicing her thoughts without meaning to, her voice far softer than it should have been. Almost as if she cared.

Their eyes met then, and something bright and profound moved through Grace, searing into her through the gloom of the rainy day and the stuffy confines of the car. She found she was holding her breath. That she could not look away from him as she knew she should.

"It was a chronological situation, nothing more," he said after a short pause, never moving his electric, arrogant gaze from hers. "I never had the opportunity to be naive or innocent." He seemed to recollect himself and looked away then, that smile sharpening as he did. Grace felt it as if he'd cut into her, as if he'd carved symbols deep into her flesh. "But I doubt innocence would have suited me, in any case." When he looked at her again, he had gone predatory. Male. Hot and knowing—and it made her melt and tremble, despite her best intentions. "I was always far more proficient in sin."

"So I have read," Grace said primly, ignoring the clamoring need in her own body. "At length. It is what makes you such an excellent choice to head up the new Hartington's campaign. All women have already had numerous fantasies about you, and all men wish they could be you. You are, yourself, the ultimate luxury brand." She smiled. Professionally. "Kudos."

"*All* women?" he asked, his eyes hard and gleaming on hers—as, she realized on some level, she must have known he would.

Had this man ever ignored a gauntlet thrust down before him? She knew, somehow, that he had not. He smiled that wolf's smile, and it connected hard with that strange humming deep inside of her that grew louder the nearer he was. He was everything she had spent her whole life fearing, avoiding. He made her into someone else, someone lost in the shimmering heat that suffused her, the flame of interest in his gaze. He made her feel things she'd never believed she was capable of feeling. She could not seem to look away. For a long, spinning moment, she could not find it in her to fight him—to fight the weakness in herself.

And she knew that was as good as the death of her.

"Does that mean you've fantasized about me, Grace?" he asked, in his seducer's voice, a low, sexy rasp that promised far too much she knew he could never deliver.

"I believe I have already asked that you call me Ms. Carter," Grace said, sounding like a starchy, stereotypical schoolmarm sort of person, to her horror. Yet it was exactly the image she strove to project, with her severely cut suits and her scraped-back hair: efficient and competent. A vestal virgin, clutching her pearls.

But what other option did she have? She was trapped in the back of a car with a man who exuded sex—long, slow, all-encompassing, masterful sex, for that matter, from which one was unlikely to recover. And Grace knew what that kind of sex meant, the damage it could and did wreak. She had seen it happen too many times. She had lived it.

"You should have said no, Gracie," her mother had said so long ago, her face hard and drawn, her eyes flashing the same censure Grace had seen everywhere else. Her own mother, who should have known better—should have tried harder, Grace had thought, to protect her daughter. But Mary-Lynn had made her choice. "You should have said no, but you didn't, and now you have to live with the consequences."

Sex like that was a threat, Grace knew, shaking off the unpleasant past. Sex like that was about power, and, ultimately, pain. She had never wanted anything to do with it after the events of her senior year—but then, she had never met a man who fascinated her on all the levels this man seemed to do. For the first time in years, since she had set her course and focused exclusively on putting the past behind her and excelling in her career, Grace felt lost.

"Is that part of your fantasy?" Lucas asked, his voice low, suggestive. He shifted closer to her, and Grace froze—her entire body, her very being, focused on the heat he generated, on the length and strength of his lean, hard body mere inches away from hers. Only inches. A breath. "I'm happy to call you anything you like."

"Thank you, Mr. Wolfe," she said in that brisk, insultingly matter-of-fact voice that had gotten her out of sticky situations in the past. She pretended not to notice how hard it was to dredge up this time, how hard it was to employ. "But I doubt very much I'm the target demographic for your particular brand of charm."

"You are a woman, are you not?" he asked mildly.

"Yes." She smiled, bright and false. "But a discerning woman, I'm afraid."

His gaze moved to her mouth, and she felt it like a touch. Hot and demanding. Sure.

"Excellent," he said softly. "Can you discern my thoughts?"

She felt herself flush in helpless reaction, and could only hope that her legendary cool kept her skin from actually turning red and broadcasting her response to him. How could this be happening? She had never had trouble in the past, keeping her feelings and any unwanted attractions safely hidden away in the parts of herself she kept locked up tight. Soon enough, they'd disappeared, subsumed into the work she'd always known would save her. Anything to pretend her past belonged to someone else.

"I'm afraid not," she managed to say, forcing

herself to sit there calmly, as if she was relaxed. "My psychic abilities only work on more…intellectual subjects."

"That is a great pity, indeed," Lucas said, not at all discomfited. "My own abilities are far more universal. Shall I tell you what *you're* thinking?"

She wanted to know what she was missing, she knew suddenly—with a deep, new need that frightened her with its intensity. She wanted him to touch her, to taste her. To mark her. Brand her. Take her. She wanted to taste that wicked mouth with her own. She wanted him in ways she'd never wanted another man—even though it made no sense. Even though it made her everything her mother had ever called her. But none of that seemed to matter. *She wanted.*

But that didn't mean she planned to act on it.

"I doubt that would be wise," she said, and mustered up an approximation of her professional smile. "Mr. Winthrop wanted me to usher you through your first project, not mortally insult you."

His gaze moved up to meet hers once more, and his smile was far too satisfied, far too aware. As if he knew that all he needed do was touch her and she would collapse at his feet, as much his to toy with as any of the hundreds of women who had undoubtedly landed face-first at his trouser cuff before. He was the ultimate predator, and that should have repulsed her utterly—but it did not, and she could not account for it. Anger and fear and something else, something too much like yearning, collided inside of her, making Grace feel jangly and breathless, unnerved.

"It seems your luck has held, *Ms.* Carter," he said at last, laughter lurking somewhere in his voice, and that dark, sensual promise in his eyes. That was when she noticed that the car had slowed considerably. He inclined his head toward the window. "We're here."

Lucas did not mind when Grace all but leaped from the car the moment it rolled to a stop at the top of the winding drive, in the looming shadow of the great house he so hated. Let her run. He had always enjoyed the chase—not that, in truth, he had ever had to do much more in the way of chasing than indicate his interest. But he'd always liked a new challenge to keep life interesting, and there were only so many times one could leap from a plane or climb a mountain when one did not, in fact, have a death wish.

He climbed out of the limousine after her, more focused on the sweet curve of her behind in the latest of her series of stuffy, corporate suits than in the fact that he was once more at Wolfe Manor.

Acquiescing to an urge he only belatedly realized was uncharacteristically chivalrous instead of calculating, he relieved the driver of his umbrella. He motioned the poor man back into the warm and waiting car, then followed the prickly *Ms. Carter* through the rain toward the front of the house, from where, he knew, she could see just about the whole of the property laid out at her feet. He loathed the very sight of it—all the picturesque British countryside spread out so prettily, with the charming little village of Wolfestone in the distance. He knew that appearances were deceiving: the prettier the surface, the uglier the mess beneath. He had not, perhaps, thought through his impulsive offer of this house for Hartington's use, much less considered that he would have to return here himself.

He concentrated instead on the woman standing with her back to him, frowning through the weather at what there was left of the once-famous view.

"You're wet," he said, close enough to her to see her start, and man enough to enjoy the flustered look she sent his way when he caught up to her. He indicated the rain, lighter now than before but still falling with no sign of stopping, and then moved even closer, shielding them both beneath the umbrella.

He doubted she knew the picture she made as she stood there, damp and inviting, her lush mouth soft, her usually sleek hair escaping from its confines and curling slightly, making her seem more wanton, more open. He felt himself harden and shifted closer to her.

"You failed to mention that this house is falling down," she said, her voice faintly accusing, her chin tilting up as she looked at him.

"Not yet," he said. He looked at the house, still regrettably upright and this time, thankfully, without his brother's disapproving presence on the front stair. While it was certainly in a notable state of disrepair, it had not been reduced to rubble and a hole in the earth, as Lucas had often fiercely imagined while still forced to live here. "Though one can dream."

But Grace was not looking at him any longer. She peered up at the house, then pivoted to look out over the wild, overgrown gardens and sweeping lawn that led down to the picturesque lake, pretty even beneath the onslaught of the rain. Her brow creased in fierce concentration, and she pulled her lower lip between her teeth as she let her gaze move from one dilapidated marker of the once-lush Wolfe estate to the next. She sighed and then turned her frown on him.

Somehow, he restrained himself from pressing his mouth into the indentation between her dark blond brows.

"I suppose we can set up a big tent on the lawn," she said. "It will be pretty if the weather is fine, and there will be enough space if it isn't. And the state of everything else could work for us. The house and grounds will add a bit of gothic splendor to the whole enterprise."

Lucas laughed, the sound more bitter than he'd intended. "This is Wolfe Manor. The ghosts here outnumber the living, I assure you, and are all known by name. And there is not a person in the whole of England who does not want to come here and see it for himself."

She looked at him, her expression warily polite, and he remembered belatedly that she was American, and was not, perhaps, as conversant on the Wolfe family and their tragic history as any citizen of the United Kingdom might be. He was not sure if he liked the possibility of her ignorance regarding all things Wolfe or resented that she might now have to learn all those terrible stories as if they were new.

He could not imagine why he should care either way. And yet he did.

"One of my ancestors supposedly drowned in the lake," he said abruptly, jerking his chin toward it. "Regrettably, not my father. He died in the house." He smiled, though he could feel it was not a very nice smile. It matched the dark memories that flew at him, each one a new knife in his gut. He shoved them all aside, ruthlessly. "The rest of us survived this place, in one form or another, but left the better part of our souls behind. I am not being poetic. There was never anything good here. Ever."

He looked down at her, unable to understand why he was speaking to her this way—as if it mattered to him that she see the truth about Wolfe Manor. He could not understand the urge.

"But it will make the perfect backdrop for your gala, I imagine," he continued after a moment. "The only thing people like more than glamour is glamour gone wrong, left to crumble into dust and disrepair and salacious old stories."

"You are so optimistic about human nature," she said, her voice as tart as ever despite the sweet honey of it, and completely devoid of any cloying compassion—or, worse, pity. She did not quite roll her eyes at him, and he felt something fierce and hot expand in him. "It is no wonder your company is so sought after."

"I am sought after because I am me," he said, arrogant and deliberate, daring her to look away, to deny him. "And because anyone seen in my company is certain to be photographed and speculated about in the next day's gossip rags. I am sought after because I am rich, sickeningly handsome and rumored to be excellent in bed." He raised his brows at her, challenging her.

"And here I thought it was for your remarkable

modesty," she replied, as quickly and as sharply as he'd known she would. As he realized he'd hoped she would.

"I don't require modesty," he assured her. "I have a mirror—and, barring that, the great and glorious British press. I am more than aware of my charms."

"Clearly." She did not look remotely impressed. Or even interested. Which, in turn, he found uncommonly fascinating. "But to return to a slightly less important topic than your vast and staggering ego, I think that we can pull this off."

She turned from him once more, to peer out across his history as if it was no more than a piece of property she was expected to transform. As if it was merely a venue.

Lucas wondered what she saw. What anyone who had not been abandoned here as a child—in his case, quite literally as well as emotionally—saw. None of it could ever be anything simple to him—never just a house, a great lawn, an old estate. His few happy memories involved his siblings, especially Jacob, and the mischief they'd gotten into with their decided lack of parental supervision over the years, but there had never been enough of those moments to tip the balance.

Wolfe Manor was where he had been discarded on the doorstep as an infant, his mother's identity ever after hinted at, but never confirmed. It was where he had come to understand as a very young boy that while William Wolfe had viewed all of his children with a certain caustic disinterest, it was Lucas who he had actively hated. It was where he had learned to be the person he was today—ever merry on the surface, ever concealed beneath, ever the disappointment to all who expected anything from him.

But Grace could see none of that. No ghosts, no uncomfortable memories, no absentee mothers and vicious, cruel fathers. For her, perhaps, this was no more than an abandoned great house on a vast property—one more British eccentricity for her to work around. In the pouring rain, no less. He watched as she worried her lower lip with her teeth, and then pulled out her PDA and began typing into it.

"We'll put lights on the house to play up its mysterious past," she murmured. "A haunted house theme, but elegant."

He realized with some astonishment that she was no longer speaking to him. She was entirely focused on her PDA, and thus the job at hand. As if he, Lucas Wolfe, the greatest temptation on two feet according to the tabloids and any number of his former lovers, was…no more than a business associate.

He found it surprisingly arousing.

"We'll have the design capitalize on the Wolfe

saga at every opportunity," she continued in that same distracted tone. "The Wolfe touch on the Hartington's brand in the eighties is widely considered to be the glory days—we'll use that. Expand it into the new era."

She continued on like that for a few minutes more, while Lucas stood idly by, holding an umbrella over her head and waiting patiently. Like one more toothless member of her intimidated staff. Like her lackey.

He was sure it spoke to the deficiencies in his character that he'd been hearing of all his life that he did not mind it as he should. That he found her deep concentration and ability to block out even him deeply, sensually intriguing. Would she be like that in bed? Would she gaze at her lover with that kind of rapt focus?

He certainly hoped so.

"What is it?" she asked, looking back at him as she slid her PDA back in her pocket, her brown eyes narrowing as they caught his expression "Why are you looking at me like that?"

The rain had picked up again, thudding hard against the umbrella and rebounding from the stones beneath their feet. They were both wet, cocooned together amid the noise of the storm. Lucas found it exhilarating. Or perhaps that was simply her presence—and the fact she was standing so close to him. Finally. She smelled like soap and rosemary and something fresher, more feminine, in the close embrace beneath the umbrella.

He could tell the very moment she realized that the pounding rain had trapped them even closer together, that she was near enough to be wrapped around him if she wished—that the only reason besides the downpour that would bring two people together like this had everything to do with the carnal heat that flared between them and nothing to do with the weather. He watched her chocolate eyes widen in alarm—and unmistakable awareness.

He reached across the scant space between them, and slid his hand along the side of her face, filling his palm with the soft skin of her tender cheek, letting his thumb scrape across her full lower lip, wishing he could test it against his teeth as she had. He was so unused to waiting. He could not recall the last time he'd had to wait for anything.

Soon, he promised himself.

"I want you," he said quietly. It echoed between them as more than a statement of intent. It was a promise. A vow.

He could read her so well, though he did not wish to analyze that unexpected ability. He heard her breath catch in her throat, saw her eyes heat with desire. He knew she wanted him. He could feel it in the fire that scorched the humid air between them, see it in the way her lips parted and the faint tremor that shook through her.

"I am afraid that *I* do not want *you,* Mr. Wolfe," she said in that brisk, professional tone, making him blink—though he did not drop his hand. The heat of her skin beneath his palm did not match the coolness in her voice.

"You are such a liar," he said, his voice low, intent on her heat, her passion. "I thought we covered this already."

He could already see them together, entwined, entangled. Her long legs wrapped around his waist, her breasts in his hands. Her lush mouth wrapped around his hardness. He wanted to take her where she stood, pull her skirt to her waist, and feel her soft heat with his hands, his mouth.

"Please do not touch me again, Mr. Wolfe," she replied. Her brown eyes were direct. Serious. She reached up and took his larger hand in hers, and pulled it away from her face. "It is completely inappropriate."

"Grace…" He let her move his hand, but he curled his fingers around hers, holding her fast. Something urgent was overtaking him, almost shaking him. He had never felt anything like it. "Do you really think I don't know you want me, too?"

They were so close, the rain pounding down all around them, stranding them beneath a noisy umbrella—the only two people in the world. Wolfe Manor, with all of its howling ghosts and terrible memories, faded away until there was nothing but the weather, this umbrella and this overly polite, overdressed woman who had somehow wedged herself under his skin.

And she was dismissing him.

She even smiled, a studiously polite, faintly pitying smile. Lucas had never seen anything quite like it—and certainly not directed at him. She tugged her fingers from his grip, and he let her do it.

"I want a great many things that are no good for me," she told him. Not unkindly, but with an undercurrent of intensity. "I want to live on nothing but red velvet cake and dark chocolate. I want to spend my days lolling about on white sand beaches, reading romance novels and basking in the sun. Who doesn't?" She tilted her head slightly, still holding his gaze. "But instead I eat healthily and I work hard. No one should get everything they want. What kind of person would they be?"

"Me," Lucas said. But there was an odd note in his own voice, and it seemed as if the rain roared in his ears. His mouth crooked to the side. "They would be me."

"Well," she said after a long, searing moment. Her voice seemed thicker—or did he only imagine that? "Life is not about *want,* Mr. Wolfe."

Something passed between them, electric and

alive, dancing in the breath of space between their bodies and jolting into him. He did not know what to make of it. He only knew he could not look away.

"You mean *your* life," he amended quietly, as if they stood in the presence of something bigger— something important.

"And in any event," she continued, squaring her shoulders as if he had not spoken, "I have a very strict policy against becoming personally involved with coworkers. I understand you've never really worked in an office before—"

"If I kissed you right now," he said, his eyes trained on hers and the truth he could see there— the truth that resonated in him no matter what words she threw out to deny it, "I could make you forget your policies. I could make you forget your own name."

That hung there like smoke for a heartbeat, then another, and then, impossibly, she laughed.

At him.

CHAPTER FIVE

GRACE thought she sounded on the verge of hysteria—and that was certainly how she felt, her chest too tight and her skin on fire—but Lucas merely stared down at her, his beautiful face looking nonplussed and not a little disconcerted. His hand tightened around the handle of the umbrella he still held above them. She could still feel the places where he'd touched her face, her hand—as if he'd burned the imprint of his hand into her flesh.

"I'm so sorry," she said, biting back the laughter before it gave her away, before he saw the truth. Before he realized she was putting on a desperate act to divert his attention. "I have no doubt you could do all of those things. You are Lucas Wolfe, are you not? You're famous for doing all of that and more to the better part of Europe."

"Never fear," he said stiffly. His green eyes burned like smoky emeralds in the wet, gray air.

"I am reckless with the feelings of others, perhaps, but never my own health."

"I'm sure you're all you claim to be," she said, injecting a placating note into her voice, which made his eyes narrow and his full lips thin. But he was no longer touching her, which meant he was no longer turning her brain and body to smoke and need, and Grace felt she had to count her blessings where she could.

"You have no idea," he murmured.

I have more of an idea than I should, she thought ruefully, pushing aside a host of dangerously vivid images that taunted her, teased her, made her yearn to throw herself headlong into the very thing she knew would destroy her. It was as if Lucas Wolfe had been created with every one of Grace's preferences and secret desires in mind. The aristocratic drawl. The quick, smart wit that suggested an agile mind he chose to hide behind his famed laziness. The lean, arrogant swagger. The narrow, beautiful face that made Grace think of fallen angels and other impossible creatures, all seduction and compulsion, magic and wonder, wrapped up in a package that was unmistakably, devastatingly male.

"And that is yet one more reason I can't possibly allow anything to happen between us," Grace said as politely as she could, speaking more to herself than to him. She forced herself to meet his gaze fully and blandly. She forced herself to smile serenely, despite the wild tumult that raged inside of her, nearly knocking her from her feet.

"Grace..." he began, but she had one more card to play. She splayed one hand over her chest, and let her smile take on just the slightest hint of something in the neighborhood of pity.

"I am, of course, very flattered," she said. Distinctly. Sweetly. Sympathetically.

She knew she'd hit the right note when he stiffened, his eyes narrowing to outraged green slits. She almost opened her mouth then to take it back, to tell the truth, compelled by a force she could not begin to understand. Why should she have the insane urge to protect him? To shield him—even from herself, at her own expense? What was happening to her?

It was the rain, she told herself with some desperation. The rain and a man she should never have met, who she could never allow herself to know in any way other than the superficial. Just the wet and the peculiarly British dampness that crept into the bones and stayed there, squatting, like a kind of grief.

It was the rain, she thought, and nothing more.

"I think we're done here," she said, when he only stared at her, affront and something else she was afraid to consider too closely written plainly across his face.

"Are you certain?" he asked coolly. "Surely you are only now warming to the subject. Just think, with some more time and energy you could flay my flesh entirely from my bones using only that sharp tongue of yours."

"Tempting," she could not help but reply, not wanting to think about her tongue near any part of him, not wanting to feel how much of a temptation he truly was, how completely he could ruin her if she let him. "But I think I'll pass." A kind of shadow passed across his face, darkening those fascinating eyes, and she felt an answering twinge in the vicinity of her chest. She cleared her throat. "I'm sorry if I hurt your feelings—"

"Please contain yourself, Ms. Carter," he interrupted her smoothly, with a touch of hauteur, all hint of shadows gone from his perfect features as if she'd imagined them. "I am Lucas Wolfe. I don't have feelings, I have sycophants. I think, somehow, I will manage to survive the disappointment."

She was surprised she was still standing, that they were still huddled together beneath the same umbrella—that she was not lying in pieces scattered at his feet after that lacerating tone of voice.

But this was a good thing, she reminded herself when she was tempted to let that affect her as it should not. When it came to this man, antagonism was the better part of valor. It was the hint of tenderness, the suspicion of emotion, that would be her downfall. But this—*this* she could handle.

She smiled her frostiest smile at him, the one that had helped earn her the title of ice queen from everyone who'd been unlucky enough to receive it.

"If you say so, Mr. Wolfe," she replied in a tone as sharp as his had been, his formal name feeling bitter against her teeth.

Then she strode toward the car, grateful for the rain against her face because it was cold. Grateful for the cold because it snapped her out of the strange spell she'd been in since she'd gotten in the car with him in London. Grateful because finally—*finally,* she told herself—she felt like herself again.

Grace would have preferred it if Lucas had reverted to his expected type over the next few days—rolling into work at odd hours, drunk and disreputable and incapable of doing more than ogling the secretaries, which was just as everyone expected him to behave—but he did not.

Instead, he turned out to be good at his job.

He threw a press conference to announce his own new position at Hartington's, deliberately starting the kind of media frenzy that would have taken anyone else a great deal of time and money to attempt to duplicate. And then he simply…went out on the town, as he normally did. He attended all the usual parties, with all the usual people. Pop stars and models, actors and Sloane Rangers. Up-and-coming artists across all mediums, and brash rockers known as much for their prodigious use of recreational substances as their music. And wherever he went, whoever he was with and whatever the event, when he was photographed—and he was always, always photographed—he talked about Hartington's.

He knew the very fact that he'd taken a job would be considered noteworthy, and so he milked the public's fascination with the idea of him at work for all it was worth. All the while talking so much about the Hartington's gala at Wolfe Manor that Grace was soon reading breathless reports on celebrity gossip sites about who was and who wasn't on the guest list, which artists were jockeying for a chance to perform—the kind of exposure and excitement she normally only fantasized about. With the centenary gala approaching so quickly, there simply could not be *enough* publicity—and certainly not of this kind and caliber.

Lucas Wolfe, it turned out, was a publicity machine, completely adept at using the press to his own ends.

"Your ability to manipulate the press is really very impressive," Grace told him at the morning meeting, the paper in front of her spread open to yet another story about the perennially shiftless Wolfe brother and his shocking newfound interest in corporate life.

Though she could not help but wonder—if he was this good at making the press do his bidding, had he been doing precisely this all along, creating the very image that even she now reacted to as if it was the gospel truth about him? Perhaps he really was as clever as she'd now and again imagined him to be, Grace thought, and could not have said why that revelation made her shiver slightly. Nor why he would have deliberately chosen to spend his life this way, to be known far and wide as this… dismissible.

"Not at all," Lucas replied with a careless shrug, though there was a measuring sort of look in his eyes when he met Grace's gaze across the conference table. Something much too commanding for a lifelong layabout. Something dark. Aware. "Paparazzi have followed me around for the whole of my life. It's long past time they made themselves useful."

"Usefulness is apparently going around," Grace said, unnerved by the way he looked at her and determined not to show it in front of her team members, all of whom still gazed raptly at Lucas as if he descended to work each morning from Mount Olympus itself, complete with a thunderbolt and a golden chariot.

Lucas, meanwhile, only watched her with an undecipherable expression that made Grace distinctly uncomfortable. Wrenching her gaze from his, she returned to the business at hand, grateful that hers was a high-pressure career that had taught her years ago how to always, always appear calm and collected no matter what fires burned inside of her or around her.

No matter if she felt scorched.

This was what she had wanted, she reminded herself more stridently than should have been necessary when she was back in her office, away from his too-incisive green scrutiny. She wanted distance. She wanted him to stay away.

She did.

So there was no reason at all for her heart to skip a beat in her chest when she looked up from a frustrating email chain regarding the florist's latest temper tantrum about the changed location to see Lucas filling up her doorway, far too broad of shoulder and smoldering of eye.

Her smile felt more forced than usual. As if that odd interlude in the rain had happened only moments ago, instead of days. As if she thought that somehow Lucas could truly see inside of her, where she still shivered for him, still wanted him, still ached for him to put his hands on her, no matter how much she wanted to deny it.

"I need a date," he said, the corner of his mouth quirking slightly.

For a moment, one panicked beat of her heart and the next, Grace wondered if this was yet another in the succession of vivid dreams she'd been having about Lucas and this very office—all of which started innocuously enough, just like this, and then quickly became shudderingly, achingly carnal.

But he merely waited in the open door, his face particularly unreadable in the gray light from the window. Grace surreptitiously dug a fingernail into her own palm and told herself she was relieved when the sharp little pain lanced through her.

She was awake. But he was still here.

"I'm sure you can auction yourself off for charity, or some such good cause," she said briskly, as if there had been no strained moment at all. She leaned back in her chair and eyed him warily. "Or, alternatively, step into the street and announce you have a gap in your social schedule. I imagine eligible ladies will tackle you where you stand."

That knowing smile flirted with the curve of his mouth. There was something especially untamed about him today, Grace thought helplessly. The suit he wore had been crafted with loving attention to every long, sinewy muscle he possessed, every hard, flat surface. His roguish dark hair fell over his forehead, begging for female hands to rake it back into place. But more than that, he seemed edgy. Determined. Words she would never have thought to associate with this deliberately languid, casual man.

But she would not have thought he could act in the interests of Hartington's, either, a small voice whispered, nor in so skillful a fashion, and he already had.

"Those are both attractive options," he said after a moment. "But my needs are more specific. You, to be precise."

Grace felt her stomach drop out of her body. She carefully folded her hands on her lap to keep them from betraying her by shaking. She ruthlessly tamped down on any outward sign, any reaction, because she knew, somehow, that it would be far too dangerous to show him any hint of what those words did to her. Any whisper of the clamoring inside of her, her heart thudding against her chest, all of her *wanting* with a force that scared her— and she would be lost.

And then what would become of her? She was afraid she already knew—and shoved aside another guilty flash of memory, resolving she would call her mother later to assuage her guilt and attempt to make amends. But that did not mean she would *become* her.

"I am running out of ways to tell you I am not available to you," she said with a great calm she did not feel. She met his gaze, her own firm. "Along with the patience necessary to keep saying it."

"I received the message, believe me," he assured her, sounding wholly unrepentant. "Though I believe it was the laughing in my face that truly drove the point home."

His green eyes gleamed with amusement. She found the sight a relief, and then immediately wondered why she cared whether he found her entertaining, on any level. She should not care if he hated her. She should not care if he was entirely indifferent to her. And yet...

"I apologize if I bruised your ego," she said, with a razor-sharp pretense of sympathy. "I will confess, I thought it impossible."

"Oh, it is," he said easily. "Which is why you can spare me a new lecture on appropriate behavior—it bounces right off my shiny, pretty surface." His mouth pulled into that self-mocking curve. "But I still need you to be my date tonight." He shook his head when she started to protest. "It is work-related, of course. I may be a desperate egomaniac, but I can, on occasion, listen."

His eyes were intent on hers, hinting at all the layers of himself he kept hidden that she could sense hovered there, just out of reach.

"Sometimes I am even capable of processing the information I hear," he continued, deep irony laced through his voice. "It is astonishing."

"There is no need for sarcasm," Grace said, trying to sound firm and in control but fearing she sounded unnecessarily prim instead.

He did not answer for a moment, and then, he casually dropped the name of the current reigning pop star sensation, the young woman who had recently taken the country by surprise with her debut album—an achievement made all the sweeter because she was the daughter of one of England's most beloved former football heroes.

Grace blinked, unable to track the change of subject. "What about her?" she asked, baffled.

"It's her birthday party tonight," Lucas said. "Quite the coveted invitation list. It should be one of the events of the year."

"And, naturally, you've been invited," Grace supplied for him.

He did not bother to address that absurdity, and Grace wondered why she'd bothered to say it. He was Lucas Wolfe. Of course he was invited.

"I thought you could accompany me and we could convince her to sing at the gala," he said instead, and there was the unmistakable light of challenge in the gleam of his eyes, the set of his chin. "I suspect she'll do it if I ask. She's had a crush on me since she was a schoolgirl."

Grace shook her head at him. Getting the current number-one pop star to perform at the gala would, indeed, be a coup—but for some reason, that was not the part of what he'd said that she focused on.

"She is *eighteen!*" she chided him, even as she was caught up in the challenge in his gaze. The dare. Even as she found herself unable to look away from him.

"I said she had a crush on me, not that I returned the favor," Lucas replied, unperturbed. His gaze grew hotter and seemed to light Grace up from within. "Besides, everyone knows I prefer my women older, desperate and married."

Grace wanted to discuss his sexual preferences about as much as she wanted to fling herself out the window behind her to the cold street below. But that did not keep her mouth from drying out, nor her pulse from leaping at her throat.

"So you are pathetic rather than predatory," she found herself saying, despite her best intentions. Despite the fact she knew it was not at all wise. "My congratulations."

But Lucas only smiled.

"Nine o'clock," he said quietly, his voice as low as his eyes were bold. He let his eyes fall over Grace's tightly buttoned jacket, then back up, and his lips twisted. "But you cannot wear one of those ghoulish suits you love so much, not in front of the paparazzi in my company. And, I beg you, do something with your hair."

His smoky gaze met hers—dared her, provoked

her, made her want to throw the nearest paper-weight at his inflated head—and then he smiled again.

No one should have a smile like that, Grace thought, hating herself for the flush that washed through her, the fire that licked into her—for her inability to tell him exactly what he could do with his sartorial suggestions.

"Anything else?" she asked tightly, furiously.

Because they both knew that she would do it. She would go to this party and she would dress more or less to please him. Because she had no choice, she told herself, because it was her job to do so, but still—she was surrendering, like all of her worst fears. His eyes gleamed with a hard, male triumph she could feel echo inside of her, making her soften instead of scream. Making her yearn.

"That should do it," he said in that insinuating voice of his, the one that tickled and teased, and crept along her skin like the softest feather, the lightest touch. "And, Grace—I have a certain reputation to uphold. Don't force me to choose an outfit for you. I guarantee that you won't like it."

She was the most irritating woman he had ever encountered, Lucas thought later that night, lounging on a suede settee in the middle of the celebrity-studded birthday party, under the all-glass dome of one of London's most exclusive nightclubs. Yet for all his annoyance, he was unable to shift his attention from Grace, who was sitting beside him and yet, somehow, managing to ignore him completely.

He might have admired her fortitude had he not had this electric current of desire and temper surging through him, making him want to take out his frustrations on her very sweet flesh. All over her flesh, again and again and again.

But that was not a productive line of thought.

"No one is convinced by this act," he told her. "The entire British press knows you are only pretending to ignore me for effect."

"Just a minute…" she murmured, not paying any attention. Not even glancing at him.

It was lowering, to say the least. Lucas almost laughed at himself. He was brooding in public, which was not like him at all. He, who was known for his ability to make all around him laugh and fall a little bit in love with his smile. But he could not seem to shift his attention from the woman next to him, as she blithely tapped away at that damned PDA of hers. She had taken him at his word regarding her attire—which perhaps he should have expected.

But he had not been prepared. He had suspected she was beautiful beneath her gloomy clothes, of course—but he'd had no idea how correct he was.

For the first time since he'd met her, she was not wearing an undertaker's suit in black or gray. Instead, she had chosen to wear a dress so red, so bright, that it was all he could do not to gawk at the way it flowed over the mesmerizing legs she'd made even longer, even more wicked, in high platform sandals. The dress clung to her breasts as he would like his hands to do, spanned her waist with a lover's attention to detail and then flared out from her body to show only saucy hints of the magnificent legs beneath. She looked like a column of fire, and he wanted to burn them both beyond recognition.

But because she was Grace, and might possibly be the death of him, she had left her hair up. In a slightly more complicated knot, to be sure, with a few tendrils of golden blond waves left hanging to tease and entice, but it was ultimately no less controlled than her usual style. He felt certain it was a deliberate act of defiance on her part.

One step at a time, Lucas thought. He was that much closer to getting her naked and beneath him, and that, really, was what mattered. It was fast becoming an obsession.

He had presented her to the pop princess who had, as he'd anticipated, eagerly agreed to perform at the gala—an agreement that Grace had immediately set out to confirm with the girl's hovering management team while Lucas suffered through a series of indecent propositions that should have appealed to him more than they did. He had smiled obediently for the cameras, and then the princess and her entourage had moved on, leaving Grace behind to email back and forth with her team members about ways to update the design concept for the party to best showcase the new talent. And leaving Lucas with nothing to do but imagine removing that silky smooth red dress from her mouthwatering curves, tasting every inch of her heated skin as he went.

"All right," she said finally, looking up at him, triumph bright in her eyes. "That was another fantastic idea. Thank you." She slid her PDA into the clutch bag she held. "I'll find my own way home, and see you in the office—"

"Home?" He tamped down on the unexpected surge of temper, but still found himself glaring at her. "You cannot be serious."

"Of course I'm serious," she said, with that calm gaze of hers that he suddenly found enraging, not peaceful or relaxing at all. "I understand that you are used to all manner of late evenings and early mornings, and more power to you. I, however, require far more sleep in order to function."

"This may very well be the party of the year," Lucas said mildly, waving his hand at the parade of celebrities, the overwrought chandeliers up above, the walls draped in deep magenta and studded with crystals. "You miss a single moment of it at your peril."

"It's a bit early in the year to be making such pronouncements, don't you think?" She shrugged. "Besides, I believe the intricacies of the London party circuit fall more within your purview than mine."

"I want you to stay with me," he said, baldly. He saw her stiffen, saw her eyes widen. He smiled. "After all, this is the perfect place to drum up excitement for the gala, is it not? Who knows what other luminaries we can rope into attending?"

Her brown eyes were wary—and furious, he noted with growing interest. Why should she be furious? But he suspected he knew. He felt it, too, the tightening noose around them. The pull of it.

The difference was, he was not fighting it. Much.

"Have I misunderstood something?" she asked in the tone of one who was quite certain she had misunderstood nothing. "I was under the impression that the collection of celebrities was your job—a job you are quite good at, actually." She waved her hand at the crowd around them. "And, of course, these are your sort of people, anyway."

"Famous?" he asked idly. "Shockingly attractive? Filthy rich and well connected?"

"Bored," she retorted with that sharp smile and a matching glint in her eyes. "Desperate. As anyone would be, were their self-worth predicated on how many mentions they received in a glossy magazine."

He eased back against the settee and watched the flush of heat that stole across her face. *Passion,* he thought with deep satisfaction. And she was not happy about it.

But he was.

"As opposed to the deep social and philosophical relevance of party planning for a department store?" Lucas asked mildly, baiting her. "I can certainly see where your exalted sense of worth comes from."

She froze, her eyes shooting sparks at him, temper storming across her normally impassive face. It fascinated him.

"I have a job," she said from between her teeth. "One that I am very, very good at. My self-worth derives from my achievements. Not my father's surname."

That might have landed a blow on a man less used to hearing such things and in far more offensive terms. But Lucas only relaxed against the settee, stretching his arm along the back and smiling at her.

"You just finished telling me that I'm good at the same job," he said, making his tone deliberately insulting, wanting to see the fire in her blaze higher. Hotter. "How difficult can it be?"

"Is anything difficult for you?" she asked, her voice scathing, her hands curling into fists in her lap. "Or do you just float through life making snide commentary and endless innuendos, forever the darling of the paparazzi and very little else? How proud you must be. How deep, indeed, your still waters run."

He was uncomfortably hard, and delighted with her temper, even though she directed it at him. He, after all, could take it. Temper did not upset him; it usually only intrigued him, since he so rarely lost his own. Still, he was a man, and her words made him long to teach her all manner of lessons. *Soon,* he thought, watching her proprietarily. *Very soon.*

"Are we discussing masks, Grace?" he asked quietly, angling close enough to breathe in her scent. "Because I've been waiting to talk about yours since the moment we met. What are you so afraid of?"

"Becoming you, of course," she threw at him immediately, with all of her customary ice and that fire that he instinctively knew was blazing bright underneath. "Becoming anything like you. A zombie with a million-dollar smile."

"That would hurt my feelings—" he began, fighting a smile.

"If you had any," she finished for him, and rolled her eyes. "I know full well that you don't."

"If I believed you," he corrected her, his voice quiet but firm. He waited until her gaze found his. "But we both know that you'll say whatever it takes to maintain this fiction of yours. That you do not want me. That you cannot feel this thing between us, this pull. What would happen if you told the truth, Grace? What then?"

The party was loud around them, a swirling cloak of laughter and music and the whirl of interchangeable faces, but Lucas hardly noticed any of it. There was only this forgotten settee in a darkened corner of the expansive room. There was only this woman. There was only this need.

"Oh," she breathed, not looking away, her eyes narrowing. "I didn't understand. This is still about your ego, isn't it? I won't fall at your feet and beg for your attention, so there must be a grand conspiracy. There must be a detailed explanation. Masks and fictions and *reasons*."

"Not at all," he said, unable to keep the laughter from his voice, though it only seemed to stoke the fire within him. "Only the truth."

"Here's the truth, then," she said, her voice dangerous, honey and fire. She shifted closer, her need to slap at him and show him her power clearly overcoming any common sense. He needed only to lean forward and he could taste her.

"I am all ears," he murmured, the laughter gone, every part of him focused on that lush, full mouth so close to his.

Her smile was like a razor, her voice like a whip. "If I were to make a list of all the things that I hate in a man, every single characteristic you possess would be on that list."

"I have no doubt," he said, raising his gaze to catch hers. Holding them both captive for a long, hot breath. "But that doesn't change the fact you want me inside of you. Right now. All night. Until you can't stand the pleasure any longer."

He saw her silent gasp as her breath fled her, saw the color flood her face, but most of all he saw the heat in her deep brown eyes. The carnal wonder. The need.

His, he thought. She was his.

"Your conceit is rivaled only by how deeply you are mistaken," she managed to say, but her voice was no more than a thread of sound, and her eyes were too wide.

"The facts remain the same," he taunted her softly.

"I don't want you," she said, enunciating every word. But he could see how it cost her, how she fought for control. "Is that clear enough for you? Is there any room for error? You bore me."

But she didn't move away. If anything, she angled her body closer.

He looked at her for a long, shimmering moment. The music pounded. The crowd surged. London sparkled and preened far below them, even as raindrops fell against the high glass enclosure above.

But all Lucas could see was Grace. Maddening, courageous, sharp-mouthed Grace. *His.*

Then, never breaking eye contact, he reached over and gently pressed his fingers against the delicate hollow of her neck. Where her skin was soft like satin and hot to the touch.

Where her pulse thumped out hard and then went wild beneath his hand.

"Liar," he whispered. Then he closed the distance between them and took her mouth with his.

CHAPTER SIX

MOST first kisses were gentle, sweet. Lucas was neither.

He simply took her mouth with no hesitation—as if it was his, as if *she* was his, as if that devastating possession was his right.

It was like a bomb detonated inside of her, exploding through her limbs, white-hot fire and spiraling need combusting again and again and again, leaving her weak. Wanting. Her breasts ached. Her nipples hardened. Her core melted. And still he kissed her, taking her mouth with an easy command that made her tremble against him.

He kissed with a carnal demand, a sheer, arrogant certainty, that shook Grace almost as much as the feel of his mouth on hers.

Hot. Commanding. As if her entire life had led inexorably to this moment, to the incomparable feel of his lips against hers, sending desire swimming through her veins like alcohol and rendering her incapable of doing anything more than kissing him back.

As if she had never done anything else. As if she would die if she did not.

She raised a hand, and then forgot why as it found the rock-hard planes of his chest, the hint of stubble on his lean jaw, each new sensation igniting a flood of desire, each stronger and more thrilling than the last.

She…forgot. Where they were. Why she was angry with him. Why she should not allow him to angle his mouth over hers with such skill and talent, nor rake a hand into her hair to anchor her head in place as he tasted her again and again and again. Everything that was not Lucas was like smoke, drifting away, signifying nothing. As if only he existed.

Without lifting his mouth from hers, without giving her even a moment to breathe, to collect herself, Lucas shifted on the small settee, his powerful arms sweeping Grace up and over him, settling her sideways across his lap. He murmured something she could not understand, could hardly hear over the pounding of her heart and the wild rush in her ears, and then he claimed her mouth once more.

It was too much. He was everywhere. Hard beneath her thighs, hard against her body, and that talented, wicked mouth of his that took and took, until she could not think at all. She could only feel the heat. The fire. The slick fit and exquisite taste of him, expensive liquor mixed with that part that was purely him. Pure Lucas. Sinful and delicious and capable of making her head spin around and around while the very core of her pulsed with need.

One of his hands remained laced in her hair, and on some dim level she was aware that he was destroying her careful twist. The pins scattered at his impatient touch and the heavy, wild curtain of her blond waves cascaded down around them, shielding them, cocooning them. She could not find it in her to care. His other hand stroked a lazy path from her cheek to her neck, down the stretch of her bare arm to settle at her hip, his big hand holding her fast on one side with his arousal stark and unmistakable on the other.

Grace's hands went to his strong, sculpted shoulders and were lost, unable to keep from testing the stark physical power he held leashed there—the fine, chiseled lines of his lean and muscular form. Once again, her hand crept to his cheek as if she could hold him, understand him, make sense of him that way. As if she could keep him there, kissing her as if he was starved for her, kissing him back as if she had never been kissed before, as if he had switched a light on inside of her and she could only glow. And glow.

She had never felt this fine desperation, this

coiling, insistent need. This fire. She was lost in him. Undone by him.

And still he made love to her mouth as if he could do so forever, as if he had all the time in the world, as if nothing existed but the two of them.

At first, the flash of light made no sense to her, though she pulled back and blinked, dazed, her breath coming in pants and her eyes too glazed to see. But then it came again, and again, and she realized with dawning alarm that it was not lightning. It was no storm. It was a camera. A flashbulb.

"Ignore them," Lucas muttered, his hands still urgent on her.

Reality came crashing back, slamming into Grace with the force of a punch to her gut. Ice and horror washed through her, and for a long moment she was frozen, incapable of movement, like a stone as she stared down at Lucas.

At that wicked mouth of his, that some treacherous part of her still longed for. At his beautiful, fallen-angel face, that she now knew the feel of beneath her hands. At his bold, unapologetic green gaze, that tore into her like knives, leaving her jagged and despairing.

She could not speak. Words flashed across her mind, harsh and accusing, desperate and pleading, and none of them came close to addressing how she felt. What it meant to be the latest in his endless parade of interchangeable females. Who she had just discovered she was, despite everything, despite all her years of sacrifice and hard work, ambition and denial.

All it took, apparently, was a red dress and the world's most shameless playboy, and she transformed into her own worst nightmare.

She lurched to her feet, putting air and space between their too-heated bodies, letting her hair swirl around her—hoping it covered her face and concealed her identity from the cameras. She wished desperately she did not have to live through the next awkward, terrible moments, that instead she could simply disappear in a puff of smoke and avoid the consequences of her thoughtless actions altogether. But when had she ever gotten what she'd wished for?

Lucas reached out and snagged her small wrist in his big, elegant hand before she could turn away, forcing her to look down at him, sprawled there on the brushed suede settee like some kind of dissolute god. She wanted to scream, to curse. To throw things at him. To ruin that handsome face, as if that could change how easily she'd fallen for him, how quickly she'd melted all over him.

She bit back what felt like a sob—but could not be. She would not allow it. Not here. Not now. Not where too many people, too many cameras—and Lucas—could see.

"Don't touch me," she managed to grit out, past the lump in her throat and the tears that threatened to further disarm and expose her. "Haven't you done enough for one night?"

"Grace," he began, his voice low, but she could not listen to him. He was all lies and seduction, and she had to go before she lost herself completely. She had to think. How could she repair the damage? It was as if a bomb really had gone off, and she was the wreckage, all splintered and shredded and strewn haphazardly about. There was nothing left of the Grace she had been before he'd kissed her like that.

And she would die before she let him see it.

She jerked her wrist from his grasp, all too aware, from the measuring gleam in his green eyes, that he allowed it. And then she spun around on her heel, ignoring his muttered curse, and threw herself into the crowd. She shoved her way past the avid gazes of the looming cameramen and bolted for the elevator that would whisk her away from this mess.

If only she could run from herself as easily.

She heard her mother's voice echo in her head, weathered from too many cigarettes and too many bad choices. "Someday you'll ruin yourself on some no-account man just like the rest of us. You'll see. Then maybe you won't be so high and mighty."

Grace felt a rolling swell of a multitude of

things—none of them *high and mighty*. Maybe no one could escape her destiny. Maybe she'd been a fool to try so hard, for so long.

It was not until she'd made it down into the lobby of the exclusive luxury hotel that she realized she'd left her bag behind on the top level—behind the tight wall of high-level security that only Lucas's famous face had managed to breach. She sighed, a noise that was dangerously close to a sob.

Her keys. Her wallet. Her PDA. How could she leave without them? Where could she go?

She came to a stop in the middle of the marble floor, her legs feeling unsteady beneath her, her breath still too quick and her heart still so loud she was afraid it echoed in the hushed space.

"Grace."

Of course he had followed her. He was the reigning champion of this particular game, and she had just forfeited. All over him and on film.

It was not possible to hate herself more than she did at that moment, but Grace tried. Oh, how she tried.

She did not turn around, but still, she knew when he drew close. Her body reacted as if his proximity was a caress. She felt an inevitable, breathless kind of heat slide from the nape of her neck to her breasts, then down between her legs where it coiled tight and bloomed into a fire. She found she was biting her lower lip and forced herself to stop. Just as she forced herself to raise her head and meet his penetrating yet oddly shuttered gaze when he stepped around to her front to face her.

For a moment, the world fell away. The glittering, ornate lobby, with its hint of tasteful music from above and the acrobatic flower displays in large ceramic vases, faded into a gray nothingness, and there was only Lucas. Only the things she told herself she did not, could not, see in him, because he was only surface no matter how he made her ache. Only the deep, abiding desire for him that rolled inside of her, the fire banked and smoldering, but too-easily kindled by the way he tilted his head to one side as he considered her, his mouth crooking slightly in one corner.

"I would almost say that you were running away from me," he said quietly, his gaze too perceptive for such a supposedly shallow man, "if I did not know that such a thing were impossible. Women run *to* me, not *away* from me."

"I must not have received that memo," she said, attempting to match the lightness in his tone, if not his eyes—but her voice betrayed her. It was too rough, too emotional. Too fragile.

Wordlessly, he held out his hand, and that was when she noticed that he held her small, glittering clutch. She swallowed and reached for it, taking care not to touch him in any way. She knew, somehow, that it would ignite that fire all over again, and she was not so foolish as to think she could walk away from this man twice. She was not even sure she could do it now.

"I never took you for the Cinderella type," Lucas said. Still that light, easy tone, but she could see something much darker, much more intense in his face, his gaze. As if he knew, too, that they danced around the same land mines, the same quicksand. That one false step would incinerate them both.

"I loathe Cinderella," Grace said, trying to firm her spine, to breathe. To retain control. "There is never any need to wear shoes so precarious that you might lose one should you need to run. And why was a ball so important to her, of all things? She'd have been much better off looking for a job instead of a prince."

"I suspect you are missing the point of the fairy tale," Lucas said in that same quiet voice. His dark brows rose. "Deliberately."

She did not know why she stood there, simply looking at him. She did not know why the moment felt so heavy, yet so breakable, and why she could not seem to make her escape as she knew she should. As she knew she must.

"Come home with me," he said, and it was a command, not a request. It licked through her, into her. She could not seem to breathe through the heat suffusing her, the tight, hot desire that coiled in her and pulled taut.

What terrified her was how tempted she was to simply do it. To give in to the demands of her body. To surrender to him and the pleasure she knew he could deliver. Had already delivered, little as she wanted to admit it.

But it was that terror that spurred her into action. She heard herself sigh, or perhaps she'd tried to speak, but then she stepped around him and headed for the grand entrance across the lobby. There was nothing to be gained by a discussion, because she could not be trusted around him. It was as simple as that. She had to get away from him—from this *spell* he'd cast that seemed to compel her to do the very thing she'd vowed she would never do.

The night outside was frigid and wet, but Grace welcomed both, gasping slightly as the cold slapped into her.

"This is absurd," Lucas said from behind her, his voice clipped with impatience. "The weather is vile. You'll contract pneumonia."

"That would be preferable, at this point," she said without thinking and heard his short laugh.

And then she was spinning around, because his hands were hot and firm on her bare shoulders, and then the world tilted again and there was nothing but the smoky green of his impossibly beautiful eyes. The ones that saw too much, however unlikely that should have been.

"You would prefer the fate of an opera heroine

to one moment more in my company, is that it?" he asked with a certain grim amusement, and were he any other man, Grace might have thought she'd hurt his feelings.

But this was Lucas Wolfe. He had none, as he would be the first to announce.

"Yes," she said, lifting her chin and wishing that alone could clear her head. "Consumption. Tuberculosis. Either is far better than being photographed as yet one more hapless female connected at the mouth to the infamous Lucas Wolfe."

The night was dark and the rain seemed to blur the edges of things, but, even so, Grace could have sworn that she'd wounded him somehow. Far more confusing than that possibility was her reaction. She wanted to apologize, to comfort him. To make that hint of vulnerability disappear.

She had no idea what was happening to her.

"Don't worry," he drawled, his eyes flashing as his fingers flexed slightly against the flesh of her shoulders before letting go. "I cannot imagine anyone will recognize you as my 'unnamed companion du jour,' or care. I doubt that it will even make the papers."

"I'm so glad," she bit out, unable to process why she was suddenly so angry with him—and not wanting to examine it, just as she did not want to examine why she felt so jagged, so messy, so ruined—as her mother had spitefully predicted all those years ago. She wrapped her arms around herself, her hands moving to absently cup the places he'd just vacated.

"Grace," he said, and her name was something between a sigh and a curse. "Come home with me," he said again. He shook his head slightly, as if he was as unnerved by his own tone of voice as she was. "Please."

"I…" But she could not seem to finish the sentence. She could not bring herself to break the odd spell between them, the enchantment—as if doing so would cause him pain. And, she acknowledged with great reluctance, her, too.

He looked at her for an age, a moment, a heartbeat. Cars skidded past them on the late-night street, the traditionally uniformed doorman hailed a cab with a shrill whistle and London carried on all around them, the city bright and noisy and shimmering in the winter rain.

And there was Lucas, brilliant against the night, as if nothing else had ever mattered, or could.

"Come with me," he whispered, and held out his hand.

She could not speak, or move. She felt herself sway slightly, as if pulled to him by some invisible chain. She knew too much now—that his body was so strong, so warm, so incredibly *male*. That he could set her on fire with only that dark, stirring gaze even as the cold rain fell down on them both.

She felt the great gulf of the loneliness she spent her waking hours denying yawn open inside of her, reminding her of all the nights she'd spent alone, all the years she'd denied she was a woman, all the vows and promises she'd made to herself about how different she would be than her mother, than her own past. Than what had happened to her. But then Lucas had touched her, and she was nothing *but* a woman.

Finally, something inside of her whispered, and that word seemed to ricochet inside of her, leaving marks. Scars.

She wanted to reach over and slip her hand into his more than she could remember ever wanting anything else.

He was far too good at this, she thought in a kind of daze—and it was that sudden spark of reality that gave her the courage, the strength, to step back from him. To really *see* him again, instead of what she felt.

To remember exactly who he was, and what he did, and *why* he knew all the right buttons to push, and how best to tempt her. He could seduce a stone gargoyle. He probably had.

And if her heart hurt inside her chest, well, that

was just another secret she would learn how to keep. And hide away, where he could never find it again to use against her.

"I can't," she whispered. "I won't."

And then she turned away from him, blind but determined, and did not breathe again until she'd hurled herself into the nearest black cab and slammed the door between them.

Walking into the morning meeting the following day, with a smile on her face and exuding all the professionalism she possessed, was one of the most difficult things Grace had ever had to do.

If she could have, she would have called in sick. But she'd suspected that doing so would be far too telling—it would give Lucas far more of an advantage than he already had, and she could not live with that possibility.

I am my own heroin, he had said, and now she was terribly afraid he was hers, too. She felt very nearly strung out, and he had done nothing but kiss her. Just imagine…

But she refused to go down that road.

"Good morning," he said, along with the rest of the team as she entered the conference room—his voice seeming to arrow straight into the center of her, kicking up echoes and vibrations.

There was no need to look at him directly, she told herself as she took her place at the head of the table and confidently addressed those gathered. There was no need for anything so foolish, and anyway, she had already blinded herself staring into that particular sun. She had already flirted with her worst fears. No need to compound her sins.

But, unfortunately, she did have to look at him when the topic of the gala's entertainment was raised. She glanced over, surprised to see that while he lounged carelessly in his seat like a pasha, his eyes were on the tablet in front of him. It should have felt like a reprieve. Instead, she felt a hollowness behind her breastbone.

"We have some exciting news," she said crisply, infuriated with her own weakness. Again. "Once again, our newest addition has proven himself to be an invaluable asset to the Hartington's team. If you'll explain your latest coup, M—"

She never finished saying *Mr. Wolfe.* She didn't even fully say the word *mister,* because his head snapped up, his green eyes fierce. Searing. Furious. Daring her to call him a name designed to distance him, after all that had happened. After they had tasted each other and burned in the same fire. *Daring her.*

There was a tense, tight silence. Grace felt herself flush. His eyes slammed into her, and she was terrified that everyone could see—that everyone knew—that she might as well have been writhing in his lap there and then, making a fool of herself, a spectacle of herself just like before, every inch the names her mother had thrown at her....

She was losing it.

"Lucas," she said, knowing as she did so that she should not have capitulated, that she should have prevented that gleam of deep male satisfaction from warming his gaze by any means necessary. That he had won something she could not afford to lose. "If you could share...?"

She could not let this happen, she told herself as Lucas began to talk. She watched him play to the crowd, with a self-deprecating smile and that wickedly funny turn of phrase that had everyone on the edges of their seats, hanging on his every word.

And she was no better.

She was, in fact, everything her mother had predicted she would become.

Grace let that sit there for a moment, a shocking and breathtaking realization, cruel and all-encompassing—but it was true. How could she deny it? Lucas Wolfe possessed not one single redeeming characteristic, and still, she had melted, become a stranger to herself, at his slightest touch. How could that make her anything but...loose? Easy? Ruined already, from within?

She thought of those strange, loaded moments in the rain outside the hotel last night. She thought of the arrested look in his eyes, as if he'd felt the same complicated rush of emotion and confusion that she had—

But she shoved that all aside, ruthlessly.

She would do whatever she had to do, but she would not let him destroy her. She would not let everything she'd worked for disappear so easily. She would not, could not, let herself be everything her mother had told her she'd be, sooner or later. Not now. Not ever.

He had expected a cold reception. He had even expected that she might pretend nothing had happened and carry on as if that was the case.

But Lucas had not been at all prepared for Grace Carter, the most determined and prickly woman he could remember tangling with, to completely avoid his gaze. To blush in public. And then to bolt toward the door when the meeting had ended, quite as if she planned to run away from him altogether.

He wanted to feel something like triumph, but did not. It was something else, something closer to temper, that surged through him.

"Grace?" he called after her, not bothering to rise from his seat, but loud enough to carry to the rest of the team as they filed for the door. To force her hand. "If I could have a word?"

He saw her back stiffen, but when she turned,

that smile of hers was firmly stamped across her mouth. Perhaps only he could see the color high on her elegant cheekbones. Perhaps only he noticed the storm in her dark brown eyes.

She waited by the door, smiling and exchanging a few words with her staff as they left, and then closed it behind the last of them, trapping them together in the great fishbowl of a conference room. It was glass on three sides, and sat in the center of the offices and cubicles all around them, so that anyone happening by in the halls could glance in and see what was going on.

He wondered if that made her feel safe. It made him…twitchy. He remained in his seat, with the whole glossy width of the big table between them, because he knew that if he stood he would put his hands on her, and if he touched her again, he did not think he would stop.

"That is the ugliest suit I have ever seen," he told her, his voice low, his careless posture at complete odds with the strange tightness that held him in a secure grip. "I cannot imagine where you find these things. It is as if you pay to deliberately obscure your figure and your natural beauty."

"Is this what you wished to discuss in private?" she asked, her voice frigid even as her brown eyes shot flames at him. Even as she retained the razor's edge version of that smile. "My fashion sense?"

"I think you mean your lack thereof," he replied lazily.

"Your concerns are duly noted," she said tightly. "And this is a world-renowned designer suit, for your information. But if that is all, I really must—"

"Grace." He liked the way her name felt on his tongue. He liked the sound of it in the air between them, the command in it. He liked how her eyes darkened in reaction. He wondered where else she reacted, and how it would taste.

"We are not going to discuss it," she told him, her full lips thinning in distress. "Not any of it. We will never mention it again. I am deeply appalled at my own behavior and can only assume you feel the same—"

"I do not." He arched his brow. She let out an impatient, aggrieved sort of breath.

"You should!" Her voice was harsh. Raw.

She cleared her throat, and smoothed back her hair with one palm. It did not require any attention—it was already ruthlessly yanked back into her typical slick twist, and all he could think of was the glorious fullness of it when it had fallen around them. The weight of it, the scent of it. Her delicate, intoxicating little moans against his mouth.

"I will thank you not to tell me how to feel," he said mildly. It was only a figure of speech, he told himself. It was only to score a point. It did not mean he *felt*.

She looked away, and he could see that she fought with herself—for control, perhaps. He wanted her to lose that control, once and for all. He had already tasted it, and he wanted more. He wanted her wild and wanton and free.

He simply wanted her. It was no more complicated than that.

"I do not have time for this," she said at last. "For you. For…what happened. I can think only of the gala."

He thought she sounded desperate. He told himself he wanted her that way. That had always worked well for him in the past. He ignored the small voice that insisted that this woman was not like other women. That she could see him. That she could know him. That she was Grace, and different.

"All work and no play…" he began, teasing her, alarmed at the direction of his own thoughts.

Her eyes shot to his. "That is not a topic I suspect you have any familiarity with at all," she snapped out. She let out a breath, and when she spoke again, her voice was smoother. "It's wonderful that you are able to help so much, that your connections are so useful. It really is. But that doesn't change the fact that my florist is a prima donna or that the security firm keeps changing its estimate, does it? And those are the things that require my attention. Not you."

"What are you afraid of?" he asked, almost conversationally.

But it was not a light question at all, and he knew it.

She stared at him for a long moment, until he felt something not unlike shame twist through his gut—though he knew it could not be that. He was immune, surely.

"Do not bring this up again," she said, her voice soft yet firm, her gaze direct. Grace, in control. Grace, in charge. Grace, locked up and put on ice. Hidden. He hated it. "It is not something I am ever going to wish to discuss."

She was lying. He knew it as well as he knew his own lies. It was as obvious to him.

But the walls all around them were made of glass, with too many eyes watching them from all sides, and so he had no choice but to watch her turn and walk away from him as if it were easy to do.

Again.

CHAPTER SEVEN

THERE were any number of flashy, spectacular parties that Lucas could have attended, from club openings to birthdays to opening-night film screenings. All of them would, inevitably, be packed with scantily clad women who would smile invitingly at him and offer him anything he might possibly want. Their attention. Their interest. Their bodies. Themselves, on any available silver platter. And yet, for some reason he could not quite fathom, he'd chosen to spend his Thursday night sitting alone in his office instead, staring out over the cold March streets rather than enjoying himself down on the pavement.

He pushed back from his desk and raked his hands through his hair, irritated with himself. That might not have been a particularly new feeling for someone as committed to his own self-destruction as Lucas had always been, but he rather thought the cause of it was.

He had done most of the work that had been

allocated to him, most of it relating to the public relations aspect of Hartington's relaunch, and the marketing and sales plans that went along with it. Lucas was as surprised as anyone else to discover that he had quite a knack for marketing, in addition to PR. It made a certain kind of sense, he supposed. After all, he had been involved in the guerrilla marketing of his own identity since his earliest days.

First, when he'd decided as a child that if he was going to be punished harshly no matter if he was good or bad he'd just as well make sure to be *really* bad. And then, of course, when he had spent his time at home diverting his father's violent attentions away from his younger siblings by any means necessary. Better he should take the hit than the younger ones, he'd thought—and anyway, he'd taken a certain, possibly sick pleasure in behaving as if he was, in fact, his father's worst nightmare.

Is that the worst you can do? he had taunted the usually drunken William, no matter how hard the blow or evil the insult. And no matter what his father came back with, Lucas had always laughed. And laughed. Even if it hurt. He'd always managed to enrage his father even more—and refocus the old bastard's attention on a target who could take the abuse.

To his siblings he had been and apparently still

was the smart-mouthed and charming ne'er-do-well: impossible to take seriously, perhaps, but quick to make them laugh and think of things other than the cruel master of Wolfe Manor. To his father, meanwhile, he had been the devil, taunting and disrespectful, and never, ever as afraid as he should have been.

Perhaps because of the roles he'd assumed so early on, Lucas had discovered quite young that one needed only to suggest a few key points, lay the right groundwork and the world jumped to the specific conclusions he'd intended as if of their own volition. It was all in the marketing, really, with a little PR polish to make it all sparkle.

He had only attempted sincerity once in his life, and that had not ended well. He felt his lips thin as he thought of the two-faced Amanda and how thoroughly she'd broken his young heart. He'd never made that mistake again. When she'd left him, he'd decided it was far easier to be what people expected him to be. Far safer, and far more comfortable in the long run.

Which meant, oddly enough, that he was well suited to the position he'd been given at Hartington's. Who would have thought it? He could not help a wry smile then. Lucas Wolfe had become what had long been his own worst nightmare: an office drone. By choice. It was the most extraordinary thing.

The iconic old building was dark and quiet all around him. What few noises there were echoed slightly down the abandoned halls. Very few employees were still around this close to midnight on a Thursday, but there was something about the emptiness of the usually busy place that appealed to him. Lucas sat behind his vast, powerful desk and stared out the window, wondering if he looked as much a fraud to the casual observer as he felt. The sudden and inexplicable businessman. The nouveau tycoon. He was certain that if he sat still long enough, he'd be able to hear the howls of derision rise from the wintry London streets far below.

And yet he could not seem to summon the necessary energy that would be required to go out on the town as he normally would, wearing his overused public face and prepared to cavort in front of the cameras as expected. It was as if the Lucas Wolfe he had worked so hard to present to the world for so long no longer fit him as it should, and he did not know what to do about it. There had always been such a fine line between the way he behaved according to the low expectations of whomever he came into contact with and what he did in private, and that line had never, ever been crossed.

No one knew the truth about Lucas, and he liked it that way. Better to remain silent and be thought a fool than to argue the point and find that one was suddenly expected to live up to a host of responsibilities that were completely beyond one's capabilities. Lucas was all too familiar with that brand of failure. That was why, among other things, he kept his particular flair for money management secret and allowed the world to speculate that he lived off the kindness of certain desperate patronesses like a bloodsucking leech.

He did not want to think about why those long-defended and maintained lines seemed to be blurring these days. He had not wanted to impress someone else in so long now that it seemed almost like an elaborate practical joke he was perpetrating against himself, this brand-new compulsion to do so. But he knew it was true. He wanted Grace Carter to think well of him. He could not think of a single reason why he should, and yet there it was, stark and impossible to deny, sitting in front of him like a wall he kept butting his head against.

It was absurd. Suicidal. And yet he still could not manage to get that woman out of his head. The cutting way she spoke to him, as if she expected better from him when she should know that he quite famously had nothing to offer. The grudging respect in her chocolate eyes when it turned out he was good at this PR game or that he knew his way around a marketing plan. The way she'd looked at him that night in the hotel lobby, as if she could see into him, into the places he'd denied existed for so long that he'd almost forgotten about them himself.

He was becoming maudlin, he thought derisively, annoyed at himself. What was next? Perhaps he could rend his garments and start talking about his terrible childhood in the streets, like all the other madmen. Perhaps he could write a self-pitying memoir and hit the talk show circuit to weep crocodile tears and garner sympathy for his poor-little-rich-boy plight. He could not think of anything more pathetic.

So instead, he thought about Grace. She remained a mystery to him, and that had not happened in a very long time. A woman was not usually much more to Lucas than a pleasant diversion, especially not after he'd tasted her. He could not understand why Grace was so different. Why she resisted him, or why she should want to continue to do so. Twice now she had walked away from him. *Twice.* He could not imagine why anyone would deny the kind of chemistry that raged between them, so explosive he had forgotten himself completely in that party—had actually forgotten where they were. What was the point of denying something so elemental? Chemistry like theirs was hardly commonplace. Surely she knew that.

Or, he considered, rubbing a hand over his jaw, perhaps she did not. Perhaps she was as shocked by it as he had been. She did not strike him as the kind of woman who had had a battalion of lovers. Perhaps she was unaware that she should be chasing this kind of connection like the Holy Grail it was. That seemed so unlikely—she was so strong, so intriguingly self-possessed—yet what did he really know about her?

He leaned back in his decadently plush office chair and considered. He was all too aware that she took her job quite seriously—so seriously, in fact, that it had begun to rub off on him in ways he was not entirely comfortable with. The fact that he was musing over Grace while seated in his office instead of in a hot tub filled to the brim with nubile women whose names he would never learn did rather tell its own story, he reflected, wincing slightly.

He knew that she was quick, and smart, and not in the least bit intimidated by either his famous name or his admittedly formidable good looks, both of which had been known to overawe those who encountered him in the past. He knew she gave as good as she got, and could throw his own words back at him as if she was trying to best him at a game of tennis. He even knew that, on some level, she enjoyed the deliciously combative relationship they'd developed, because he found it surprisingly addictive—and he'd seen the look in her eyes that indicated she did, too.

He knew that she buttoned herself up like a

latter-day Victorian maiden and reacted with the same level of overblown outrage when called on it. He suspected she did it deliberately, to hide the mouthwateringly perfect body he had now seen in clinging silk and felt with his own hands. He knew that she unfairly concealed her glorious mess of hair from view, which he felt was an offense against every aesthetic he possessed. Why would a woman allow her hair to grow like that, so wild and free and sexy, and then spend most of her life scraping it back and wrestling it into submission?

Grace was a mystery, and Lucas discovered that he did not much care for mysteries. *Not knowing* left too much to chance, and left him far too unsettled.

Before he knew it, Lucas found himself typing her name into the search engine on his computer, just to see what other tidbits he could come up with. There were pages upon pages of links to her name, most having nothing at all to do with the Grace Carter, events manager for Hartington's, that he knew. There were images of all kinds of Grace Carters, none of whom were *his* Grace.

He scrolled idly through the list, trying to imagine the Grace he knew as a production assistant in Los Angeles, a concert pianist from Saskatchewan, a book-writing missionary in the Côte d'Ivoire. And then his eyes fell on one link that did not seem to go along with the others. *Gracie-Belle Carter,* it read. It made Lucas laugh, even as he clicked through. *Gracie-Belle* sounded absolutely nothing like the Grace he knew—in fact, it sounded a lot more like the kinds of women, soft and smiling and always submissive, who had helped him solidify his reputation over the years.

But then the picture loaded on the screen in front of him, and Lucas froze in his chair. Desire and curiosity combined, rushing through him like something heady and illicit.

Because it was—yet also wasn't—the Grace he knew.

The woman before him in full-color photography was more properly a girl, all coltish limbs and ripe curves, hair flowing all around her, sexy and rumpled, wet and lush. One picture showed her in nothing but a pair of bikini bottoms, looking coquettishly over her shoulder at the camera with big eyes and sultry lips, the line of her bare back an enticing, mesmerizing curve. Another featured an even smaller bikini, and a whole lot of sand plastered in interesting places, as she knelt on a dark rock and stared moodily at the camera, holding back her wild, wet hair with both hands. A third showed her lying on her back in some kind of hammock, eyes closed, a wet T-shirt showing the full swells of her breasts while her thumbs were hooked in her bikini bottoms as if she were about to tear them from her body and bare all.

She was delectable. Shockingly sensual in ways he had not imagined she could be, and he knew how she tasted.

It took Lucas longer than it should have to realize that he was looking at an old American sports magazine with a swimsuit photo shoot. It took even longer than that for him to accept that he was, without a doubt, looking at Grace. *His* Grace, listed as Gracie-Belle Carter from Racine, Texas. She could not have been eighteen when these pictures were taken. She was flushed with youth, yet still somewhat unformed—beautiful in the way young girls could be, but not yet as mesmerizing as she would become with the passing of the years.

His Grace, the born-again Victorian, a swimsuit model? That went against everything he thought he knew about her—and some deep, male part of himself loved it.

Alone in his office, Lucas smiled. He'd known it, hadn't he? He'd known that she was wild beneath that prim, severe exterior. He'd sensed it, and he'd tasted it. And now he knew for certain.

What would it take to bring the real Grace out of hiding? What would she be like if she let this part of herself free? He felt himself harden just imagining her fierce and unfettered, bold and sexy, hiding nothing.

He sent all the images he could find to the printer. His Grace, a wanton. His Grace, unrestrained and unbound by propriety. He was deeply, darkly thrilled. He couldn't wait to get under her skin and taste the truth of her, at last.

Grace slammed open his office door without knocking, which was his first clue that he'd riled her considerably. She was halfway across the room before he had time to react at all. When he did, he found he could only watch her as she stormed toward him, the file folder he'd left on her desk gripped tight in one hand.

She was furious.

And glorious, he could not help but notice, with the flush of temper high on her cheeks and the light of battle in her eyes. She had hidden herself away in one more dreary corporate suit, a depressing gray with a long hem and a high collar, and he could not help but imagine her in nothing but her bikini instead. She stopped in front of his desk and slapped the folder of photographs down in front of him.

"I expected you to be contemptible," she told him in a low, angry voice. "After all, you quite famously have the moral standards of an alley cat in heat, but this is over the top, even for you."

"I don't know what you mean," Lucas said easily, leaning back in his chair and eyeing her. She was like a high-octane narcotic, a rush and a thrill, and he could not help the fact that he enjoyed it when she fought with him. "I am excoriated daily for photographs of me, many of which are taken without my consent. You, on the other hand, posed for these, did you not?"

"I was *seventeen!*" she gritted out from between her teeth, her hands in fists at her sides. "And *I* have not courted public opinion and infamy every day since!"

"*I* do not have to court attention, Grace," he replied, smiling slightly. "It finds me whether I want it or not." He indicated her presence before him with a languid wave of his hand, and was rewarded by the sparks that flashed like lightning in her eyes.

"That might have been more believable before you proved yourself to be a master manipulator of the press, the marketing department and anyone else you come into contact with," Grace seethed at him. She shook her head fiercely. "I don't believe your lazy playboy act any longer."

Lucas did not speak for a moment, watching the play of emotion across her face instead. There was fear behind her anger, fueling it. He found it fascinating—and disconcerting. Something turned over in his gut.

"What happened to you?" he asked her quietly, his eyes searching her flushed face.

He took in the inevitably sleek and perfect bun she'd wrapped her hair into, the severe and overly conservative cut of her suit. All she was missing was a pair of clunky black eyeglasses, and she could have completely embodied the stereotype. Why was she hiding? What was she hiding *from?*

And why was he so compelled to find out the truth about her?

"If you mean what happened to me *this morning,*" she snapped at him, vibrating slightly with tension and fury and that incomprehensible fear, "I came into the office to discover that the resident Don Juan spent his free time digging around in a past I leave buried for a reason!"

"I mean, in your life," he said, shaking his head slightly. The look in her dark eyes made him feel restless, made him want to do things that were anathema to him—like try to save her, galloping in on a gleaming white horse and pretending to be someone who could. But he had stopped rescuing people a long, long time ago. "I could hardly believe these were pictures of you. Why do you hide all your joy, power, beauty? Why do you pretend that part of you never existed?"

"Because she never did!" Grace threw at him, her hands rising and then dropping against her thighs, her voice much too rough, too raw.

And then, to his horror, her dark brown eyes filled with tears.

* * *

She could not cry. She would not cry—not in front of this man, who had managed to expose her darkest secret with the same lackadaisical smirk and easy carelessness as he did everything. Not here, not now, where she was already far too vulnerable.

She had almost passed out when she'd opened that folder after the morning meeting. Shame and horror had slammed into her with too much force, too much pain, and the fact that it had been Lucas who had found the pictures, Lucas who had seen her like that…It made her want to sob. Or scream. Perhaps both.

Thank God she'd been alone in her office! Of all the things she'd expected to see in a folder from Lucas, the very worst mistake she'd ever made had not been on the list. Sometimes, eleven long years later and a world away, she even let herself forget about it for long stretches at a time. She would tell herself that everyone had things they would prefer to forget tucked away in their history, that it hardly bore thinking about any longer.

That her mother had not been right. That she had not been ruined so long ago, when she had let it all happen. That she was not beyond the pale, as she'd been treated. That her mother should have believed her—and should not have disowned her.

But she had been kidding herself, apparently.

He had presented the glossy reminder of the worst

year of her life to her in bright color photographs, in her office, the one place where *Gracie-Belle* had never existed. Could never exist. *Gracie-Belle* had died the moment those pictures were published, and she'd been so young and so stupid it had taken her far longer than it should have to recognize that fact. She'd needed money desperately enough to forget everything she'd learned about the way men were, and the way the world worked—and she'd paid for that. She was still paying.

Grace's hands curled into fists at her sides. How dare he throw those pictures in front of her as if he knew something about them—about her?

"I do not expect you to understand," she said coldly, stiffly, desperately fighting to sound calm—no tears, no sobbing, no shouting—and not quite succeeding. "You have never *needed* anything in your privileged, aristocratic, yacht-hopping life, have you?"

"Grace," he said, his green eyes growing dark as he stared at her, that confidence he wore like a second skin seeming to slip before her eyes, "you are taking this the wrong way. I only meant—"

"To humiliate me?" she interrupted him wildly. "To punish me because I refused to sleep with you?"

He looked appalled. Shocked. "What? Of course not!"

They stared at each other for a searing, tense

moment. He swallowed, then shrugged, visibly uncomfortable. "I only wanted to remind you. Of who you are. Who you could be."

"Who I am?" she asked, hearing the bitterness in her own voice. She tried to shake it off, turning away from him toward the wall of windows and the lush little seating area grouped before them. "How could you possibly know who I am?"

"It's funny, isn't it?" His voice was deceptively mild in the quiet office. "We all think we know someone because we've seen them in pictures. Isn't that how you knew I was so contemptible?"

She did not want to admit that he had a point, throwing that word back at her, and she told herself it didn't matter, anyway. Rich men acting badly made the world go around. They could, like Lucas himself, wake up one morning wishing for a change, and just like that, executive positions were doled out like candy.

It was different if one happened to be born dirt poor. And a woman.

"Let me tell you a story," she managed to say past the lump in her throat and the tight ball of anxiety in her gut. "You'll have to use your imagination because it takes place far, far away from a sprawling estate in the English countryside or the glamorous Christmas windows of Hartington's."

She shot a look at him over her shoulder, not sure how she felt when she saw how he watched her, as if he really did know her—something almost tender in his expression. But what did that really mean? He thought the pictures he'd unearthed were a good memory, that they were something other than desperate. He did not, could not, know her at all.

"I grew up poor, Lucas," she said as evenly as she could. "Not 'Daddy refuses to pay my bills this month' poor, but real poor. 'Having to choose between rent and food' poor. A trailer park in a dirty little Texas town that nobody's heard of and nobody ever leaves, because there's no money for dreams in Racine."

"Grace…" he said, but she was too far gone to stop. She could hear the emotion in her voice, could feel it pumping through her. She did not know why she was telling him this, only that she had to.

"Mama didn't understand why I couldn't just settle down with whatever boy would have me and live the same kind of life that everyone we knew lived, that she lived, but I couldn't." She shook her head, as if that would help ward off the accent that returned when she talked about Texas, her words sprawling, her drawl thickening. "I read too much. I dreamed too hard. And even though there was a part of me that loved Racine more than words, because it was home, I knew I had to leave."

She swallowed, as if she was still standing in

that dusty trailer park, so blisteringly hot in the summer, and the wheezy old air-conditioning forever being turned off to save pennies—even though she could see London in front of her, sparkling and cosmopolitan through the windows.

"So while the other girls my age were making out in backseats and getting ready to marry their high school sweethearts," she said quietly, as if remembered dust and despair were not choking her even now, "I was banking everything on a college scholarship."

She could hardly bear look at him then, so beautiful and impossible, high-class and expensive, like a male fantasy made flesh. *Her* fantasy. The only man who had gotten under her skin in eleven long years. She didn't know why it made her ache to see him as he sat there behind his big desk, as far away from her now as he had ever been. She told herself she wanted it that way. That the kisses they had shared, the odd moments of communion, were no more than an elaborate game to him, and she was not at all the worthy player he seemed to think. That he simply hadn't known it, but he would now.

She told herself she was glad.

"It was one thing to be bookish," she said, looking at the folder of the photographs that had damned her. "And something else to be pretty." Her mouth twisted in remembered shame and trembled slightly. "And I was much too pretty. Mama's new boyfriends were always quick to comment on it. Some of them tried to get too friendly when they were drunk. I kept my head down, hid in the library and studied. I was the top of my class—the top of the state, even. I knew I'd get some kind of scholarship—but I also knew it very likely wouldn't be enough to cover my expenses. I'd have to do work/study, at the very least. Maybe more than one job, if I wanted textbooks. Or food. But I was destined for better things. That's what I thought."

"You were clearly correct." Lucas's voice was cool, crisp. His aristocratic accent seemed to cut through her memories of those hot Texas days like a knife through butter. But it only served to remind her how vast the gulf between them was, and how little he could ever understand her.

She did not want to think about why she wanted him to understand her in the first place.

"That fall my class took a field trip to San Antonio to see the Alamo," Grace said, forcing herself to continue, however little she wanted to keep talking. "And that was where Roger discovered me."

She didn't want these memories. She wished she could excise them from her head and throw them away as easily as she'd gotten rid of all the other things that had held her back from the future she'd so desired. Like her accent. Her roots. Even her mother, who hadn't wanted her enough, in the end. And it had all started with Roger Dambrot.

"He was a photographer," she said. She could feel Lucas looking at her, and she had no one to blame but herself. She had started this, hadn't she? "Quite a famous one, actually."

She had decided to share this story of her past, but that didn't mean she had to share all of it. Like her doomed, childish love for Roger, who had been as happy to sleep with her as he had been to disappear the moment she veered toward any emotion. She thrust the memory of that first, last heartbreak aside. She had been a colossal idiot, but wasn't every teenage girl? She'd been so pleased with the attention. So delighted that he could make her look like that with his camera. She'd thought she'd found her calling—her ticket out of Racine and into the bright future she'd always believed she'd deserved.

"Thanks to him," she said, fighting to stay calm, "I was offered a lot of money for a modeling contract, and it never even crossed my mind to refuse it." She smiled, unhappily. "I was proud of it! I thought it proved that I was different—that I was special."

"Grace…" Lucas's voice was a caress. She shook it away.

"What I did not expect," she said tightly, "was

that appearing in a bathing suit in a national magazine meant that every one in Racine would consider me a whore. The teachers at school. The other kids. My mother's boyfriend."

She could remember it all so clearly, no matter how hard she'd tried to forget it over the years. Travis, her mother's latest boyfriend, with his copy of an American sports magazine in his hands and that knowing, lustful look in his mean black eyes. The tiny bedroom in the trailer that Grace had always considered her refuge. Travis's hands, touching her. His big body, reeking of stale beer and old cigarette smoke, pressing her back, pushing her down, making her freeze in panic and confusion.

And then her mother's appearance in the doorway—to save her, Grace had thought. *Thank God,* she'd thought. It had taken so long, too long, for her brain to accept that her mother's rage and fury was directed at *her,* not Travis.

"I should have known you would pull something like this!" Mary-Lynn had screamed at her. "This is how you repay me? After all these years?"

And the names she'd called Grace. Oh, the names. They were still lodged like bullets beneath Grace's heart. She could still feel them when she breathed.

"Once they think you're a whore," she said quietly, "that's how they treat you. Even my own mother. And more to the point, her boyfriend."

All the things she did not say hung there between them, and Lucas only looked at her, as if she was not more naked, more vulnerable, than she had ever allowed herself to be before. Grace felt a deep trembling move through her, climbing from her feet to her neck, and fought to breathe.

"I'm sorry," Lucas said, his voice too soft, so soft it made her eyes heat with the tears she refused to shed. "As it happens, I understand completely what it is like to be judged on photographs, and the conclusions about one's character that so many people draw from them."

"So one would imagine," she said. She turned around and met his gaze fully, not sure when he'd climbed to his feet and not certain she liked the reminder of his height, his surprising grace.

"Why do you care so much what so many ignorant people think?" he asked, still in that soft voice.

"Because they were *my* people!" Grace blinked to keep the wet heat from sliding down her cheeks. "Racine was the only thing I ever knew, and I can never go back. Do you understand what that feels like?"

"I cannot understand why you would wish to return to a place that scorned you," Lucas said, his voice low.

"Those pictures are the reason my mother threw me out of the house when I was seventeen," she said, as evenly as she could. "I hate them and everything they stand for. I wanted to make some money for college, and instead I lost my family, my hometown and, for a long time, my self-respect. That's all you need to understand."

"But that was then," Lucas said, smiling slightly, encouragingly. "Now they are an acknowledgment that you were always, as you are now, a beautiful woman."

"I don't want to be *a beautiful woman,* whatever that is!" Grace cried, old and new emotions boiling too hot, too wild, inside of her. Why couldn't he understand? Her looks had never done anything but cause her trouble. She would have removed them if she could. The life she'd built had nothing to do with her body, her face. It had everything to do with how well she did her job, and she couldn't let go of the panicked notion that if everyone knew what she looked like half-naked that would be *all* they knew about her, ever after. Again. What would she lose this time?

"Why should you hide yourself away?" Lucas asked, in the same light tone, because what wasn't light to this man?

And it was just too much. Over a decade of anguish seemed to well up within her, threatening to spill over and drown her. She had already been down this road—she knew what happened. Let a man see her as a piece of meat and he would treat her that way, too. This was the truth about men. This was what Grace inspired in them. Hadn't she spent all these years completely immersed in her job, her career, to keep from having to face the uncomfortable truth? The loneliness? Why had she wanted so desperately to believe that Lucas was any different?

"Did you really believe I would be delighted to see these pictures?" she countered. Her eyes narrowed. How had she tricked herself into believing there was more to him than this shiny surface? When would she learn that she knew nothing of men—especially not men like Lucas, who wielded sex as just one more weapon? "Or was this one more of the sick little games you play that mean nothing to you, because you are completely heedless of the damage you cause to the people around you?" She was unable to hide the hurt from her voice. "Because you can be?"

He stood there against his desk, an arrested look on his face, his smoky green eyes changing to something much darker, much grimmer. It was as if she watched him alter before her eyes. Gone was the sly, insinuating good-time guy, made of sin and rumor and utter carelessness. And in his place was this…man. Different. Darker.

Tortured, she thought, her heart pounding like a drum, too fast and too hard. But how could that be? How could he be hurt?

And why should she care?

He is like all the rest! that old voice inside of her cried, still nursing the wounds her mother and Travis had inflicted so long ago. *Don't listen to a word he says—don't believe the things you think you read on his face!*

But she could not bring herself to move.

"You have no idea of the damage I can do," he said, his voice thick with what could only be self-loathing, the lash of it making her blink and sway slightly on her feet. "And ferreting out a few perfectly tasteful pictures from a decade ago hardly match up to the destruction I can wreak. You should count yourself lucky, Grace."

She did not want to care about this man. She did not want to feel that unwelcome tug in the vicinity of her heart, or want to soothe away the darkness that had overtaken him. She wished she did not know that he could feel pain, that he could react at all to the things she'd said. She wished he was no more and no less than the flighty playboy she'd believed him to be.

But if she'd truly believed that, why, the relentlessly logical part of her brain asked, had she told him the story she'd never told another living soul?

"Do not show those pictures to anyone," she said, her voice shaking slightly, trying hard not to notice the way his mouth twisted, as if she'd wounded him again.

"They are only pictures," he said softly, with a bitterness she could not understand. He swept the folder into his hand, and then pitched it into the wire trash bin that stood next to his desk. "And now they are gone. No lives ruined. But I am Lucas Wolfe, after all. I'm sure there are six or seven other lives I can destroy before the evening news."

Grace knew she should have walked away then. She should have turned on her heel and left the offensively luxurious top-floor office he'd done nothing to earn. She should have considered the matter finished, and comforted herself with the knowledge that he was the person she'd believed him to be from the start—shallow, conscienceless, empty.

But she did none of those things.

"Why do you want me—the world—to think the worst of you?" she asked before she knew she meant to speak. That odd tension that had gripped her in the lobby of the hotel and out on the street the other night returned, hovering between them, making the air feel heavy with portent and meaning. Regret and fear. Secrets. *Hope.* Or perhaps that was no more than the way he looked at her.

"It saves time," he replied, his voice strained, almost harsh. "There is nothing here, Grace. Nothing beneath the pretty face. Isn't that what you think? What everyone thinks? Congratulations. You are correct."

His pain has nothing to do with you! she cried at herself, but it was as if another person inhabited her body. Another person who swayed closer to him, whose hands itched to reach over and touch him—a person who could not let that much raw pain go unacknowledged. Especially when it was his. A person who could not believe he was who he said he was. Who would not believe it.

God help her.

"I think," she said, very quietly, unable to look away from him, unable to hide herself as she should, as she'd meant to do, because something about the way he was talking made her think he was grieving and she could not ignore that, she simply could not, "that your looks are quite probably the least interesting thing about you."

"Grace—"

He bit out her name, but she could not stop. She lifted her chin and did not so much as blink as she gazed at him. As she *saw* him.

"I think that you could teach lessons on how to hide in plain sight," she said. "That you do it all the time. That you are doing it even now."

CHAPTER EIGHT

THE following afternoon, Grace forced herself to unpack her things from her suitcase and put them away in the wardrobe of her cozy room at the Pig's Head, the only inn and tavern in the quaint little village of Wolfestone—just down the road from Wolfe Manor. The honey-colored beams above her head and the cheerful fireplace in the corner should have made her feel relaxed, as if she was on holiday, but she could not seem to keep the wild tension swirling inside of her at bay.

In fact, she was not sure she'd breathed fully since that stark, upsetting scene in Lucas's office. She did not know what might have happened had they not been interrupted by Charles Winthrop's pursed-mouthed secretary, who had taken no notice at all of the crackling tension in the room and had invited Lucas to visit Mr. Winthrop at once.

It was only after he'd left that she had retrieved the photographs from his waste basket, because she could not leave them lying around, and certainly not in his office. She had shredded them with great relish in her own office, shoved the past back down into the vault where it belonged and told herself she'd had a lucky escape.

But somehow, she did not feel lucky at all.

She should be jubilant, she told herself now and not for the first time, that they had been stopped before they could go any further along that road of personal revelation. She had a feeling that they had hovered perilously close to a great disaster, and disaster was something she could not afford with the gala so close. It had been a relief to depart for Wolfestone this morning, knowing that this last stretch of time before the party was crucial—and that living immersed in the venue and on hand to deal with the inevitable issues that would crop up was necessary.

Necessary and convenient, Grace acknowledged ruefully. There would be little time to deal with the mysteries of Lucas Wolfe. Much less her own confusion regarding her reaction to him. So far she had discovered that she could neither keep her hands off Lucas nor her mouth shut around him. Even his own behavior failed to give her pause. What was next? She shuddered to think.

There was a sharp knock at her door, and she walked over to wrench it open. A jolt of awareness shot through her when she found Lucas himself standing there, as if she'd summoned him.

Were they both thinking about those photographs? Grace wet, wild, debauched? She swallowed with some difficulty and felt herself flush.

Lucas smiled.

Up close, all hints of the tortured, wrecked man she'd seen the day before were gone. He lounged in the doorway as if he was the local gentry—which, of course, she reminded herself, he was. His wicked mouth crooked invitingly, making his lean and clever face seem positively sinful. One arm was propped up over his head against the door-jamb. His dark hair was artfully tousled, as if he'd just woken from a nap or had raked his fingers through the mess of it. Repeatedly. He was wearing a soft-looking shirt in bright blue that clung like a lover to the planes of his hard chest, thrown carelessly over a pair of denim trousers that fit him like paint, and Grace could not pretend to herself that he was anything but the most gorgeous man she'd ever beheld. He made her mouth run dry.

Or maybe that was her fear about what might happen next.

"Invite me in." The crack of command in his voice dragged her attention to his eyes, which were far darker and ripe with the tension between them than the rest of him let on.

She was doomed.

"Why would I do that?" she managed to ask crisply, as if she was affected neither by his stark male beauty nor the darker truths she could see move through his gaze. "Do you plan to suck my blood?"

"Is that a request?" he replied, but his customary easy charm was gone. She sensed it before she understood it—a whisper of trepidation that danced across her skin, snuck down her spine. *Something is different,* a small voice whispered in alarm. He seemed edgier. More dangerous. Less controlled. She remembered that dark fury she'd sensed in him the first morning he'd walked into her office. *Everything has changed,* she thought. But she cast it aside.

If she pretended she didn't notice that the balance had shifted between them, that every breath and every moment seemed taut and terrifying and much too unwieldy to be borne, would that make it so?

"I had to see it for myself," he drawled, his eyes like green fire as they traveled over her, making her feel scorched. Making her *want.* Making the air seem to hum with everything that had changed, everything that was new and dangerous. "Up close."

"I have no idea what you're talking about," Grace managed to say over the catch in her throat. She left him standing in the doorway, because it was that or risk much more than she dared, and moved back over to the bed as if she meant to finish unpacking. But she was aware only of Lucas.

"You do." He stepped inside the room and let the door swing shut behind him, which was not at all what she had planned. She jumped slightly and then turned to face him, her stomach dropping. The room seemed much smaller, suddenly, constricting around her. Trapping her—and yet she couldn't bring herself to run.

Worse, she did not want to run.

She meant to speak, to deny him again, to keep up the civil, professional pretense—but she couldn't seem to do it. It was the hungry look in his eyes as he moved closer, lean and big and more commanding than he should have been. More intense. More compelling. She could not tear her gaze away from him. It was as if, having seen a glimpse of what was behind the mask he wore, she could not see that mask any longer. She saw the man. Electric and consuming, and so much more real than he had seemed before—more real than was at all healthy for Grace. Her heart began to beat low and deep, the pace quickening—becoming ever wilder, more frenetic—the closer he came.

"I had no idea you even owned a piece of clothing that was not strictly stodgy and office appropriate," Lucas continued, that mocking note in his voice, the one that suggested he was being playful when she could all but *see* the tension shimmer through every tendon, every bone of his lean body. "Other than that one red dress."

"There is nothing in the least bit outrageous, or even interesting, in anything I'm wearing," she said, trying to sound authoritative. In control. She had chosen the crisp denim jeans and smart black cashmere sweater deliberately, knowing that while her team might choose to dress more casually while away from the conservative head office, she could only allow herself to unwind so far. Her version of *casual* involved dry cleaning and clothes she would be comfortable wearing to business meetings with her superiors.

Was she really thinking about her clothes? With this man so near? So unpredictable? Did she think that would work?

He ignored her, and prowled closer, peering at the clothes stacked in her open suitcase and beside it on the thick white duvet. Grace felt frozen in place. She did not dare to move. He was much too close, so close she could smell him, heat and man and something expensively spicy. So close she could seem to do nothing at all but think of how his mouth had fit against hers—how demanding, how sure. Or recall how warm his skin was to the touch, or think about how she felt so shivery now, so hot and cold.

And he knew everything. There were no secrets.

Why should that make her feel even weaker? Even more aroused?

He leaned back against the bed, far too close to where she stood, crossing his long legs at the ankle and tucking his hands into the pockets of his jeans. His green eyes were hooded as he gazed at her for a long, hot moment while Grace could do nothing but panic. Her heart sped up and her pulse pounded. Her eyes seemed to glaze over with heat, while her mouth stayed far too dry. The very air in the room seemed to crackle.

"Will we talk about it?" he asked, that dark edge to his voice, as if he fought the same demons that Grace did. "Or will we continue this game of cat and mouse until we end up in bed? I love to verbally spar with you, Grace, do not doubt it. And I intend to take you to my bed. But I rather think there is more to this than that."

"More?" She did not *quite* stammer. Not quite, though her voice went up an octave or two, and she flushed.

"I am afraid you've seen behind the curtain," he said in a low voice, with that odd, stirring current beneath. The corner of his mouth flirted with a smile, though his gaze was far too direct, too disconcerting. Too dark. Was this the real Lucas? The man behind the mask? Because Grace knew, beyond a shadow of a doubt, that he was not joking. Not this time. "There are penalties for that. Taxes that must be levied. Those are the rules."

She could not breathe. She moistened her lips and then clenched against a shocking flood of heat when his gaze dropped to her mouth and a stark, purely sexual hunger cast his face into wickedness. The kind of wickedness she wanted to taste, despite everything.

"I came to find you yesterday, after meeting with Charlie Winthrop," he said, coiled there, just out of reach, about to pounce. And still, Grace could not bring herself to move away as she knew she should. His head tilted slightly to the side, his gaze measuring her. "But you'd gone."

"I had a meeting," she said faintly. An electric current was buzzing through her, skimming along her skin, burning through her veins. She felt almost light-headed. Almost dizzy.

"I do not understand this," he said in the same quiet, serious tone he'd used yesterday. The same stark, brutal honesty. The same directness, with the same undercurrent of something like despair. The room seemed to contract, trapping them both in the same tight, bright grip. "I do not understand why I feel compelled to tell you things I normally do not speak of to anyone. I do not understand why I cannot stop thinking about you. I can't seem to stay away from you." His smile turned wry. "And the truth is, I do not want to."

"You must," she said, but her voice was insubstantial, the barest breath, and he ignored it, anyway.

"I have never been very good at doing what I must," he said, a hard amusement flashing through those smoky green eyes. "It is among my many and varied character flaws."

Grace did not want this. She could not want this—it was too much. *He* was too much. She felt as if the world shook, as if she shook with it, though nothing moved.

"I am not interested in your flaws, many though they may be," she said, fighting desperately to return to familiar ground. *She could not do this.* "We have a job to do. Nothing more."

"Yes," he said. "Our job. That has brought us here, to this village of the damned I vowed I would burn to the ground before I'd return to it, and all I can seem to do is wonder."

His voice was deceptively light, completely at odds with the intensity and fire in his gaze.

"Wonder?" she echoed, as if she did not take his meaning, but she knew.

She wondered the same things. She wondered so much and so heatedly, so breathlessly, that she had barely slept in days. Even the invocation of her past, of what had happened to her, had not changed the wondering, the imagining. And that was only the physical part of this. The easy part. The only part she planned to acknowledge. The inn seemed to spin and tilt wildly at the corners of her eyes, but at the center of it all stood Lucas.

And an uncomfortably reasonable voice inside of her whispered, *Why not?*

Grace fought to keep her breath even. She had told Lucas the truth and he had not looked at her differently. He had not reacted like a long-ago almost-lover in college had: he had not looked at her in that calculating way and asked if, in fact, she *had* been seducing her mother's boyfriend that day. If she had that scarlet letter blazoned upon her face, the way she'd always believed, Lucas had not seemed to see it. And if he already knew the worst but didn't believe the worst of *her*—what was the point in denying herself the pleasure that might go with that kind of uncomfortable honesty? The spoonful of sugar to sweep away the taste of the bitter pill?

And who was to say that this time she couldn't be the one to take control—to beat the player at his own game? Why not be the seducer instead of the seduced? Why not call the shots? *Why not,* indeed?

She blinked, dazed by her own trail of thought. And all too aware of the heat and sleek beauty of him, standing near enough to touch, watching her so closely.

If she'd learned anything from her mistakes,

from her mother, from her own hard-won successes, Grace thought with a dawning sense of certainty, it was this: it was always better to be the one in control.

So if she was already doomed, she might as well dance.

It was as if a great weight fell from her then, and disappeared into the tense air between them.

"If you keep looking at me like that," Lucas warned, his expression hard with hunger, "I will not be held accountable for what happens next."

"I already know what will happen next," she said. She faced him—and herself—head-on, clear-eyed and somehow completely ready for what had been, only moments before he'd walked in this room, unthinkable. He'd had no compunction about throwing those photos in her face, so why should she worry about using his own weakness against him now? She raised her brows at him in deliberate challenge. "I only hope that after all of this talk and all these promises, you can live up to your reputation."

He was not in the least bit fazed. His eyes seemed to see straight through her, to all the places where she ached for him, yearned for him, dreamed of him at night. All the places where she was made of nothing save the want of him. And she would use that against him, she thought. She would get her own back. She would be the one to laugh when it was done, and leave, too.

He did not move from his position at the bedside, lounging there, watching her as if cataloging her every move, her every thought. It was almost too much. It was almost too real. He was quite obviously not a fantasy at all, as someone who looked like him should be—he was a man.

"I have to check in with the team," she said, teasing him, feeling the tension and electricity roll through her. It made her feel powerful. As if it really was hers. To wield. To use. To enjoy.

But he only laughed.

"The team is in the pub, and the last thing they need is the intrusion of their ice queen boss to force them into tediously good behavior and stilted conversation," he said. "The best thing you can do for them is give them tonight to blow off steam. You'll be in one another's pockets for the foreseeable future as it is."

"Well," she said, momentarily discomfited by his unexpected insight—not to mention the fact he knew the whereabouts of her staff when she did not. "That works out, then."

For a moment she did not move. He was the only thing she could see, green eyes and that crooked smile, as if nothing else existed. She let that wash over her, through her. Then she stepped toward him, closing the distance between them with a single step.

Surprise warred with desire in his gaze, on his face, but his hands moved to her hips—anchoring her against him as she moved to stand between his legs. She rested her hands against his sculpted chest, tested the softness of his shirt and the muscles beneath with her palms, eliciting a faint, rough laugh from him.

"Do you know what you're doing?" he asked, threading one hand into her bun and starting to pull the pins out, one by one, with an easy confidence, as if she was already his. His other hand tucked beneath the soft hem of her sweater, then moved hot and hard against the small of her back, urging her even closer.

She could do this. It might even be easy.

"Do you?" she countered. She leaned into him, pressing her heavy breasts against the wall of his chest, letting her body slide against his, bringing their mouths within a scant inch of each other.

She had the impression of scorching green fire and hectic color. Of exhilaration pounding through her like wine. And a sense of absolute rightness that might have scared her, had she not already decided to take him—on her terms.

And then, finally, she leaned up and kissed him, *taking control,* she thought, and everything burst into flame.

* * *

Lucas allowed himself to remain surprised for roughly three seconds, and then desire took over. He did not care why she was doing this, only that she was doing it.

Finally.

He slanted his mouth over hers, determined to make her his, determined to prove that she was no more than any other woman, no different, no matter what yesterday's uncomfortable conversation had indicated.

He had been alone forever, and he liked it that way. It was simple. Easy.

But she tasted like honey, like her Texas drawl, warm and sunny and sweet. She went straight to his head, until he could not seem to care about protecting himself as he knew he should, as had always been second nature to him before.

He did not like the feelings she aroused in him. The need to protect her, even from her own past. Yesterday's searing need to unburden himself. This obsession, this need, to lose himself in her. He hated it, he told himself, and so he kissed her again and again, deeper and harder and longer, surrendering himself to her exquisite taste, her scent, the sweet perfection of her body pressed against his.

This was sex, he told himself. Nothing but sex. And he happened to be particularly talented in that arena.

She pushed him back on the bed, and he let her,

CAITLIN CREWS 173

bemused by this sudden show of assertiveness. But who was he to argue? He lay back and watched appreciatively as she climbed up on the bed with him, straddling him.

He hissed in a breath as the core of her came up flush with his groin, making him harder than he could ever remember being before. *More.* He wanted more. He wanted to bury himself inside of her and lose himself entirely. He wanted to make her scream his name. He wanted to taste every inch of her body, every freckle, every moan. He wanted her in every possible way, all night long.

Only then, he told himself, could he exorcise her. Make these uncomfortable feelings disappear as if they had never been. Make her no more and no less than another conquest, indistinguishable from the rest. That was what he wanted. He didn't know how to want anything else.

She settled against him, her wild blond hair falling forward, making her look like some kind of goddess. *His goddess,* he thought and stretched out his hands to test her hips, the indentation of her waist. He pulled a long strand of hair to his mouth, rubbing it over his lips. She smelled like rosemary and wine, and the feel of the long blond waves was like raw silk. But she batted his hands away, and then frowned down at his shirt as her fingers started to work the buttons.

Her fierce concentration, her focus on the task

at hand, kept him from flipping her beneath him as every instinct shouted at him to do. That stern frown of hers made him stir against her, made the fire blaze even higher, even hotter, within him. She finally bared a swathe of his chest and bent over to taste it, him. Her tongue was soft, wet, maddening. He tangled his fingers in her hair and urged her up to eye level, taking her mouth with a swift possession that made some kind of bell toll, long and true, deep inside of him.

He ignored it, because he was tasting her—hot and female and deliciously, undoubtedly Grace—until he felt drunk from her. Wildly, fantastically drunk, and more than happy to stay that way.

But she had other ideas. She reared back up, and pulled her lower lip between her teeth as she returned to work on his shirt. When he moved to pull her close again, she shook her head at him. He was mesmerized by the silken fall of her hair across her shoulders, the way it teased her breasts, the way the length and wave of it softened her face, making her seem more flushed, more open, more *his*.

"Just lie back," she said, bracing one hand on his abdomen, as if she thought she could keep him there against his will.

"And think of England?" he asked dryly. "I'm afraid that's not my style."

"It can be a brand-new experience for you," she

said in the prim voice that drove him crazy with need, her attention drifting back toward the bare skin she'd uncovered. "I doubt you have many of those."

Lucas did not. But he had also never been one to wait.

He sat up, holding her flush against his hips, and only smiled against the delicate skin of her neck when she made a sound of protest. When she had settled against him, her arms loose around his shoulders, he let his hands skim down her back to slip under her sweater. The soft cashmere was almost harsh compared to the warm silkiness of her skin beneath. He tugged the sweater up and over her head, baring her to his view, then threw it aside.

She was perfect. Taut, full breasts encased in decadent black lace that said far more interesting things about the real Grace than the depressingly austere suits she preferred. Lucas cupped her breasts in his hands, dragging his thumbs slowly across the peaks, making her head fall back as she moaned out her pleasure. The sound was like petrol on a bonfire—he ached to be inside of her. He reached behind her, expertly unhooking the bra with a single hand, then caught a hard nipple with his mouth as he pulled the garment free of her flesh.

He heard her breath stutter as her body tensed and then shook beneath him. He tasted one breast, then the other, taking his time, learning her. He traced a path from her breasts to her collarbone, pressing kisses against her as he went, tasting her with his tongue, his lips, his teeth. He reached her mouth and took it in a hard, deep kiss, holding her face between his hands, his fingers deep in her wild mane of hair.

"Wait," she whispered, pulling away. She shifted against him and then lifted shaky hands to his shoulders to push his shirt off, so that when she pressed back against him they were skin to skin.

Yes. So hot. So soft. So perfect.

He was delirious. He wanted more. And then still more.

Growing impatient, he swung her around and then rolled her under him in a swift, simple move. She blinked up at him, her chocolate-brown eyes molten with passion, her generous mouth faintly damp from his.

"You are not letting me take control of this," she scolded him through lips swollen from his kisses, her breasts full against his chest, the taut peaks sending pinpricks of desire shooting through him, straight to his hardness.

"No," he agreed, his voice rough with desire. "I am not."

He propped himself up on one elbow, then traced a lazy pattern down her torso with his hand, stopping to worship each breast in turn. He continued on to her navel, testing that shallow valley, before he reached the waistband of her jeans. He had them unbuttoned and unzipped in a heartbeat, and she let out a shaky laugh.

He tested the upper edge of her lacy panties, pulling slightly on the elastic that held them in place. She let out a slight moan, her legs moving restlessly against the coverlet. He looked down at her, smiled—then slid his hand beneath the lace, to hold her wet heat in his hand.

She gasped and shuddered, bucking her hips against his palm, her eyes drifting closed. She was so wet, so soft, deliciously, meltingly hot. She burned into him, making him sweat. Yearn. *Need.*

Soon, he told himself. *So very soon.*

"Are you sure?" he taunted her gently, his fingers learning her most intimate secrets, stroking her silken folds, then pressing inside. "I know you had some doubts, did you not?"

She made an incoherent noise, her head moving against the bed linens, her hips meeting his hand, matching him stroke for delicious stroke.

He wanted more. God help her, he wanted everything. He'd forgotten why. He only wanted.

"I want you to come," he whispered, his mouth against her ear, delighting in her long, slow shudder, the way her hand speared into his hair, holding him as he held her.

He used one hand deep in her heat, his fingers moving to an age-old rhythm within her, and his mouth bold and demanding against her breast. One breath, another. Her head tossed back and forth against the pillows while her body tightened, her back arching and her hands curling into fists.

"Now, Grace," he whispered, moving to her other breast and circling the nipple with his tongue. "Now."

One tug on her nipple with his mouth, one hard rocking motion against her molten femininity with the palm of his hand, and she convulsed around him, shattering into pieces, her face flooding red and her mouth parting on a long, high sob.

She was the prettiest thing he'd ever seen. *His*. And he was only getting started.

CHAPTER NINE

GRACE barely had time to breathe, and no time to compose herself, before Lucas sat up and stripped her boots, jeans and panties from her body with more of that consummate skill that should have worried her deeply, but instead made her thighs clench against another thrilling wave of desire.

He removed the rest of his own clothes as quickly and then moved back over her as she lay, shattered, on the bed. Her heart was still pounding too hard, her breath still uneven.

She was supposed to be the one in control! She was supposed to be the one leaving him this undone!

"Lucas," she began, not knowing what she might say. Not knowing where or how to begin. Not even recognizing the sound of her own voice.

"Shh," he replied, and then he moved down the length of her body to rest between her legs. He slid his strong arms beneath her hips, and before she had time to react, to take back the lead and use it, he lifted her and settled his mouth against the hot core of her.

Passion exploded inside of her, a white-hot, searing heat that blanked out her plans, her fears. He licked her, teased her, took her—his mouth more wicked, more clever, more confident.

She arched against him, into him, as he kept her anchored beneath him, his mouth glued to her heat. She heard her own voice, moaning wordless sounds of desire, of pleasure, of ecstasy, as if from far away. Her breath came in hard, shallow pants, and she could not quite catch it, she could not calm down. And still he built that fire, stoking the flames with every swirl of his tongue, pushing her higher and higher until she toppled over the edge and dissolved all around him.

When she came back to herself, he was braced above her, surrounding her, his wide shoulders blocking out the world. She felt turned inside out, exposed, made more vulnerable than she had ever been before. She did not know if she wanted to burst into tears—or kiss him.

"Pay attention, Grace," he murmured, amusement and passion in his low voice, bringing himself down against her chest, his skin like hot satin over steel, rubbing against her taut breasts, making her sigh as the aftershocks still rolled through her.

And then he thrust inside of her.

Grace felt the leftover pleasure from her last

climax coalesce and shiver through her, kicking into her as he began to move, slow and sure, building her up again when she would have thought she was more than sated.

Lucas rolled over, keeping himself deep inside of her, but bringing her on top of him. Dazed, Grace could only stare down at him for a moment.

"I thought you wanted control," he said, pressing kisses to her jaw, the corner of her mouth, her neck. "By all means, take it."

"Your concept of control is a bit more elastic than I'd intended," she said, amazed that she could speak at all—astounded that she could hang words together, no matter how breathless her voice sounded.

He laughed, and she felt it inside of her, as deep as he was. She felt it radiate through her, pleasure coursing outward from where they were joined, lighting her up from within.

"I don't much care for boundaries," he said, pushing her hair back from her face, teasing her lower lip with his teeth. "Unless I set them."

He was so hot and hard within her, so uncompromisingly male, and Grace felt suddenly restless, urgent. Unbelievably, she felt that tightening, that coiling desire, begin to pull taut inside her all over again. All that mattered was that feeling. She sat back, settling herself against him. Then she rolled her hips into a slow, steady pace and watched his eyes go dark with passion, reveling in the power she had over him just as surely as he could wield it over her.

But she didn't care about the power. Not anymore. Not after what had just happened between them. She knew she should care about that, but she shoved it aside. She cared only about the pleasure, about the slick slide of their bodies, the thrust and the pull that made her feel wild, insatiable. She forgot about the photos, forgot about the past and the pain, forgot about the lessons she'd decided she'd teach him. The truth was his hard length within her, his wild hands on her flesh. The truth was she wanted him with a desperation that should have terrified her, but instead made her yearning all the more intense. She was more hungry for him than she had ever been for anyone. Than she had ever imagined it was possible to be.

She was too hungry for him to protect herself. Perhaps she had known that from the start.

At a certain point, his hands gripped her hips, and Grace could no longer think, she could only feel. And when she shattered one more time, he spurred her on, his thrusts wild and urgent until he, too, fell over the edge.

She thought he even called her name.

Lucas knew how he was supposed to act. Smoldering, arch, easy. Hadn't he played the role a thousand times? He knew how to perfect the postcoital scene. He knew how to make a woman who had just bedded him feel like a queen, as if she'd never made a better decision in her life. He knew how to leave them wanting more.

But none of them were Grace.

Outside, the night had long since fallen, casting the room in shadows. Only the lamp on the antique desk shed any light, and it was the barest halo, yellow against the gloom.

He was still deep inside of her. She was still sprawled over his chest.

He had no idea why he felt a great sense of melancholy when he considered his next move, almost as disconcerting as the unusual sense of well-being that washed over him when he did no more than hold her and breathe.

So much for the exorcism.

She stirred. He had the strangest urge to pretend he was asleep, to keep her there against him, the perfect, soft weight of her holding him down, as if she anchored him to the world, to herself. But instead, he let her move away from him and disposed of the condom as she pulled herself to her feet on the opposite side of the wide bed.

She looked over her shoulder at him, thoroughly disheveled, and he felt a fierce stab of a kind of pride. Her hair was a wild cloud around her face, her lips still slightly swollen, her eyes not entirely focused.

"I am going to shower," she said, her voice still rough from passion. There was something awkward in the way she held herself, something uneasy. She did not quite meet his gaze, and he knew as she pulled an arm around herself that she felt the heaviness, the weight, that hung there between them.

He was a master at this scene. He should have sorted it out already, made her laugh, flattered her and teased her into pleased satiation. But his happy manners, his notorious charm, seemed to have deserted him completely.

"Grace." He did not know why he said her name like that, why he felt it reverberate through him, why he wanted to reach for her for no reason at all but to hold her close. To stay in this moment, not to let it go. He did not know why every part of him felt that could be disastrous to move forward, to keep going.

To admit that he was back in Wolfstone, with all that entailed.

He was descending into melodrama, and she was not even looking at him.

"Why don't you order room service?" she asked lightly, her tone not fooling him at all. But what could he do when he was not even sure what held him in this odd, tight grip around his chest? "We could use some food, I think."

And then he watched her walk across the room to disappear into the en suite bathroom, naked and more beautiful than any woman ought to be, her head held high and regal, the culmination of fantasies he hadn't even known he'd had.

He was in trouble. More trouble, he understood, than he had ever been near before.

"You accused me of hiding yesterday," he said without turning around, not moving from where he stood in front of the big bay window. "In plain sight."

He had heard the water shut off, had heard the old pipes cease their chattering and clanking. He'd heard her move around in the bathroom, and then emerge. She brought a cloud of fragrance with her, something floral with a faint kick of spice. Her soap, shampoo, perfume. It teased his nose and made him harden again in the jeans he'd thrown back on to answer the porter's knock when their food had been delivered. Lamb with buttery mashed potatoes and peas. Hearty fare befitting a cold March night—and yet he could not seem to summon up an appetite.

"It was an observation," she replied in an even tone, closer to him than he'd expected, though he still did not turn. "Not an accusation."

"It was astute, either way," he said. "But I cannot seem to do it here."

He turned to find her just beyond his shoulder, her face carefully blank, her brown eyes noticeably wary, her hair piled haphazardly on the top of her head and curling at the ends. She was wrapped in a thin silk wrapper of a deep royal blue, her skin flushed pink and rosy from her ablutions. Or perhaps from what had happened between them.

She looked like candy, sweet and damp and all too edible. And he could not understand why tasting her again, though he yearned to, was not the urge that drove him. Why something else battled to take him over instead.

It was the ghosts again, he thought darkly. There were too many, especially in Wolfestone. Hadn't his run-in with Jacob taught him the folly of revisiting the past? And yet here he was, back in this village, as if he'd learned nothing at all. He'd even been the one to suggest coming here, so full of himself, never considering the consequences. The story of his damned life.

"I don't know what this is," he muttered. "If it is you—or this damned place. It brings back far too many memories. None of them good."

Her wary eyes searched his face, and he saw her swallow, as if fighting for calm. Oddly, that small sign of discomfort eased him. It made him realize that this woman—who knew something about hiding herself in plain sight just as he did—could understand. That he wanted her to understand.

"What happened to you here?" she asked in a soft voice, as if she feared he would not like the question.

He looked at her for a long moment, and then back out the window. The night was dark and blustery, with no hint of moon or stars. He could see only the wind-tossed branches of the trees across the lane, and the impenetrable country blackness beyond. But he still knew precisely where he was. He still knew that the Wolfe estate began just on the other side of the deceptively bucolic river that wound through the town, that the manor house hunkered out there in the dark, empty and brooding and marked, as far as he was concerned—forever marked as soulless and evil as its former owner had been.

What had he been thinking, to return here?

"I had the misfortune to be born William Wolfe's son," he said, a hollow laugh escaping him. "That is what happened to me. Do not let the tales of his fame, his great charisma and cult of personality fool you, Grace." He shook his head. "I've managed to put him from my mind for vast swathes of my life—but that does not work here, apparently. The things he did and the kind of man he was hang in the air in this village like smoke."

She was quiet for a long moment, and Lucas felt

that ache inside of him expand. As if he had never known loneliness, not really, until this moment. But then she brushed past him, and sat down on the couch just beside the window and faced him, tucking her long, bare legs beneath her. She tilted her face toward him, and he saw…nothing. No judgment. No arch, inside knowledge she might use against him. Nothing but her warm, steady gaze.

"He was a monster," Lucas said baldly. He felt his mouth twist and turned away, staring out the window once again, though what he saw was the past. He shrugged, as if he could will it away.

"And…" Her voice was hesitant. "Your mother?"

"I never knew who she was," Lucas said, on a sigh. Funny that the truth could still sting, when he should have long since ceased caring about a relatively meaningless fact like that one. "He told me only that she could not stand the sight of me, and that was why she'd left me on his doorstep." He smirked a little bit then, ignoring the small noise she made. "I grew up rather amazed that what people saw when they looked at me was this remarkable face I'd been awarded in the genetic lottery, when I knew the truth about how ugly I was. So ugly it repulsed my own mother, who was never heard from again. So ugly it made my father hate me. Quite a dichotomy."

"And you had only your father's word on that?"

Grace asked, and it was the lack of pity, the simple calm in her voice that made it all right, somehow, that he was telling her all of this. No matter that he still did not know why.

Lucas remembered then, unwillingly, the night he'd confronted William in his study with the birth certificate he'd found after hours of searching. He'd been a mere teenager then, angry and bitter that all of his siblings knew their parents—even Rafael, the other bastard son who lived in the village yet out of William's view, had the comfort of his mother's presence to ease William's rejection of him. But Lucas had nothing. Only William's lifelong loathing and a birth certificate with the mother's name blanked out.

William had reacted predictably when Lucas had waved the document in front of him, and Lucas had still been too emotional, too small yet to fight back as he might have done later. It was only when William had him pinned to the wall that he'd relented at all—in true William Wolfe fashion.

"Your mother is a difficult woman to forget," he had said, in a vicious sort of tone, designed to wound, confuse.

He had thrown a photo album at Lucas's feet, sneered at the nose he'd bloodied with his own big fist and left Lucas to page through photographs of his uncle Richard's wedding—to a woman who had Lucas's own unusual green eyes. If what he had seen was true, it meant William had slept with his own sister-in-law. Lucas had been sick right there on the study floor.

The subject of Lucas's mother had never been raised again.

"Yes," Lucas said now. "I never discovered who she was. Not really." He could not believe how much William's behavior could still get under his skin, even all these years later. When it could not matter to anyone, not even to him. When the man had been dead for nearly twenty years. "Not for certain."

"My father disappeared before I was born," Grace said matter-of-factly, wrapping her arms around her knees. "There are any number of John Benisons in the world, and none of them were interested in claiming me. I don't even have his name." She looked at him, her dark eyes intent on his. "There is no shame in being an accident, Lucas. There are only parents who are not up to the challenge."

"William was not up to any kind of parental challenge," Lucas said. "He was not what I would call a parent at all, aside from his biological contribution."

He looked at her then, taking in the way she gazed at him, his own near-overpowering urge to touch her, to hold her, to pull her close to him again and make him feel that fleeting sensation he'd felt in the bed, that he'd never felt before. He was afraid to name it.

"I told you before that there are ghosts here, Grace," he said quietly, but in that moment he did not know if he meant in Wolfestone or in himself.

She smiled slightly, seemingly unperturbed by his warning.

"Will they rattle their chains and scare the guests away with all their moaning?" she asked.

"They are more likely to dress in designer labels and behave as if they are normal human beings," Lucas replied dryly. "When they are not. Not one of them."

She searched his face for a moment, then twisted around to look out the window, as if she, too, could pierce the darkness with her gaze and see the dilapidated manor house in the distance.

"Is that why it was abandoned?" she asked, and he knew she meant the house, not him. "Too many ghosts?" She frowned slightly, as if trying to make sense of it. "Was it easier somehow to let it crumble into the ground?"

"If it were mine," Lucas said with a quiet ferocity, "I would demolish it and salt the earth on which it stood."

Her brows arched then, and another near-smile played over her generous mouth, drawing him like a moth to a flame. He could not bring himself to look away.

"That seems unduly dramatic," she said. "Surely you could simply choose not to visit. Or donate the place to English Heritage. It is only a house." When he did not speak, she shrugged. "And surely not all of your siblings share your opinion of the place?"

"We are not close," he said. He laughed slightly, a hollow sound. "Or perhaps it is more truthful to say they are not close with me. And why should they be?"

"Because you are their brother," Grace said quietly, as if she believed in him. As if she knew him. And he could not let her, could he? He could not let her think he was something other—something better, something less worthless—than he was. Not even if it felt as if she'd wrapped him in sunshine. This was meant to be an exercise in exorcism, not in intimacy.

He sat down next to her on the plush, bright couch, confused by the urge to be near her even when he planned only to disabuse her of any positive notions she might have of him. Then, even more confusing, he reached over and took one of her pale, slender hands in his. He did not understand himself, when he thought he had looked into every dark corner he possessed, and more than once, leaving no surprises. He had never been more of a stranger to himself than he was tonight.

"One night when I was eighteen," he said, striving for an even tone, "William got drunk. This would not have been of interest to anyone, you understand, except that on that particular night he worked himself into a temper over my sister, Annabelle." He smiled, though it was the barest sketch of a smile. "He brutalized her," he said, his voice growing raspy. He indicated his face with his free hand. "Slashed her face with a riding crop."

"Why?" Grace breathed, her eyes wide.

"He was a bully and a drunk," Lucas said caustically. "Did he need a reason?" He shook his head slightly. "My brothers tried to stop him," Lucas continued. "But they were too young. When my older brother, Jacob, came home, he waded right into it." He paused and looked at her, hard. "I was not there, of course. I was chasing a set of twins through Soho."

But she did not flinch, nor look away. So he did.

"When Jacob pulled William off Annabelle," he said, concentrating on their linked hands, "he punched the drunken bastard as he richly deserved. Hard."

Grace's hand tightened around his, as if she knew. "And then?" she asked quietly.

"He died," Lucas said matter-of-factly. "That was

always the William Wolfe way." He let out a derisive sound. "He always did get the last laugh."

"I am so sorry," Grace murmured. "For all of you."

"It is my younger siblings you should feel sorry for," Lucas said, that jittery feeling washing over him, as it always did. Muted, somehow, but still there, making him restless. Making that old self-loathing glow and expand within him. "Once Jacob was cleared of any charges, he, of course, put his life on hold to be a guardian to us all, because that was Jacob. Generous to a fault. The perfect older brother. But he could not live with himself." Lucas shook his head. "What did that vile old bastard ever do to deserve regret? What did he do besides make us all miserable?"

He could hear the echo of his voice, raw and rough, and was glad there was no mirror nearby. He felt certain he would find himself unrecognizable. His heart was hammering against the walls of his chest and he felt unhinged, untethered, as if he might explode. But then Grace brought their linked hands to her mouth and kissed his knuckles, one by one, and Lucas let himself breathe.

"I dreamed every night for years that I'd killed William myself," he said quietly. He turned to meet her troubled gaze. "I hated him. I would not have lost a single night's sleep if I'd been the one to kill him, accidentally or otherwise, nor would the weight of him on my conscience, such as it is, have caused me a moment's pause."

"Then what does?" she asked, and he had the most uncomfortable feeling, once again, that she could read him. Much too easily, and far too closely. "Because," she continued, "it is clear that something weighs on you, Lucas. Heavily."

"It's only myself," he answered, with unflinching honesty. "When Jacob left, the role of guardian fell to me." His smile felt like acid. "I was unfit for the position, to put it mildly. I abandoned them, too. Deserted them. That is the kind of man I am."

The room was quiet. The enticing scents of the food set out on the room service tray perfumed the air, and the wind rattled the windowpanes.

"How old were you?" Grace asked after a moment, her gaze unreadable, her face calm.

"Eighteen." He made a bitter sound. "A man."

"Or, perhaps, a boy who had been brutally treated the whole of his life," she said quietly, holding his gaze. "A boy who knew nothing at all about how a parent should act. I think you expected far too much of yourself. Unfairly."

He looked at her for a long moment, his history shimmering between them, his failures and flaws lying out there with nothing to cover them. Not his charm, his wit, his face—none of the usual tools he'd used his whole life to prevent a moment like this from ever occurring.

And what was most unreal was that he had done all this himself. He had thrown all of this at her feet. And he still could not allow himself to think about why he had done it. He did not dare.

"This is what I was talking about earlier," he said, reaching over to cup her jaw in his hand, his body thrilling to the feel of her soft skin, the way her lips parted slightly. "No one has ever expected anything of me, Grace. Least of all me. Why should you?" He stroked his thumb along her soft cheek. "Why do you?"

Her eyes were luminous. Deep and unwavering as she stared back at him.

She shrugged slightly, though her gaze never left his. "Perhaps it's time you started."

And then she turned her head, pressing her lips into the palm of his hand, and that simply ruined him.

CHAPTER TEN

GRACE felt all the blood drain from her head, fast, as she stared at the tabloid newspaper in front of her. Her stomach twisted into a complicated pretzel and she thought for a moment she might simply pass out from the shock. Her knees wanted to give way beneath her. Her mind wanted to simply succumb to the spiral of dizziness.

But she did none of that, much as she might have wished otherwise. Instead, she could do nothing but read the paper the visibly embarrassed member of her staff had handed her when she'd arrived at the team breakfast meeting prepared to go over the last-minute details before the gala—which was tonight.

"I'm so sorry," Sophie murmured in an undertone—or perhaps she shouted. Grace could hear nothing over the kettle-drum pounding of her heart.

The headline screamed in block letters: *LUCAS RELAUNCH? WOLFE UP TO USUAL TRICKS*

WITH AGING SWIMSUIT MODEL. The article that followed featured not just the pictures of Grace kissing Lucas at the pop princess's birthday party— fully identifiable despite her hair swirling around her and her eyes dazed with passion, sprawled over his lap as if she were made of syrup—but also the old American sports magazine photos that Lucas had unearthed. In full, unavoidable color.

Grace stood there like a stone and stared at the paper in her hands. This was what it felt like to have her entire life fall to pieces, she observed from an odd, stunned distance. This was how it happened, then: all of her years of hard work came to a screeching halt in a place called the Pig's Head, while her entire body was displayed in a trashy newspaper for the whole of Great Britain to pore over. She was sure she would have some feelings about that, but for the moment she felt paralyzed, aware only of all the eyes fastened to her, waiting for her reaction.

How could this be happening?

The biggest party of her career was in a matter of hours, and her half-naked body was plastered all over the tabloids. Not exactly the classic yet modern sensibility Hartington's wished to portray, she was certain. And even worse than the swimsuit photos, everyone in the entire world—including the entire staff, all the executives, and the board of directors of Hartington's—would now know that she was sleeping with Lucas Wolfe.

She waited for that anguish to spill over, as it nearly had in Lucas's office, but it did not come.

"Sorry, Grace," Sophie muttered again, red-faced with embarrassment, as everyone else pretended to be absorbed in their morning tea and full English breakfasts. "But everyone was reading it and I thought you should know."

A quick glance around showed Grace that there were, indeed, copies aplenty of this particular tabloid rag—seemingly one on every table in the restaurant. No doubt on every breakfast table in all the world. Her mother was no doubt reading it even now in Racine, Texas, and nodding knowingly over Grace's behavior and patting herself on the back for stamping out the viper in her nest. *Terrific*.

"Thank you, Sophie," Grace said with every stitch of poise she could dredge up from inside herself.

It was her very worst nightmare, broadcast in lurid color, in the shape of her seventeen-year-old bikini-clad body. She knew what happened next. She knew how this scene played out. She felt her gorge rise in her throat, and wondered, still as if from a distance, if she might actually get sick in full view of her entire staff and half the village of Wolfestone, all of whom were packed into the Pig's Head to watch her with avid gazes only some tried to hide.

She simply could not allow that to happen.

Especially not when Lucas sauntered in from the lobby, looking sleepy and rumpled and as if he'd just rolled out of a decadent bed—which she happened to know that he had, as she had been in it with him. Every head in the room swiveled to track him as he wound his way through the tables toward her. Grace could hear the whispering, the muttering. She could feel the speculation heat up the room, as if gossip were an electric current and she was being slowly, surely electrocuted.

Grace watched him approach, noting that easy lope, that careless swagger that called so much attention to his inescapable masculine beauty. She'd spent a week learning every last detail of his long, lean body, and melting under the sorcery of his clever hands, and her body wanted more. Now. It readied itself for him as if on command, melting and shivering, as if he had not been thrusting deep inside her, kneeling over her with his hot mouth fastened to the nape of her neck, one wicked hand wrapped around her breast and the other at her core, not twenty minutes earlier.

She had to clench her thighs together and force her bland, professional smile. Apparently, he was irresistible, even when the worst had happened. *Was happening,* she amended. *Right now.*

But something occurred to her then, as Lucas walked toward her. This had already happened. Lucas had seen these photos, and nothing had changed. He had still wanted her. *Her,* not some fantasy photograph of her. He had not called her names, or looked down at her. The world had not ended—if anything, the photos had been the catalyst for a whole new world of possibility she'd never imagined.

Why do you care so much what so many ignorant people think? he had asked.

And she could not help but ask herself, why did she?

Grace watched him read the room as he moved through it. She saw the cool calculation in his green gaze as he drew close, and could now tell the difference between the real Lucas and the self-mocking, lazy and careless Lucas he produced on cue, as he did now, smirking slightly as he reached the team's table.

She preferred the real one, but she was deeply grateful for his easy mask today.

"Has it finally happened?" he asked mildly, yet in a voice that seemed to accidentally carry throughout the room. He smoothed a hand down his chest, calling attention to his excellent physique, and the phenomenal way he'd chosen to package it today in a tight-fitting green designer T-shirt beneath a fashionable black sport coat and a pair of distressed denim jeans that transformed his delectable behind into sheer poetry. "Have I become better-looking overnight?"

A wave of laughter swept through the room. Because everyone loved Lucas, Grace thought. How could they not? He was so good at pretending to take nothing seriously, least of all himself, and it was impossible not to laugh when he did.

Their eyes met, held. Something almost painful flared between them, silently, and she felt her practiced calm sweep through her. She saw that fierce light gleam in the depths of his gaze, the one she wondered if only she could see. The one that showed her the truth of him, that she craved more than she should. But she was forced to ignore it in front of so many interested gazes. She handed him the tabloid, keeping her face expressionless.

"Not yet," she said. "Though you are, apparently, as interesting to the press when you are shilling for Hartington's as when you are romancing minor royalty on the Continent."

She could see the nearly imperceptible way his body tensed. She could almost see, as well, the anger roll off him in waves. Was it the fact that they were in the tabloids, or the offhanded way she'd introduced the topic, as if she thought what had happened between them had something to do with Hartington's? She could not tell. And either way, no one else seemed to notice anything in his body language at all. All they could see was scandal, and the bright shining light that was the presence of Lucas Wolfe.

"Unfortunately, I grew bored of me years ago," he said in his everyday, mild and languid tone. He tossed the paper aside without so much as a glance at it, as if the article held no interest for him. He then sat down at the table with every appearance of relaxed ease, signaling the hovering waitress for hot coffee—the topic clearly closed as far as he was concerned.

Grace swept a quick look over the table as she took a seat opposite him, confident she exuded nothing but her usual competence in the face of all the averted eyes, the speculative glances. She would not give them the reaction they clearly wanted. She would not let them see her crack. She would be nothing but her usual ice queen self, ready for another day's work with a calm smile and a no-nonsense approach to even this.

They were only pictures, and the truth was, before Travis and her mother had sullied the experience, she'd *liked* them. They were gorgeous pictures, and just happened to be of her. They'd paid for her college education and, one way or another, they'd made her the driven, successful woman she was today.

Why should she be ashamed of them?

And what went on between her and Lucas was nobody else's business.

So she ignored the damned tabloid, and the too-beautiful man who watched her with hooded green eyes and a disconcerting intensity, and snapped open her event notebook instead.

"All right, then," she said briskly, as if this was any other morning. Any morning meeting on any normal day. As if everyone at the table had not seen what she knew they'd seen. Her nearly naked body, in so many suggestive poses. Her passion-flushed face. But there was nothing she could do about that now, and she'd be damned if she'd apologize for herself, so she shoved it aside. "We're in the final countdown, people," she said. "Tell me where we are and what needs to happen before tonight."

The irony, she thought as the staff member nearest her launched into his spiel, was that before she'd walked into the breakfast room this morning, she had been on track to thinking this had been the most magical week of her life.

The week in Wolfestone had passed like some kind of delicious, wickedly sensual fever dream. For the first time in her life, Grace had not analyzed, plotted or planned out her every last move. Nor had she let the past keep her locked down, hidden away. Once she had accepted the fact that she would not be beating Lucas at his own game, that she wanted him as much as he wanted her, and could neither fight it nor summon the will to try, she had simply…lived.

The days were full to bursting with all the last-minute details involved in transforming the long-forsaken Wolfe Manor into the appropriate spot to celebrate the new Hartington's. Grace traipsed over every inch of the site with the designer and various contractors, nailing down the final details of placement, construction, access and out-of-bounds areas, parking and security. She had coordinated all the reports from her staff regarding the floral arrangements, the dramatic ice sculptures and their delivery, the many food stations that would have to entice the guests yet never overpower the tented area with long queues—all stocked with delicacies available in the revered Hartington's gourmet food hall.

She went over set lists with the DJ and the band, debated the placement of the dance floor and spent hours placating both the talent and their often far more excitable representatives. She made sure the details of transportation for all of the A-list guests, talent and executives were nailed down and agreeable to all parties. She held the caterer's hand during a brief breakdown over the mini-Cornish pasties. She did her job, and she did it well.

And then, every night, she lost herself in Lucas's arms.

He was the least inhibited, most adventurous

lover imaginable. He knew no boundaries, had no hang-ups and always maintained his wicked sense of humor. He was as happy to have her standing up against the wall as slippery and wet in the deep tub. He was as interested in exploring her body as in having her test his hardness in her mouth. He reached for her again and again, but he also held her so tenderly, and kissed her so sweetly, that it made Grace ache in ways she knew better than to consider too closely. He was not at all the man she'd thought he was when he'd first walked into her office, and Grace hardly knew how to reconcile all the different images she had of him in her head—much less in her heart.

It was easier, somehow, when they were both naked, and her body hummed with an overload of pleasure after another demonstration of his boundless enthusiasm for all things carnal in general and Grace's body in particular.

"I may require a stiff drink," she had said one night as they lay on the thick, soft rug before the fire, smiling as he toyed with the ends of her hair, curling the waves around his finger as she lay sprawled across his chest. "Perhaps several."

"To dull the pain?" he had asked in his mocking way, but she'd known him better by then and had known that he was teasing her—and more, that the mockery he used so skillfully was perhaps the only form of affection he knew how to give. It made her feel warm.

"To see which is more potent," she had said softly, propping her chin on her stacked hands and looking at him, as if she could memorize the artistic dream that was his beautiful face, so close to hers. "Hard liquor or you."

There had been a moment then, a heartbeat or two too long, when he had gazed back at her with an almost arrested look in his smoky green eyes, as if he could not quite work her out. She loved such moments—when she knew she was looking at the true, unadulterated Lucas. The real man, not the act.

"I imagine it very much depends on the bartender," he had said, but she had the sense he had wanted to say something else entirely. His smile sharpened. "I did used to be one, as it happens. In a former existence."

"What?" She had wrinkled up her nose as she gazed at him. "Yet another job? You continue to destroy my faith in your terrible reputation."

"Keep your faith," he'd suggested dryly. "I had no choice but to get a job—any job. I'd already blown through the first part of my inheritance with a group of disreputable malcontents all over London, and I was all of twenty-three."

"Only the first part of your inheritance?" she'd asked in the same dry tone. "Not the whole of it? That seems to lack commitment." She had not wanted to think about the amount of money that might have been, nor how he had managed to throw it all away. It might have sent her fiscally conservative heart into cardiac arrest.

"My father perhaps anticipated that his children might take his profligate, hard-partying example to heart," he'd said, with that challenging gleam in his eyes, daring her to swallow yet another example of how terrible he believed he was. "Or that I might, anyway. My inheritance was split in two. Half on his death, and half again should I survive to my thirtieth birthday. He expressed his doubts about the latter in his will."

"And you lost the first half by the age of twenty-three," she had said, forced to shield her gaze from his at that point. She'd looked at the hard muscles of his chest instead, the tempting valley between his pectorals, the steel-hewn strength of his shoulders.

At twenty-three, she had used her carefully chosen, prestigious summer internship as a springboard into her first events management firm, and had been working on her first parties. She had never wasted a single penny in all her days. Her modeling money had paid for what her scholarship had not and then some, because she had always been obsessed with savings accounts, a retirement fund and the careful stewardship of conservative investments. She could not allow herself to imagine the kind of money Lucas had frittered away.

But then, she could not imagine the childhood he had had to live, either.

"I managed to charm my way behind a bar in one of the casinos in Monte Carlo," he'd said then, holding her to him as he'd shifted slightly beneath her.

"Monte Carlo," she'd echoed, shaking her head at him. She thought of the famous sweep of tall buildings cascading toward the yacht-studded marina, all of it huddled there between the craggy French mountains and the sparkling Mediterranean. "Of course. Where all the paupers naturally congregate."

He'd ignored her, though his eyes gleamed and he ran a possessive hand along the length of her spine, making her arch against him, feeling like a fat and satisfied cat.

"It was my first job, and I was shockingly good at it," he'd said with his usual modesty. "I was showered in fantastic tips, no doubt in enthusiastic recognition of my keen knowledge concerning all things alcoholic."

Grace had laughed, and had pulled herself up to sitting position, pulling her mess of hair over one shoulder to rake her fingers through it like a makeshift comb.

"No doubt," she'd agreed. But when she'd looked

down at him he had a strange expression on his face. "What is it?" she'd asked.

"Do you remember the first time you fell in love?" he'd asked then, his expression unreadable. But she'd had no doubt it was not an idle question. Or, at least, it had not felt in the least bit idle to her.

Grace had felt the fine hairs on the back of her neck stand at attention, and had had to look away, to focus on the flames dancing merrily in the fireplace, crackling and popping. She'd told herself she was tired from all their lovemaking and the insanely busy days—that there was no other reason her face should feel warm, or there should be that worrying wet heat behind her eyes.

"Of course," she'd said quietly. "I was a teenager, and I was mistaken."

But his hand on her bare thigh was kind, and somehow she had found herself telling him the rest of the story about Roger Dambrot. How she had thought giving him her virginity was the same as giving him her heart, and how devastated she had been when he had been so contemptuous of both. How utterly destroyed. How her mother had spoken to her, and what she'd said. And then, so soon afterward, the scene with Travis. All those predictions, those curses. And worst of all, how Grace had always believed them—how she'd always thought falling in love and sex and emotion were inextricably linked with shame, loss, pain.

"I thought if I could keep myself apart, removed, I could escape the future she'd always predicted for me," she'd told Lucas. "Blood will tell, she said. Carter women were fated for heartbreak and misery." She'd bit at her lip. "And then, later, she said I was fated for far worse."

"Perhaps you were simply seventeen," he'd said gently. "Gorgeous and new, while she was simply jealous."

"Jealous?" It wasn't that Grace had never considered that possibility before; it was the way he'd said it. So matter-of-fact. As if, contrary to everything Grace had always believed, there had never been anything wrong inside of her. As if she'd never had any reason to be ashamed.

"Jealous," he'd said again. "And you were too young to know better." He'd met her gaze. "I was no better, let me hasten to assure you. The bar manager's name was Amanda, and I fell madly in love with her. She had the most adorable little girl." He'd smiled the kind of smile that made Grace want to weep, without even knowing why. "Her name was Charlotte, and I worshipped every angelic curl on her head with all the weight and gravity of my twenty-three-year-old heart."

"Why do I sense this does not have a happy ending?" Grace had asked.

"Because love stories never do," he had replied, his eyes crinkling in the corners as if he meant his words lightly. Grace had not been fooled. "Amanda started working all night shifts, but I hardly minded. I took care of Charlotte. I was dependable, stable. Good."

His voice had taken on that self-mocking lash again, harsher this time, deeper. Grace did not say a word; she merely laid back down beside him and pressed her lips to the place where his shoulder met his arm. And then against his lean, hard jaw, not sure he would speak again.

"It turned out she was having an affair with a wealthy older man," Lucas had said eventually, with a derisive smirk. "It was such a cliché. I believe I was no more to her than convenient child care. Poetically, I had been planning to tell her my true identity the very night she confessed."

He had not gone into details, but the bleak look on his face told Grace all she needed to know about Lucas and love. It was not necessary for him to draw her a picture. He had never had love, nor security, nor family, not really. He had felt responsible to his siblings when he could be the punching bag in their stead, but he was so convinced that there was nothing good in him, nothing worthwhile, that he had gone out of his way to prove it, again and again—even when his siblings could actually have used him as something other than the most convenient target. And then he'd found a brand-new family, and had dared to hope—only to have that hope cruelly crushed. Again.

She would have cried for him, had she not suspected he would hate her for it.

"Things did not end well for Amanda," he'd said, with evident satisfaction. "This may come as a great shock to you, as it did to me, but her marriage did not work out. Neither did any of her subsequent ones. I confess that I take greater pleasure in that than I should."

"And Charlotte?" Grace had asked, running her hand along his chest, letting her palm rest over the hard plane of muscle that covered his heart, broken though she knew it must be beneath.

"She was far luckier," he had said after a moment. His mouth curved. "It turned out she had a very generous and anonymous benefactor, who made certain that her mother's many reversals of fortune over the years never affected her. She is currently at a Swiss boarding school, where, by all reports, she is thriving."

"Lucky Charlotte," Grace had said, hiding her smile against his warm skin. "But I thought you had lost all your money?"

"I made back my squandered inheritance, and then some," Lucas had said, eyeing her with that air of challenge again. "By the time I was twenty-five. I found being discarded for a wealthier and far less attractive man exceedingly unpleasant. I much prefer to be cast aside for the defects in my personality, thank you."

"As do we all," she'd agreed, humoring him.

He'd smiled then, showing her that beloved dent in his lean jaw, that irresistible sparkle in his eyes. The sheen of vulnerability behind them. "But these are all deep, dark secrets, Grace. Can you be trusted to keep them?"

"You will just have to wait and see," she'd said lightly, her heart aching for this man, who would have argued if she'd suggested he was a hero to the little girl he'd loved and still protected. Who could not allow himself even the smallest shred of compassion. Who was so convinced he was damned.

Who had, she'd understood that night with a deep, searing certainty that might have frightened her if she hadn't felt the rightness of it, stolen her heart without her even having been aware of it.

"If I must wait," he'd murmured, pulling her closer and twisting so that he came over her on the rug, settling in between her legs with his arousal jutting hard and proud against her, "then we really ought to while away the time more amusingly."

"I can't think of anything to do," she'd whispered, caught by the emotion darkening his eyes, so at odds with the smile on his face, the lightness of his words.

"Neither can I," he'd replied, and thrust into her, riding them both into oblivion.

Grace finished the morning meeting with her trademark minimum of fuss, and sent her staff off to attend to their duties. Her temples ached from the effort of maintaining her usual serenity, and she had an extremely unpleasant phone call to make to Charles Winthrop before she could head out to the manor house and oversee the final preparations for tonight. She gathered up her things as the team left and strode from the restaurant as if she could not see the patrons still looking at the tabloid and then measuring her against it—and as if she was unaware of Lucas's golden, impossibly beautiful presence at her side.

"We should talk about this," he said in a low voice as Grace headed up the inn's stairs toward her room two floors above.

"There is nothing to say," she replied, clutching her mobile in her hand as it vibrated yet again—announcing, she knew, one more no doubt increasingly tense message from Charles Winthrop's secretary, ordering Grace to call in. "What's done is done," she continued. "The only thing to do now is minimize the damage—"

"Grace." It was the snap of command in his voice, or perhaps the darkness beneath it, the edge in it, that had her slow her steps and turn to face him.

They had rounded the corner of the stairwell, and stood in the no-man's-land between the floors. Though the bustle of the inn below them floated up the stairs, they were for all intents and purposes hidden away from all the eyes that had watched them so closely in the restaurant. Grace felt that same sweet, hot cocoon close around her, the way it always seemed to do when she was near him, as if there was some kind of bubble that they could disappear into when they were together. She did not know why she should feel it now, when she knew in the worst possible way that it was not true at all. That there was no bubble, there was nothing safe—there never had been. His world involved spies with cameras and was always monitored. She should have expected it.

"I have to call Mr. Winthrop," she said, her voice little more than a whisper.

She was too caught in his troubled green gaze, too afraid that if she stepped any closer to him she would melt against him as she always did, and if she melted, she would let out all the emotions that she knew must swirl around inside of her somewhere. And she could not let that happen. Not with this phone call to handle somehow, and the gala to pull off—assuming she was not summarily fired for indecency.

"I did not do this," he said, his voice fierce, his hands clenched into fists at his sides. "I did not hand those pictures over. I am capable of many things, Grace, but not that."

She was stunned. She blinked, and swayed toward him, putting a hand out to grasp his arm before she knew what she was doing. Before she remembered that she could not touch him without causing the very melting she was trying to avoid.

"That never even occurred to me," she said, emotion beginning to flood in from wherever she'd been keeping it. Perhaps she should have suspected him—perhaps she should have imagined that Lucas might betray her, but she had not. It had not even crossed her mind. What did that say about what had happened to her in the past week? Since she'd met him? Did she really trust him? *Should* she? Or was this precisely the same path she'd watched her mother tread a hundred times—leading straight to Travis, the biggest liar of all? Was this the ruin that had always been her destiny?

The mad part was, she was not at all sure she cared.

"This is my fault," he said in the same low, angry voice. "I will take full responsibility. I'll ring Charlie myself—"

"I appreciate the offer," she said, cutting him off. She shook her head, more at herself than at him. More at the panic she did not feel, the terror that was not dragging at her. Her lack of shame and despair. When had she stopped fearing what he could do to her? When had she decided to enjoy him instead? "But this is my mess, Lucas. I'll handle it."

"I am a great seducer of women," Lucas said, the self-loathing crackling in his voice, turning his eyes nearly black. "I am sure he will have no trouble at all believing that I led you astray. That is what I do, after all."

His pain, his toxic hatred of himself, was like a live thing pressed between them, electric and dangerous. It pushed against Grace, crowding her, making her want to fight back. To fight *him*. To show him the truth.

"You did not seduce me," she reminded him, her hand tightening on his arm. "It was the other way around, if you remember—and anyway, it is none of Charlie Winthrop's business, which I intend to make clear to him. I notice your mobile is not ringing off the hook. Why should mine be?"

"I am a pollutant," he said bitterly, his eyes grim and focused on her, as if he was desperate for her to understand. As if his world hung in the balance. "I destroy everything that crosses my path, sooner or later. None of this would have happened to you were it not for me. This is what happens to the people I care about, Grace—and heaven help you if you care about me. Then I'll rip your heart out and make you regret you ever met me." He let out a hollow bark of laughter. "You need only ask my family."

"Nothing has happened," she said very distinctly, searching his face for the Lucas she knew, the Lucas who could be tender, gentle. Funny. Wry. Not this dark, angry man who she well believed could destroy himself and anything else in his path if he chose. "They are pictures, Lucas. Just pictures and nasty speculation. Who cares?"

"You do," he gritted out. "Charlie Winthrop does."

Grace considered him for a moment, and let her hand drop from his arm.

"I should care," she said, focusing once again on what was happening within her—and what was not. "I should care deeply. I keep waiting for it—I'm anticipating a tsunami of shame, anger, fear. All the things I felt when you left that folder on my desk."

"Because I am a prince among men," he said acidly. "And still you allowed me in your bed. Do you not understand this yet, Grace? The only thing pretty about me is this godforsaken face. Everything else is rotted and ugly. Putrid. Corrosive."

"That is ridiculous," she snapped at him. "The point is, the wave has yet to crash. I am worried about an embarrassing conversation with my boss, but that's about it." She shrugged, her eyes locked to his. "Those pictures were taken of me when I was very young. And I was, in fact, kissing you at that party. I never claimed I did not do those things. I never lied. I won't apologize for any of it."

"You should." It was stark, brutal. It hung between them.

Grace felt something move through her then, akin to the wave she'd been expecting, but so much different, somehow. It was as if something had been ripped away from her, exposing her to a truth she'd been bending over backward to avoid.

She did not want to hide anymore. Not from herself. Not from life. Not from anything. She had been wearing a mask for years, but no more. The tabloids had made certain her past and her present were exposed, laid open before the world, and why had she been so convinced there was something wrong with that? Why did she feel she had to hide who she was, what she felt, what she'd done? Why was she so ashamed? Why couldn't she simply show her true face to the world, at last?

Why had she let her mother's fears, Travis's lies, control her for so long?

If being around Lucas had taught her anything, it was this: once someone saw behind the mask, it was impossible to go on wearing it. It no longer fit in the way it had. Once she had been seen—*known*—how could she settle for anything less?

And once she knew what she was hiding, how could she allow it to remain hidden?

"I'm falling in love with you," she told him matter-of-factly, because that was the only secret she had left. And he knew all the rest of them. She had turned over every last stone she had and showed him all the dirt she'd hidden away beneath. She laughed slightly, at her own daring, and her own folly. "Who am I kidding? I've already fallen."

"You don't mean that." There was an edge of something like panic in his voice, a certain shock in the way he looked at her then. "You are far too intelligent for that kind of nonsense."

"I am not telling you this because I expect anything from you," she told him quietly, holding his gaze, her head high and proud. "But because I suspect you believe you are inherently unlovable, as if you were somehow born undeserving of it, when nothing could be further from the truth."

"I've told you more about my past than I've ever told anyone else," he gritted out, moving closer and grasping her shoulders in his hands, holding her tightly—but not hard. Gentle, even now. "Damn you, Grace! You know more than enough to run!"

"I have no intention of running," she said, her voice crisp, despite the emotion she could feel searing through her, making her eyes glaze over. Despite the waves of deep emotion and long-denied truths that washed through her, over her. Changing her completely even as she stood there. Shaking her. Rendering her maskless forever.

No matter what happened.

"Then I will do it for you," he growled, but he did not let go of her. He did not back away. He did not, in fact, run.

"Are you saving me from yourself?" she whispered. "Is that what a man as bad as you claim to be would do, Lucas? Or is that a bit more noble than you normally allow yourself to be?"

"You have no idea how bad I can be," he insisted, a wildness to his voice, his gaze. "You have no idea what real ugliness is, Grace. But I do—and I have his blood running in my veins!"

He let go of her then, as if the invocation of William Wolfe brought his ghost between them to shove them apart.

"He is dead," she said, her voice low, intense. "And even if he were not, you are nothing like him. You are a good man, Lucas. A decent man. A man worth loving."

She heard the way her voice cracked with emotion, felt the way she shook where she stood, but all she could see was Lucas. All she could see was the shock on his face and the heavy curtain of denial that fell across it, obscuring him.

For a moment he only scowled at her, his big body vibrating with tension and fury, his green eyes gone black with all of his self-loathing, all his years of self-destruction, his whole lifetime of loneliness. She could see all of it.

She wanted to fight all the ugliness, all the darkness, all the lies he'd made truth over the years to fulfill his own prophecies. She knew about that. And now, today, she knew truths she should have seen long ago. She wanted to reach inside where he was so cold, so alone, and warm him. But she knew she could not do any of that, not really. Not without his help.

She had only one weapon in her arsenal. Only one chance.

"I love you," she said, letting the words hang there, strong enough, she hoped, to battle his ghosts. Because they were all she had. "I do."

"Then you are a fool," he said, his mouth twisting.

He brushed past her on the stair, turned the corner and was gone.

CHAPTER ELEVEN

LUCAS saw the solitary figure standing away from the scaffolded manor house and the commotion in and around the gala's big tent that commanded the better part of the grand lawn. He knew who it was. The figure stood down near the lake, facing away from the gathering crowds, and Lucas moved toward him before he could think better of it—before, in fact, he could fully register what he meant to do.

Lucas had been wandering aimlessly for hours, stamping about the property like some kind of wraith. He had made his way through the over-grown reaches of the estate, all of it so much the same and yet so different from the grounds he remembered combing every inch of as a child. Had there only been moors, he thought, he could have done an impression of Heathcliff to put his brother Nathaniel, recently awarded his first Sapphire Screen Award to international acclaim, very much to shame.

He had walked and walked, as if he could outpace his demons, as if he could leave his past behind him simply by remaining in motion.

He should never have returned here. He should have known better.

Grace was not the first woman to tell him that she loved him, but she was the only one he'd ever believed. The only one he knew had nothing to gain, everything to lose and absolutely no reason to lie to him. He wanted to deny it, even to himself, but he'd seen her face. He'd seen the truth in her deep brown eyes, heard the quiet conviction in her honeyed voice. Worse, he'd felt something shift inside of him, as if in answer.

It should have been impossible. Grace was determined and intelligent, resourceful and strong. She was more beautiful than she wanted anyone to notice, and far kinder than she should be. She had worked her whole life to get where she was, against the kind of odds Lucas could hardly imagine. What could she possibly see in a wastrel like him?

Was there anything to see? After a lifetime insisting there was not, why was he suddenly so worried that he was exactly as empty as he'd always declared he was?

"Jacob," he said in greeting when he reached his brother's side. They both stared out over the deceptively placid water, watching it gleam in the late-afternoon light. Lucas thrust his hands in his pockets, aware as he did so that he and Jacob moved in concert. As if they still knew each other as they once had. It nearly made him smile.

"How thoughtful of you to ask for permission to throw an event here," Jacob murmured, an ironic undertone to his voice. "In this house which, for better or worse, I own."

"Oh, good," Lucas said mildly. "You received your invitation." He pivoted toward Jacob. "I did wonder, having only tossed it through the door." That had also been his version of requesting permission. He looked back over the water, and pretended he did not care about the next question. "Does that mean you are staying?"

"I'm happy that Wolfe Manor could be used in such a creative manner," Jacob said, with something like a smile, avoiding the question. Lucas felt the other man—the grown man and near-stranger who had taken the place of his long-lost brother— look at him, then away. "And that you took my advice so closely to heart."

"I believe it was more a shot *to* the heart," Lucas said dryly.

He did not press Jacob about his plans. He tried to summon the anger he had felt before, the dark fury that had propelled him away from this house, from his brother, but he realized in a dawning sort of amazement that it was no longer there. Where there had been all of that bubbling, simmering resentment and despair, there was now only Grace. He was not at all sure how to handle that knowledge. Nor how she had managed to become the thing that haunted him, even here.

"I never thought I'd see the day you held down an honest job," Jacob said in a quiet voice.

"You are certainly not alone," Lucas said. He smiled slightly, rocking back on his heels. "Though I think I might be rather good at it."

"That does not surprise me at all," Jacob said. Lucas let that sit there, afraid that if he looked at it too closely, paid it too much attention, it might disappear as if he had imagined it. He did not want anything to mean so much to him, especially not one man's opinion. But then, this man's opinion was the only one that ever had.

Jacob shifted his weight, frowning, and Lucas instinctively braced himself for the inevitable blow. Would Jacob throw the latest tabloid report in his face? He would deserve it. Would he mention William Wolfe's rather notorious reign in the same position Lucas now held at Hartington's, fueled by cocaine and intemperate rages? He could certainly draw some pointed comparisons. There were so many ways Lucas could disappoint him without even trying that it was pointless to try to pick one on his own. He could only roll with whatever punch might come his way.

The way he always had.

Jacob turned so he faced Lucas, his dark eyes unreadable, his mouth a serious line. "You deserve more from life than to make yourself over into his ghost. That is all I meant."

Lucas thought of Grace's wide brown eyes, filled with emotions he dared not name, could not accept—even though he longed to do so. He thought of the peace he felt when he held her, the fierce, unexpected loyalty she showed no matter what story he told her, no matter how often he expected her to register her disgust with him. He thought of her bravery, her dignity in the face of a scandal that could have—should have—taken her to her knees.

He thought about her voice, all Texas heat and that sweet, Southern honey, saying, *I love you.* He thought about the way the words seemed to loosen things inside of him, open him up, make him feel as if there was light where there had only been dark and decay before.

"Do you know," he said conversationally, as if the world had not shifted beneath him, as if he was the same man he had been before, as if the very concept of *hope* was not foreign to him in every way, "I think you may be right."

The late-afternoon sun dipped closer to the land, casting shadows all around them. Behind them, lights blazed from a thousand clever lanterns Grace had placed every few feet, and the closed-off yet well-lighted manor house gleamed like a gothic wonderland, beckoning guests to venture near. Inviting the whispered stories, the half-recalled legends, the tragic and celebrated and mythical history of the Wolfe family. *His* family.

Meanwhile, the rather less mythical truth was two men who might one day be friends again, but were in any case still brothers, standing quietly near an old family lake, putting ancient ghosts to rest.

"I will see you at your gala, then," Jacob said after a moment.

"Indeed you will," Lucas agreed. He felt some of his old mischief rise to the surface, and grinned. "I will be performing the role of Lucas Wolfe, England's favorite playboy, for all the assembled guests. Prepare yourself. I am quite good at it. No less than three-quarters of the crowd will end the night desperately in love with me."

"They always do," Jacob said, in the lightest tone Lucas had heard from him since his return. He reached over and clasped a hand on Lucas's shoulder, briefly, then let go as he turned toward the house.

They had not been a demonstrative family at the best of times, whenever that might have been, and Lucas felt the gesture for what it was. An olive branch. A bridge. It was not the twenty years they'd lost, but it was a start.

"Jacob," he said, staring ahead at the lake, as if all the answers lay just beneath the gleaming surface.

He heard Jacob pause behind him, and smiled then, more focused on the future than the endless, dreary past. More interested in who he could be than in who he'd been.

At last.

"Welcome home," he said quietly into the coming night, and was not at all surprised to discover he meant it.

Lucas shook every hand, posed for every picture and flattered every guest who ventured near him. The great tent was filled with golden, glittering light and hung with tapestries and chandeliers, and the people who filled it were strictly the crème de la crème of Europe. Celebrities, socialites, aristocracy. All mingled with the expected corporate kings, basking in the past and future of Hartington's with the members of the Wolfe family who had made an appearance.

Jacob, the mysteriously returned heir, was at least as interesting to the gathered press corps as the current reigning Hollywood idol, Nathaniel, and the brand-new fiancée he had on his arm. Even Annabelle, who was photographing the event and hid behind her camera and her great reserve as was her way, was a Wolfe and therefore noted, no matter how little she might have wished to interact with the guests. Or, for that matter, her brothers. And Lucas, of course, who the press could not help but love, so skillfully did he manipulate them at their own game, was always a paparazzi favorite.

"No more pictures," he told his least-favorite photographer with a smile—when the man deserved his fists for taking those pictures of him and Grace. "Haven't you caused enough trouble this week?"

But he laughed, as if there were no hard feelings, because that was how best to avoid having his next intimate moment broadcast to the entire world. It was better to work with them than fight against them, he knew. It was wiser to let them think they had control. He was certain there was a lesson in there somewhere, should he care to search for it.

It was, Lucas thought as he moved away from the photographer, straightening his tuxedo jacket with an expert jerk, a perfect night all around. Old Charlie Winthrop looked jovial and well pleased, sitting with the rest of the board of directors as they basked in the celebration happening all around them. The marketing and publicity departments had had their moment to shine and present the relaunch to great applause and many pictures, and Lucas had even said a few words before yielding the stage to the pop princess herself.

Yet Grace was nowhere to be found.

Lucas could see the other members of her team on the fringes of the crowd, weaving their way through the brightly clad groups to fix problems, relay information or put out the odd fire. But no Grace. Eventually, after he'd looked for her in vain for far too long, he flagged down one of the interchangeable girls who had always spent the morning meeting making cow's eyes at him.

"Where is Grace?" he asked, impatient with the starry way the girl blinked at him. *You do not even know me,* he wanted to scold her, but did not.

"Oh…" the girl breathed. She gulped. "Well, Mr. Wolfe, uh, she's been sacked."

The words did not make sense. Lucas stared at the girl before him, aware that he had lost his smile, that he had gone too still, that he was glaring ferociously at the poor creature.

"I beg your pardon?" His tone out-froze the towering ice sculpture nearby, and made the girl flush scarlet.

"M-Mr. Winthrop met with her just before the first guests arrived," she stammered out. "No one knows what he said, but she told Sophie to take charge and then she left." She sucked in a shaky breath. "That's all I know!"

But Lucas had already stopped listening to her. Temper roared through him, thick and vicious. He scanned the party, his eyes narrowing in on Charlie Winthrop, who was laughing merrily with his band of cohorts, completely unaware of the danger he was in. He wanted to rip the round little man apart with his hands, but there was a greater urgency moving through him then, something much closer to fear. He felt his hands clench into fists at his sides, and could only imagine what expression he wore when the girl before him made a squeaking sound and melted away.

He forgot her immediately. He looked around the glittering party, taking in all the famous faces, all the rich and the bored, the infamous and the outrageous. They were all the same. The same faces he had seen again and again, in every party, from London to Positano to Sydney and back again. The same gossip, the same stories, the same old game.

But he had no interest at all in playing, not anymore.

He had changed. He was not the same man he had been when he'd staggered up the drive to Wolfe Manor, battered and bleeding, all those weeks ago. He was not the same man he'd been pretending to be the whole of his life, and the pretense, the mask, no longer seemed to fit him as it should.

And the reason for that was not here, as she should be.

The great well of emotion, black and terrible, vast and unconquerable, that he had tried to outrun all day today swelled in him, nearly knocking him from his feet, so intense he wondered if he could beat it back and maintain his balance. He did, but barely. In his whole life, only three people had mattered to him so much that their loss had altered the course of his existence. His mother. His brother Jacob.

And now, tonight, the woman whose absence seemed to alter the very air around him, making it impossible to breathe.

He had suffered through the other losses, had even accepted them. But not this time. Not this one.

Not Grace.

For the first time in a long time, maybe ever, Lucas wanted to—*had to*—fight for what he desired, what he needed, what he could not imagine living without. He had no other choice. He could not let Grace leave him, could not let her disappear, could not let her go. He could not.

Because for the first time in his life, he realized as his heart beat too hard and the panic raced through him like an electric charge, he had far too much to lose.

Grace sat in her room at the Pig's Head for a very long time, staring at nothing.

"We wanted you to *manage* Lucas Wolfe, Grace," Charles Winthrop had said, his round face screwed into a contemptuous sneer, right there in full view of the staff and Wolfe Manor itself. Grace had had no recourse but to stand there and take it. "Not manhandle him in public view."

So disgusted. So disdainful.

"Act like a whore and you'll be treated like a whore!" her mother had shouted years ago, as all of Racine gathered around their copies of an old American sports magazine to condemn Grace and whisper about her behind their hands. As Mary-Lynn threw Grace's meager belongings out the door into the dirt and screamed at her to stay out.

Charles Winthrop had not actually called her a whore, of course. He had murmured about propriety and reputation. He had made it clear that a woman who had had the bad taste to allow herself to be photographed in such a compromising position—he did not clarify if he meant on Lucas's lap or in her bikini at seventeen—was by definition no longer the appropriate choice to represent Hartington's interests, much less their corporate events. He might as well have handed her a brand-new scarlet letter to wear on her forehead—perhaps even affixed it himself.

She had seen the way he'd looked at her, the way his eyes flicked over her professional demeanor, as if looking for the cracks in her veneer—as if, were he to look at her in exactly the right way, the whore would seep out and show herself.

Just as her mother had always predicted.

What was surprising, Grace thought now, rising to her feet and looking around the room, though she hardly saw it, was that she'd been furious, not upset. She hadn't been *hurt* that Charles Winthrop thought so little of her when faced with those pictures—she'd wanted to throw something at his head. That fury and indignation had carried her in an outraged silence all the way back to her room at the inn—where the reality of the situation had settled around her like a suffocatingly heavy cloak, and had forced her to sit there on the couch by the window for much longer than she should have.

Because she had lost everything.

Again.

The truth of that was starting to sink in now, the longer she stood in the room, still and silent. The more time passed. She knew the gala was happening even now—could even hear the music on the wind—and she was finished. It was all as she'd feared it would be. She'd lost her career. The respect of her peers. Everything she'd worked so hard for, all these long years. Hadn't she warned herself? Hadn't she had her memories of her mother's voice to chime in when her own had wavered? Hadn't she understood from the start that this very thing would happen?

She needed to go, she knew. She needed to pack up her things and head back to London. She needed to come up with a new plan for her life—a new direction. But every time she told herself it was time to get moving, she remembered some other bright, captivating moment that had happened in this room, with Lucas, and she could not bring herself to budge from her position. As if she was paralyzed.

He was the reason for her downfall, and even so, she yearned for him. He had thrown her love back in her face, disappeared without a trace, and still, she longed for him. How could that be? How, even now, could there be a part of her that whispered fiercely that it did not matter what she'd lost, that she would do it again—that he was worth it. That all of this was worth it.

This was it, she knew, with a sickening certainty. This was the exact ruin her mother had foreseen. Grace just hadn't expected it to feel like this. So… encompassing.

She had always known she would pay a high price for touching a man like Lucas Wolfe. She had never been in any doubt on that score. He was the proverbial rocky cliff, and she understood, now, why the hapless ship hurled itself against those rocks, again and again, until all that remained were splinters and painful memories, churning waters and the remains of what had once been a proud, sleek vessel.

She was surprised when she felt the wetness on

her cheeks, and it was not until she raised her hands to her face that she realized she was crying.

Just as it took her long moments to realize that when the door opened and Lucas stormed in, it was really him, not just a convenient fantasy tossed her way by her desperate imagination.

He was breathing heavily, almost as if he had been running in his elegant black-tie evening wear, and his eyes were burning with a light that made her stomach clench in automatic response. Desire. Despair. Both.

"What are you doing here?" she demanded, furious that her voice was hoarse, that there were tears on her face, that he would see her like this, brought so low. "The gala is happening right this minute!"

"How can you possibly care about that now?" he asked in the same tight voice, as if he fought to keep himself under control.

She should have left ages ago. Why was she still here? Had she lingered deliberately, hoping for exactly this? His reappearance? What did she imagine would come of this? She had told him she loved him, and he had walked away. What more was there to say?

She wished there really were rocks strewn in front of her, so she could knock herself oblivious upon them. It could only be an improvement on the agony she felt coursing through her, making her feel weak. Making her want to be the kind of woman who begged. But she was not. She could not allow herself to be, not even for him. Not even now.

"I must pack," she said in a low voice, not daring to look at him as she jabbed at her eyes with the backs of her hands. She already felt too much. And she had already shown him too much, left herself too vulnerable. She was afraid there was nothing left. "And you must go back to that party. They need you."

"I am sure they do," he said, in a voice she did not recognize. Uneven. Rough. "But what about what I need?"

She jerked her eyes to his, and caught her breath, not at all sure she recognized the Lucas who stood before her, his fists clenched and his green eyes so bright with emotion.

Out of control, she thought, in a kind of wonder.

"Are you all right?" she asked, frowning.

He moved farther into the room, his big, lean body more tense than she had ever seen it, his beautiful face in an uncharacteristic scowl.

It occurred to her that she had never seen him like this. That this was, finally, the maskless, artifice-free Lucas Wolfe, all rampaging emotion and driving need—and he was in a towering rage.

She should not find that exhilarating. She should not allow that to let her...*wish.*

"All right?" he asked, his tone murderous. He shook his head as if he could not understand her, and crossed the room until he was right in front of her, inches away, and still scowling. "I cannot live without you, you idiotic woman! How could anything ever be all right again?"

CHAPTER TWELVE

"THAT's lovely," Grace replied, stung, her eyes heavy with tears yet again. "Poetic, really. Thank you."

"Is this what you wanted?" he continued as if she hadn't spoken, in the same thick, rough voice, the volume increasing even as Grace stared up at him. "Did you do this deliberately?"

"Did I...?" She shook her head, fighting back the tears, wanting to reach over and shove him away from her—but too afraid that if she touched him, it would be to drag him closer. "What are you talking about?"

"What am I supposed to do now, Grace?" he demanded, outraged. "How am I supposed to carry on with my life? Have you ever thought of that?"

She felt her own temper kick in, the one that urged her to wreck things, punch things, cause damage and destroy her own property. The one she usually tamped down. It was better than the tears. Anything was better than the tears.

"I've been a little bit busy today, Lucas," she threw at him, suddenly, deeply furious. "There was the invasive tabloid article, complete with photographs, and the gala I still had to prepare for while awaiting my boss's arrival. Then I was summarily fired because of my whorish behavior. So, no—I'm afraid I have not spent a lot of time wondering what *you* might do with your life. I'm a bit preoccupied with my own!"

"You can't just *do* this!" he cried wildly, throwing his hands out as if she'd wrecked him, somehow. As if he, the man who defined *ease,* was at a loss. He moved closer, to glare down at her. "You can't show up in my perfectly constructed life, turn it inside out and then vanish into the night! Were you even planning to tell me what had happened? That you were leaving?"

"Was I supposed to?" she demanded, fire and anguish twining inside of her, making her stomach tense—as powerful as the urge to reach over and touch him. Hit him. Caress him. She could not tell. "Before or after you stormed off and left me standing on that staircase? I told you that I loved you, Lucas, and you ran away."

"I had to think!" he shouted, completely unhinged, and Grace stopped breathing.

Lucas Wolfe...yelling? Truly out of control? Was this really happening? This was Lucas stripped down, laid bare, she realized. This was no more and no less than…a man. Not the legend. Not a collection of pretty words and practiced smiles, one for every occasion, whatever the situation called for. This was just a man.

An angry, emotional man.

Mine, a small voice whispered, reigniting that flame of hope she'd thought he'd extinguished when he'd walked away from her.

"I had to think," he repeated, his breath coming fast, his eyes hard on hers. Almost desperate. "Because I need you, and I have never needed anyone. Ever. It is not an easy thing, to change the habits of a lifetime—"

"Because, of course, it was so easy for me," she interrupted, feeling unhinged herself, as if the world was starting to spin, around and around, drunk and erratic.

"I am not a good bet," he threw at her, almost snapping out the words. "Quite the opposite, especially for someone who has achieved all that you have achieved, and all on your own. I have actively discouraged anything so much as masquerading as a commitment—even a second night in my company. I have never known any other way to be."

"If that is your résumé, it leaves something to be desired," she said, trying to sound fierce, tough, though she could hear the shake in her voice. The quake. And everything that was not Lucas tilted and whirled—or perhaps that was only her stomach.

He considered her then, seeming to take in her wet eyes, the slight tremor that shook through her, for the first time since entering the room.

"I may crash and burn at any moment," he said, his voice softer, though not necessarily calmer. "There is nothing to suggest that I am not exactly the waste of space everyone believes me to be. Everyone including me." His green eyes searched hers. "Everyone save you."

She was afraid to breathe. Afraid to move. Afraid that she was imagining this wild, electric moment.

"Are you?" she asked softly.

He let out a breath that was very nearly a laugh, and suddenly his nearness was overwhelming. She wanted to touch him more than she wanted anything else, wanted to burrow into him and hold him, even if it was to her own detriment. Even if it ruined her more than it already had. She did not care what that said about her, what that made her. A broken ship against the rocks. Her mother. None of that seemed to matter.

The closer he was, the more she felt free.

"No one else has ever seen beneath the surface," he said, his voice low, intense. "But you—you saw through me from the start." He reached over, taking her shoulders in his hands and bringing her flush against him. "If you give me a year, Grace, I will give you everything I have. I cannot promise it will be much, but it's yours."

She tilted her head back, and saw the warring emotion in his smoky green eyes, the fear and the hope. And something unfurled inside of her then, something strong and hard. Something right and true. Undeniable.

Because she could recognize truth when she saw it, when he shared it. When he offered her what she had given him earlier today, no matter what words he used.

The only words he knew, she thought. The only words he could.

"Are you offering me a test run?" she asked, over the sudden lump in her throat. "A year to see if you can work out all the kinks?"

"I could tell you that I love you," he said in a low, intense voice, his eyes fixed to hers. "And it might even be true. I believe it is. But what does the word even mean to one such as me? What context do I have for it?" He leaned close, placed his forehead against hers, as if he needed her to help him stand. Grace felt herself shake against him, into him. With him. "I know that I should let you go—it's the only thing I've ever been any good at—and instead I am here, making promises I have no idea at all if I can keep."

"Qualified promises," Grace pointed out, emotion tangling in her throat, in her voice. "What every girl dreams of, I'm sure."

He let out a breath, and ran his hands up and down her arms, in an easy rhythm, building heat, spreading fire.

"My brother Nathaniel is getting married to his Katie next month," he said. "Will you come with me?"

She laughed then, unexpectedly, the tears spilling over, and she didn't care.

"Have we downgraded from a year to a month?" she asked, sneaking her arms around his narrow waist. "How much testing do you think you require?"

"I don't know who I am!" The words seemed almost torn from him. He pulled back and stared down at her. "Don't you understand? I want to give you the world, Grace, but I have no idea how to do it."

"I do not want the world," she said simply, sliding her hands up to hold his beautiful face between them. "I can get that for myself, if I wish it. I only want you."

"I am yours," he said, his words ringing through her, around her, with the force of a vow. "In every way."

"Then what else do we need?" she asked, and pressed her mouth to his.

Fire and wine. Lucas's wicked mouth, and her

own needy little moan. He pulled back, his eyes dark with passion and something else, something she knew might take him some time to accept as truth. To truly believe.

But she was more than happy to wait.

"A date," he said, tilting his head back, his mouth crooking up in the corner. "I need a date to the gala. And you no longer work for these people, Grace, so really, no more of these appalling suits. I cannot bear it."

She did not ask how he managed to produce a midnight-blue gown from nowhere, one that clung to her breasts like a lover and then swept all the way to the floor, fitting her perfectly. And she did not argue when he only looked at her when she emerged from the en suite bathroom, her hair in a French twist, and ordered her, in that dark, demanding voice, to take it down.

"Enough hiding," he said, and then held out his hand. And this time, she took it without hesitation.

She walked into the gala she had planned for so many months with her head held high, her hair swirling around her shoulders, no longer pretending to be anything but what she was. A woman. A competent and confident woman who did not need to hide any part of herself away, no matter what Charles Winthrop might think.

"Grace," her former boss said when he saw them come in, his round face creasing with concern. "What are you doing? I thought you understood that you were not welcome here."

"She is with me," Lucas bit off with absolutely no sign of his famous charm, and perhaps a shade too much of the seething danger she had always seen in him. "And by definition always welcome, is that not so?"

The other man paled. Grace put her hand on Lucas's arm, and smiled her cool smile at Charles Winthrop.

"Don't worry," she said in her best calm, cutting way. "I am only a guest. But you can be sure that as of Monday morning, I'll be your competitor. Who knows where? Perhaps I'll go out on my own. But rest assured, I have no intention of simply drifting off into the ether because you fired me."

She had enjoyed the look on his face more than she should have. But then, she had never claimed to be a good person, had she? And in any case, Lucas was smiling at her, in a way she knew he had never smiled at anyone else. In a way that was only hers. Theirs.

It heated her up like the Texas summers of her youth. The man was lethal, and she loved him.

"Come, Cinderella," he said quietly, smiling as he drew her toward the dance floor. "It's coming up to midnight. Do try to keep your shoes on."

She did not care about the cameras, the staring and whispering former staff members, the entire rest of the world. She moved into his arms, and let him lead her into the music.

"I'm beginning to understand the point of the fairy tale," she said, smiling up at him, losing herself in the hot, bright gleam in his green eyes. "Who cares if I lose a shoe?"

"Who, indeed?" he asked softly, and swept them both away.

Much later, when the party had ended and most of the guests had dispersed, Lucas led her away from the tent and out onto the great lawn, where she could see the moon was just starting to rise over the trees. For a moment they stood there, side by side in silence, and gazed out over the darkened grounds. She shivered slightly when he turned to look at her, and told herself it was from the chill in the air.

"I walked around these grounds for hours today," he said quietly. "I thought I would confront myself—or my father's ghost. Perhaps I thought they were the same. But there was nothing here. Only an angry fool tramping about in the cold."

"It is just a house," she said softly. "Just some land. And he is only here as long as you keep him here."

He looked at her for a long moment.

"The only ghost I seem to be haunted by these days is you," he said, his voice a rasp against the thick night all around them.

"I am no ghost," she assured him, feeling a rush of heat to her eyes and fire to her core, an ache behind her ribs. "I am real and I am right here, Lucas."

"I have no idea at all how to build a new life without burning the old one to the ground," he said. "But I suppose we do not all need to be phoenixes, rising from the ashes, do we? Some of can simply walk on. Change."

"We can grow," she agreed in a whisper, heedless of the tears that overflowed and tracked down her cheeks, basking only in the great white heat of the joy that moved through her. "Live. Without ghosts and without fear."

Grace nestled against him, tucked into his side as if she'd been made to fit him that precisely, that well. As if she was meant to be his, and there, in the dark and facing all of his ghosts full-on, he let himself believe it.

The manor house stood behind them, covered in scaffolding, drenched in the past and lit up by the rising moon. Lucas took one last, hard look at it as the lights from the gala went off, one by one, leaving nothing to see but stone and brick and memories.

It was just a house. And he was free of it.
Finally.

"Yes," he said, kissing her again. "All of that, Grace. I want all of it. And you."

He took her hand in his, and together they walked down the great lawn toward the lane, toward the village and the world beyond, away from Wolfe Manor at last.

And straight on into their future.

LARGER-PRINT BOOKS!

◇Harlequin *Presents*

PASSION GUARANTEED SEDUCTION

GET 2 FREE LARGER-PRINT NOVELS PLUS 2 FREE GIFTS!

YES! Please send me 2 FREE LARGER-PRINT Harlequin Presents® novels and my 2 FREE gifts (gifts are worth about $10). After receiving them, if I don't wish to receive any more books, I can return the shipping statement marked "cancel". If I don't cancel, I will receive 6 brand-new novels every month and be billed just $4.80 per book in the U.S. or $5.49 per book in Canada. That's a saving of at least 13% off the cover price! It's quite a bargain! Shipping and handling is just 50¢ per book in the U.S. and 75¢ per book in Canada.* I understand that accepting the 2 free books and gifts places me under no obligation to buy anything. I can always return a shipment and cancel at any time. Even if I never buy another book, the two free books and gifts are mine to keep forever.

176/376 HDN FER2

Name _____ (PLEASE PRINT) _____

Address _____ Apt. # _____

City _____ State/Prov. _____ Zip/Postal Code _____

Signature (if under 18, a parent or guardian must sign) _____

Mail to the **Reader Service**:
IN U.S.A.: P.O. Box 1867, Buffalo, NY 14240-1867
IN CANADA: P.O. Box 609, Fort Erie, Ontario L2A 5X3

Not valid for current subscribers to Harlequin Presents Larger-Print books.

**Are you a subscriber to Harlequin Presents books and want to receive the larger-print edition?
Call 1-800-873-8635 today or visit us at www.ReaderService.com.**

* Terms and prices subject to change without notice. Prices do not include applicable taxes. Sales tax applicable in N.Y. Canadian residents will be charged applicable taxes. Offer not valid in Quebec. This offer is limited to one order per household. All orders subject to credit approval. Credit or debit balances in a customer's account(s) may be offset by any other outstanding balance owed by or to the customer. Please allow 4 to 6 weeks for delivery. Offer available while quantities last.

Your Privacy—The Reader Service is committed to protecting your privacy. Our Privacy Policy is available online at www.ReaderService.com or upon request from the Reader Service.

We make a portion of our mailing list available to reputable third parties that offer products we believe may interest you. If you prefer that we not exchange your name with third parties, or if you wish to clarify or modify your communication preferences, please visit us at www.ReaderService.com/consumerschoice or write to us at Reader Service Preference Service, P.O. Box 9062, Buffalo, NY 14269. Include your complete name and address.

HPLP11B